ADVANCE PRAI

This sensitive memoir about the war in Bosnia in the 1990s will quickly make readers think about the current conflict in Ukraine: stories of families torn apart by the horrors and atrocities of war; the miracle of love finding new hope in mountains of despair. Aida Šibić's war tragedy, *Luck Follows the Brave*, recalls another Bosnian writer, Nobel Prize winner Ivo Andrić, who, in fiction, crafted sensitive portraits from the galleries of Bosnian history. Šibić draws deep from her own well of experience to paint an accurate portrait of contemporary Bosnian history. Read it to weep. Read it to learn. Read it to find your own pathway through life's trials to dreams of hope.

—**B. William Silcock**, PhD, Emeritus faculty and former Assistant Dean for International Programs at the Walter Cronkite School of Journalism and Mass Communication at Arizona State University

Luck Follows the Brave will remind readers of frightening current events now repeating themselves in Ukraine. As an immigrant myself, I deeply felt Aida Šibić's pain, cried alongside her over losing loved ones, and laughed at the crazy immigrant jokes. Despite being robbed of her childhood, getting divorced, being a single mom with two young children, and losing her mom, she still managed to make peace with the past, becoming grateful for the life she lives today. "There are no knights in shining armor that will ride in and rescue the princess in distress," she writes. "The princess rescues herself and writes her own happy ending."

—**Maria Jones Esq.**, Founding Attorney and CEO of Maria Jones Law Firm, author of *Deportation Impossible*, Former Chair of the Immigration Section of the State Bar of Arizona

It's unimaginable that one woman could not only survive multiple traumas but also rise above her experiences with courage and resilience. As a fellow survivor of suicide loss, I could identify with Aida's story. It resonated with me. By telling our stories, we can heal and, in turn, inspire others to not give up, regardless of the circumstances. Aida's love for her children reminded me of my own motivation to keep going, despite the emotional turmoil. I highly recommend *Luck Follows the Brave*. You will be touched, moved, and inspired.

—**Cathie Godfrey**, author of *Your Suicide Didn't Kill Me: Choosing to Live and Love Again After Loss*

Aida Šibić's *Luck Follows the Brave* is a well-written book that includes important life events from the genocide in Bosnia, though difficult to read at times. Anyone like me, and the millions of others who have survived genocide or violence in any form, will find it comforting to read about someone who has gone through a similar experience. Aida's memoir proves that life doesn't have to be only about pain. While sorrow is essential to human life, it can, and should be, overflowing with joy. Aida's life is a living witness to that possibility.

—**Oksana Kushaliieva,** from Ukraine, Crimea; BA in international studies with a minor in French from Brigham Young University Idaho

LUCK FOLLOWS THE BRAVE

Aida Šibić

From Refugee Camps,
Abuse, and Suicide Loss
to Living the Dream

LUCK FOLLOWS THE BRAVE

Aida Šibić

From Refugee Camps,
Abuse, and Suicide Loss
to Living the Dream

PEACOCK PROUD
P·R·E·S·S
Phoenix, Arizona

Luck Follows the Brave: From Refugee Camps, Abuse, and Suicide Loss to Living the Dream
Copyright © 2022 by Aida Šibić

First Published in the USA in 2022 by Peacock Proud Press, Phoenix, Arizona
   ISBN 978-1-957232-05-8 Hardback
   ISBN 978-1-957232-06-5 Paperback
   ISBN 978-1-957232-04-1 eBook
Library of Congress Control Number: 2022907452

Editors
   Laura L. Bush, PhD, PeacockProud.com
   Charles Grosel, Write4Success.net

Cover and Interior Layout
   Jana Linnell

Portrait Photographer
   Elaine Kessler, elainekesslerphotography.com

DISCLAIMER:
This is a work of nonfiction. The information is of a general nature to help readers know and understand more about the life of the author, Aida Šibić. The stories in this book are the personal opinions and experiences of the author. Some names, characters, and places have been altered to protect the privacy of individuals. Readers of this publication agree that neither the publisher nor the author will be held responsible or liable for damages that may be alleged or resulting directly or indirectly from their use of this publication.

This book is not intended as a substitute for the medical advice of qualified health care practitioners, nor to provide legal advice. All matters regarding health require prompt medical attention and supervision. All matters related to the law require legal expertise and qualified advice. The author has no professional training in medical or legal fields. Neither the publisher nor the author shall be held responsible or liable for any alleged loss or damage arising from information provided or suggestions in this book. All external links are provided as a resource only and are not guaranteed to remain active for any length of time. Neither the publisher nor the author can be held accountable for the information provided by, or actions resulting from accessing these resources. The sole purpose of the information provided in this book is to inspire and provide hope and strength for those who are coping with grief, loss, or trauma.

CONTENTS

Introduction 1

Chapter 1 – The Crumbling of Hopes and Dreams. 3

Chapter 2 – Children of War 14

Chapter 3 – A New Life in the New World 32

Chapter 4 – The Working Life 52

Chapter 5 – Husband Material. 63

Chapter 6 – Carpe Diem. 72

Chapter 7 – Patience and a Condo. 81

Chapter 8 – Faith and Fights. 89

Chapter 9 – The Gift of Life 102

Chapter 10 – A Mostly Blissful Time 113

Chapter 11 – Trouble in Paradise. 127

Chapter 12 – The Gift of Life: What's in a Name? 140

Chapter 13 – Dissolution, End of Illusion 154

Chapter 14 – Anger Management 177

Chapter 15 – Miserability. 191

Chapter 16 – Running from Reality. 212

Chapter 17 – The First Attempt 223

Chapter 18 – "Mens Sana in Corpore Sano". 241

Chapter 19 – Surviving Grief 253

Chapter 20 – The Many Roads to Healing 268

Chapter 21 – Back to Bosnia: We Went, We Saw, We Loved 278

Chapter 22 – Home is Where You Feel the Most at Home. 289

Epilogue – Living a Blessed Life. 308

Acknowledgments. 311

About the Author 313

For my children, Mia and Tony. I want them to know only love.
And for my best friends:
My mother, Elbisa, who taught me strength and perseverance.
My father, Zaim, who instilled in me a sense of eternal optimism.
My sisters, Azra, Lejla, Aida and Sue-Ellen, who showed me loyalty,
friendship and unconditional love.

For anyone struggling with abuse—substance, physical, emotional, or verbal—
I hope you find strength and inspiration to persevere and fight the good fight.
National Domestic Violence Hotline
TheHotline.org or 1-800-799-3224

For anyone struggling with mental health issues or emotional distress,
I hope reading my story helps you find your way out of darkness.
The 988 Suicide & Crisis Lifeline
988lifeline.org or 988

With Much Love,
Aida Šibić

INTRODUCTION

Young children are filled with wonder. As children in Bosnia, we all had our hopes and dreams. We believed in magic with childlike innocence and created grand plans for the future. Like kids everywhere, my Bosnian friends and I aspired to be teachers, athletes, artists, astronauts, entrepreneurs, engineers, doctors and scientists. None of us ever dreamed of becoming genocide and abuse survivors, Muslim refugees in America and single parents raising two kids on their own, with no family to lean on, while coping with the grief of suicide loss.

Yet here I am. That has been my life in a nutshell. But my life has also been so much more. Along with tragedy and trauma, I've experienced love and laughter, great friendship, and career success. I have two beautiful children whom I love more than life itself. I've travelled to many beautiful parts of the world, eaten and prepared delicious foods, listened to great music, and danced with friends. In short, I've lived life in all its sadness and glory, and I'd like to think I've learned a few things along the way.

Until my early teens, I didn't even fully comprehend what it meant to be a Muslim. When I was a child, it simply meant the boys in our family were circumcised and we didn't eat pork. It was not us versus them, Muslims versus Christians. We were all kids, absolutely equal before God. Kids with dreams about the future, with hopes of our crushes asking us to a school dance. Happy kids who played hide-and-go-seek together in the neighborhood. Smiling kids who kicked a soccer ball around a field, cooled off by the river in the dog days of summer, spending summer breaks vacationing with our parents on the Mediterranean coast.

Then it all changed in the cataclysm of war. Seemingly overnight our peaceful country was ripped apart by an aggressor. There was violence and killing, mass executions and torture, rape and genocide. As a Muslim family, we were in the wrong place at the wrong time, but we were luckier than some—we made it out alive as refugees and eventually settled in the United States.

I'm not going to lie. We faced hard times in our new lives in our adopted country, exiled from everything we had always known. Many of my childhood dreams were shattered, and some turned into outright nightmares. Other dreams have come true, however, and exceeded my expectations in ways I never could have imagined. For the fulfillment of these dreams, I am eternally grateful.

✦

It was on the eve of my fortieth birthday, beholden to no one but God and those I cherish most, that I solemnly reflected on these thoughts and the fact that I was simply happy to be alive, to have survived. I sat outside on a hot August evening, amidst palm trees and saguaro cactus of the Sonoran Desert, waiting for the clock to strike midnight and mark my forty years of life on this planet. A life both ordinary and extraordinary, a life that has straddled two worlds, a life filled with tragedy and triumph. And though I've been filled with grave doubt and teetered on the edge of the abyss of despair, I've always come back to this: the human spirit, fueled by love, cannot be held in check. We are all capable of great feats of courage and love. And if I can do it, so can you.

That's why I'm telling my story.

CHAPTER 1

THE CRUMBLING OF HOPES AND DREAMS

I was born in 1978 in Banja Luka, Bosnia and Herzegovina, a small country on the Balkan peninsula in southeastern Europe, then one of six republics in the Socialist Federal Republic of Yugoslavia. The five others were Slovenia, Croatia, Serbia, Montenegro, and Macedonia. Bosnia and Herzegovina is a mouthful, even for those of us born there. We call it simply Bosnia.

Nestled between the clear blue Adriatic Sea, the magnificent Alps, and the blue Danube immortalized by Johann Strauss in his famous waltz, Yugoslavia is abundant in natural riches and fairy-tale landscapes—lush green mountains and valleys, turquoise rivers and crystal-clear lakes. At the crossroads where West meets East, Yugoslavia's history, heritage, and culture was as rich as her landscapes, with influences from the Roman, Turkish Ottoman, and Austro-Hungarian empires to resistance movements in World Wars I and II. Religious beliefs included Roman Catholicism, the Orthodox Church, Islam, Judaism, Buddhism, and just about any other religion you can name. This mix of cultures peacefully coexisted for centuries.

I didn't know this as a child, but Bosnia is one of those rare countries in the world where one can stand at an intersection and see a mosque on one corner, a Catholic church on another, and an Orthodox church on yet another. At a certain time of day, the sounds of azan—the Islamic call to prayer—and church bells are married in perfect harmony. I grew up in that harmony, maybe even took it for granted, like many of us who grew up there. It's just the way things were. Neighbors looked out for one another, and friends let themselves into each other's house without knocking because everyone was always welcome, as my grandmother used to say.

The post-WWII in Yugoslavia was a time of unity and brotherhood. This was a time when students and the elderly alike worked together to rebuild the nation's war-torn infrastructure, all the while singing patriotic songs of love for country and fellow countrymen in celebration of defeating fascism. This was a time when youth was celebrated in a national holiday, the Day of Youth. This was a time when higher education and cultural achievements were encouraged and revered, a time when etiquette was practiced by all.

As reward for outstanding academic achievements, young people from every region were hand-selected by their schools to run in the annual Youth Relay, connecting cities and regions throughout Yugoslavia. The runners passed the Youth Baton, a symbolic gesture meaning the future of the nation rested on educated youth. Proud parents, along with people from all over the country, lined up alongside flower-decorated streets and waved flags as they merrily cheered the passing of the baton.

The mastermind behind it all—the one who took the best principles of Marxism, socialism, and communism to govern the Socialist Federal Republic of Yugoslavia—and biggest advocate of brotherhood and unity as a way of life was President Josip Broz, known more commonly as Marshal Tito.

To us kids, Tito was larger than life. Every classroom had his picture hanging above the chalkboard. Every man, woman, and child celebrated him. On Republic Day, every seven-year-old took a solemn oath to unity and joined the Pioneers Union of Yugoslavia. Becoming a Pioneer was the highest honor bestowed upon a child. We all wore our white button-up collar-shirt, navy blue pants or skirt, red scarf, and navy-blue hat with a red star pinned to the front. With parents proudly watching from the audience, each of us kids solemnly recited our oath:

Today, as I become a Pioneer,
I give my Pioneer's word of honor
That I shall diligently study and work,

Respect my parents and elders,
And be a loyal and honest friend,
who always keeps their promise.
That I shall love our country
Self-governed Socialist Federal
Republic of Yugoslavia,
That I shall spread brotherhood and unity,
And the principles for which Tito fought
And that I shall value all people of the world,
Who wish freedom and peace.

We were born in unity, and we swore to protect it. In return, Tito ensured that all families had access to free healthcare and higher education, affordable housing, six weeks of vacation a year, and holiday trips to the Mediterranean.

To the outside world, Marshal Tito was an independent, but fierce and celebrated leader who had commanded his Partisan troops to victory against the Nazi German invasion and stood up to Stalin. He was a charismatic man who ruled with an iron fist against corruption and social injustices. He was also one of few heads of state to light a cigar in the White House during his first full-dress state visit with President Richard Nixon.

+

Tito died on May 4, 1980. Yugoslavia died a little over a decade later.

+

In the early 90s, I was just another kid filled with hopes and dreams, about to graduate from middle school. I took enrolling into my local high school and attending college in Banja Luka as my birthright. I watched older kids from my neighborhood grow up and move out of their parents' homes, with most of them staying in Banja Luka and visiting their parents frequently. I assumed I would, too.

Like many of my childhood friends, I dreamed of becoming a doctor, one who delivered babies, to be precise. I always believed there was something magical in witnessing new life come into this world. Being part of new parents' joy and happiness was my dream job.

My parents were over the moon when their daughters Anela (yours truly) and Amila were born. According to Mom, Dad bought drinks for everyone at the bar each time (men weren't allowed in the birthing rooms back then). My sister Amila is two and a half years younger than I am. We call her Ami, and I go by Annie. The best way to show our relationship as kids is through situations like this: Ami would break a jar of honey in the cupboard below the sink, for example, and leave the mess for Mom to clean up.

Although Mom knew the answer well before she asked a question, she would yell for both of us. "Annie! Ami! Which one of you did this?"

At the sound of Mom in distress, we both would drop everything we were doing and run to the kitchen to face her. Ami would look at me, then look back at Mom, and shrug her shoulders. I would wait for Ami to confess, and when she didn't, I would reluctantly tell Mom that I broke the jar. Ami and I both knew the punishment for me would be far less severe, since Mom already knew that Ami broke the jar and that I was protecting her. Mom would still punish me by making me do chores for lying and to teach me not to take blame for others. Ami would go back to playing, showing no remorse for her actions. It took me a lifetime to learn to hold people accountable for their actions. As a seven-year-old, however, and later as a young adult, I protected those I cared about, regardless of the consequences.

In the fifth grade I realized I had my first crush, Igor, when our schedules got rearranged, and I missed seeing him at school every day. I was in the sixth grade the first time I sat on his lap on a school field trip to a movie theater. The first time we kissed was in seventh grade, sitting on the stairs by the Vrbas river, after we both ditched school to spend a day together. By eighth grade, I couldn't imagine my future without him.

Igor was an aspiring rock star who played bass in a heavy metal band. He had a bulging vein on his forehead and piercing blue eyes—the kind of eyes that glowed and sparkled with genuine love each time he snuck a secret look at me in class. He gave me butterflies and made me giggle. His short, dirty blond hair reminded me of faraway places and soft, sandy, exotic beaches. In my innocent little-girl dreams of our fabulous future together, we would be married with a family of our own, and our loving parents would guide us through life's ups and downs with their wisdom, but only if we needed them to.

I drew pictures of the house we would live in during that imagined future. I recall dark blue ink on white construction paper and crooked out-lines of a two-story house with five bedrooms, three bathrooms, a pool, and a tennis court. Growing up, we didn't have a pool or a tennis court, nor did my family know anyone who did, even though we were considered an affluent family who lived in a four-story house. But who's to say a girl can't dream about having a pool when she grows up?

An entire room of my imaginary house was dedicated to pets. During playtime, I'd often say to my mother, "I'm going to have a house full of pets when I grow up."

"I hope you can keep up with all of them," she'd tease.

The house might have been imaginary, but my love of animals was not. I rescued pets at every corner. If I saw a sad looking puppy on the street, cold and hungry, I had to bring it home, feed it, and give it shelter. Given all the puppies, kittens, rabbits, turtles, and a myriad of fish I adopted, my room resembled a miniature zoo.

Mom constantly made excuses for why we couldn't keep another pet, but she's the one responsible for my love of animals. For my eighth birthday, she gave me my first and favorite pet, Coco—a budgie parakeet with a yellow tiger-striped body and a splotch of green under his wings.

I spent countless hours playing with him, teaching him tricks, and how to talk. He quickly learned to say mama, hello, and his own name. My friends adored him, oohing and aahing at his skills, and admiring his wit and our special bond. We kept his cage door open. His favorite perch was the chan-delier in our first-floor dining room, where he enjoyed an aerial view of the entire downstairs.

Coco and I had our favorite game. If I was sitting in the living room and wanted to play, I snapped my fingers twice and extended my index finger in the air. On my mark, Coco flew across the room, landed on my finger, and gave me little bird kisses. For his treat, I rubbed the back of his head while he fluffed his feathers and purred like a kitten. He was part of the family. I couldn't imagine a day without him.

As a young girl with stars in her eyes, I had my whole life planned out—my future husband, house, and pets. I'd be a baby doctor and live close to my family. We'd have lots of dinners and parties and laugh and dance and play music. My parents would be our model couple, and Ami and I would someday plan a party for their sixtieth wedding anniversary. Our kids and grandkids would be there in Banja Luka, along with our many cousins, aunts, uncles, and friends.

I did not know at the time—I could not have known—that I was setting myself up for a world of hurt, disappointment, sadness, and feelings of failure in adulthood.

I even had a name picked out for my first-born son: Namik, after my grandfather, my father's father. Dad's family had a longstanding tradition of naming their first male child after the grandfather, but that's not the only reason why I wanted to name mine after Grandpa Namik.

Grandpa Namik was my favorite grandparent. He and I had a very special bond, and my family always said I resembled him the most of his four grandkids. As a professor of Work Health and Safety at the University of Banja Luka, he was a prominent man in our hometown, and beyond. He had a master's degree and had begun his doctorate around the age of fifty.

In Bosnia, it's common for the extended family to live in the same house, often called simply, "the family home." Ours was a big brick house, four stories tall, with white stucco façade and a red shingled roof in the heart of Banja Luka. It squeezed in between surrounding houses and five-story buildings set off by old linden trees and narrow alleyways. Old willows stood guard in the street in front of the house. With three separate living rooms, eight bedrooms, and three bathrooms, the house was large enough for all of us: Mom, Dad, Ami, and me; my father's parents; Dad's grandmother; and his older brother, who was also married and had two kids.

Grandpa had turned one of the rooms in the family home into a study, where floor-to-ceiling shelves, filled with books and encyclopedias, decorated three of the walls. We called it Grandpa's library. As kids, my cousins and I loved hiding in the study to look through his medical encyclopedias, trying to find the rarest and weirdest diseases. We couldn't keep ourselves from falling about laughing. We weren't laughing so much at the diseases, but at the fact that we weren't supposed to be there in the first place.

Grandpa also had an old, oversized, brown cedarwood chest in the study, which without exception he kept under lock and key. To us kids, it looked like a treasure chest. He frequently travelled around Europe and faraway places, bringing back gifts for the family, which he stored in this chest. One of our favorite pastimes was snooping around the library, scheming ingenious new ways to pick the lock. We never succeeded in our quest.

Since we were a Muslim family, we didn't celebrate Christmas. Instead, we celebrated New Year's Eve, which was a time for our family to gather around the dinner table, reflect on the year, celebrate the good, bid farewell to the bad, and wish each other good health, joy, and cheer in the upcoming year. When the clock struck midnight, Grandpa showered us with the gifts from his worldly travels.

Instead of wrapping the gifts, Grandpa stuffed them in oversized black garbage bags, one for each of his grandkids. We couldn't see what was inside the bags until midnight, which added to the suspense of eager children who had been waiting an entire year to get a sneak peek of their presents. Grandpa was a big kid himself and loved the game. He lived to see the ear-to-ear smiles across our faces when he outmaneuvered us with his surprise each year.

I remember our last New Year with Grandpa. I opened my bag to discover a white cashmere sweater with green and lavender hearts, which he found in Italy. It became my favorite sweater. He also gave me a globe and a pencil holder from England, made of artificial leather and embellished with blue images of Buckingham Palace and a matching blue zipper. After asking myself out loud where I wanted to travel, I spun the globe and stopped it with my finger landing on San Francisco. That made everyone laugh. I dug farther into my bag of surprises and found a talking doll with curly blonde hair and blue eyes. Back in those days, talking dolls cost a small fortune, but

Grandpa was a generous man. He also gave me a coloring book and pencils, other school supplies, my favorite wafers and snacks, and an assortment of candy.

Jumping with excitement, I didn't know what gift to play with first. I couldn't wait to show off the presents to all my friends. I hugged Grandpa hard and held on to him for a good fifteen minutes while he radiated pure love and joy.

Grandpa was a well-travelled, worldly, and intellectual man. He treated everyone with the utmost respect and kindness and had friends all over Europe. Everyone who knew him held him in high regard. His word was his honor—come hell or high water, Grandpa always kept his word with me until one hot mid-August night on the eve of my eighth birthday when he sat me on his lap and said, "I know it's your birthday tomorrow sweetheart, and I did not forget. Grandpa has been busy lately, my dear, and your birthday snuck up on me. I wanted to get you something very special. Will you be mad at me if your gift is a few days late?"

"Of course not, Grandpa," I said smiling. "You really don't even have to get me anything. You gave me enough presents to last a lifetime. I can't wait for tomorrow, so all of us can try the yummy cake that I helped Mama bake."

He squeezed me tightly, gave me a big kiss on the cheek and looked at me with eyes full of love when he said, "My sweet child, you are so smart and kind. Always stay this beautiful. I love you all the way to the stars and back! I feel bad about your birthday present, but I promise I will make it up to you very soon."

"Grandpa, it's okay. I can wait. You always get the bestest presents for us. I love you all the way to the stars and back too."

He smiled and replied, "It's getting late. Go get some sleep now, so we can have an awesome birthday party tomorrow for the bestest girl in the world. I can't wait to try that yummy cake too."

"Thanks Grandpa. Sweet dreams."

We hugged and kissed once more before he said good night. Then I ran upstairs to my room and went straight to bed, excited for my birthday.

The next morning, the day of my birthday, I woke up early and heard Mom in the room. She seemed to be sniffling while she opened and closed the closet doors as if she were rummaging for something. I jumped out of bed full of energy, excited about my party later that day. That's when I saw a stream of tears running down her cheeks and realized she must have been looking for a handkerchief. I grew anxious when I heard other voices in the house that sounded like friends and neighbors. They, too, seemed to be crying.

"What's wrong Mama? Why are people at our house so early? And why is everyone crying?"

Mom sat on the edge of my bed, gently took my hands into hers and softly said, "Baby, your grandpa Namik passed away this morning. I am so, so sorry."

"But... But... Mama, what do you mean?" I was completely baffled and in a state of shock, thinking this must have been a bad dream I couldn't wait to wake up from.

"Grandpa went to sleep last night, baby, and never woke up. He went to Heaven."

This was my first experience with death. I burst into tears as I realized that my favorite grandpa was gone forever, and he didn't even get to try my birthday cake. Instead of celebrating my birthday, my childhood friends gathered at my house to mourn with me. Instead of eating cake and drinking Pepsi, I gathered my friends in my room so we could read a book and keep quiet because the adults were sad. It was later that day that Mom brought Coco home to put at least one smile on my face that day.

Soon after, I decided if I ever had a baby boy, I would name him Namik after my beloved grandfather.

✦

But life doesn't always go quite the way we imagine.

First, my parents split up. Then the war came. This all happened four or five years after Grandpa Namik died.

Mom and Dad truly loved each other. They were sweethearts while still in high school. Mom lived in Prijedor, about thirty miles from Banja Luka, and when he was still courting her, Dad often rode his bicycle in rain or snow after school from his house to hers. He would bring her flowers and over the course of four years before they married, he wrote her poems and the most romantic love letters, which she cherished. But Dad was also a privileged young man doted on by an affluent family, and though he was friendly and warm, after he lost his father, he did what he wanted with little consideration for others, least of all Mom. He was charismatic and good-looking, and females flocked to him, especially when he was the one buying round after round of drinks in this bar or that. He didn't turn these women away as he coped with his grief. I imagine many of the women he met didn't care at all that he was married with children. Some may have preferred it.

Mom caught wind that he was spending time in the company of other women and decided to catch him in the act. It was a cold and snowy January night. I was a tender and impressionable age of twelve. That night, Mom took me by the hand for a walk to the other part of town, where we hid behind bushes, waiting. I wasn't exactly aware of our purpose for being there until a scene played out before my eyes like a bad movie.

After a while, I saw a vivacious blonde enter my father's car and give him a lusty kiss on the lips. I screamed and charged at the car from the bushes. Mom ran after me. Startled by a screaming child, both my father and his mistress got out of the car. I ran right at the mistress and body-slammed her. In defense, she picked me up by my shoulders, and I kicked her in the shins as hard and as much as I could with my pointed-toe Heidi boots until one of my parents pried me away.

You'd think Mom would be the angry one, but she was simply in despair. Dad was furious, madder than I'd ever seen him. As he drove us home, he berated Mom for bringing me with her, calling her judgment and qualities as a mother into question, and told her he would soon file for divorce. He said he could never forgive her for bringing me with her that night.

I remember her crying that night, as well as many other nights during their separation. Mom loved Dad and was heartbroken. She stayed in Banja Luka for the sake of my sister and me, though my parents lived in separate rooms.

Soon after my parents split up, the war broke out in Bosnia and many Muslims lost their jobs, including Mom. With nothing to keep her in Banja Luka, she returned to her hometown of Prijedor to live with her mom, taking my sister Ami with her. I was deep in puppy love with Igor and couldn't imagine living without him, so I stayed in Banja Luka with Dad to finish eighth grade. Mom didn't like it, but she was too tired to argue.

CHAPTER 2

CHILDREN OF WAR

If you could call my childhood ordinary (in the best sense), my teenage years were far from it. In 1992, when I was thirteen going on fourteen, war came to Bosnia. Our family would never be the same again.

I still don't fully comprehend how my birth country went from brotherhood and unity to hate and exterminate practically overnight. All I remember is one fateful day while our nation was still busy peacefully coexisting in perfect harmony, disgruntled Bosnian Serbs woke up on the wrong side of history. Chanting a 500-year-old slogan about the oppression of the Turks during Ottoman Empire times, Serbs weaponized past ethnic grievances and took out their centuries-old resentments on their Muslim and Catholic brothers and sisters in the twentieth century in the form of ethnic cleansing, a fancy word for raping, pillaging, and exterminating. In short, genocide. This all unfolded in the heart of Europe as the world stood by and watched, wondering if they should get involved.

I can read the histories and get the facts, but you had to witness the magnitude of gaslighting and terror firsthand to get a true sense of what really transpired in Bosnia.

Dating back to World War II, two distinct guerilla factions detached from the Yugoslav People's Army—the Serb Orthodox Četniks and the Croatian Catholic Ustashe. Both factions indoctrinated their members against every-one who was non-Serb or non-Croat. Both groups carried out terror attacks and massacres against civilians, and each other, in WWII. Both groups bred hate, chauvinism, and nationalism. As such, they were a threat to Brotherhood and Unity. Nationalism and affiliation with either group was considered a political crime sanctioned by Tito's regime and persecuted.

A few years after Tito's death, Serbian political leader Slobodan Milošević[1] began his efforts to reform the 1974 Constitution of Yugoslavia, limiting the powers of Serbia's autonomous provinces and moving the country from a one-party system to a multi-party system. Those efforts allowed him to rise to power and claim the Presidency of Serbia and also laid the foundation for the rise of nationalism. After Tito's death in 1980, nationalism began to run rampant, and as a result, Yugoslavia began to break up in the early nineties, with wars of independence erupting in Slovenia (briefly) and Croatia.

Bosnia and Herzegovina might be the only nation in the world where being Muslim is considered a nationality more than a religion. In other words, being Muslim was more an affiliation with a country and its way of life—a life of peace, humility, hard work, cleanliness, and don't do onto others what you wouldn't wish to be done onto you. And although Bosnia was predominantly Muslim, with over 40 percent of families identifying with Muslim nationality, the religious aspect was never obligatory or imposed. Bosnia was cosmopolitan.

Bosnian Serbs and Croats represented 31 percent and 17 percent respectively. By the early 90s, Bosnian Serbs began illegally arming under a false allegation that Bosnian Muslims were arming for war and attempting to establish an Islamic state.

By October 1991, a shadow Serb operation began creating centralized plans and preparing jingo Serbs for the takeover of various municipalities within Bosnia and eastern parts of Croatia. Their aim was to seize territory and unify Bosnian and Croatian Serb communities into a "Greater Serbia," in an effort to prevent the two republics from secession from Yugoslavia. The architects and masterminds behind the takeover were a team of nationalist political and military leaders.

Radovan Karadžić[2] was one of these nationalist leaders. He was born in 1945 in Montenegro to a father who was part of Četnik terrorist forces.

During the better part of Radovan's childhood, his father was incarcerated for the crimes he had committed during WWII. Radovan studied medicine and began his career as a psychiatrist. He was barred from practice after abusing his position to issue false evaluations to friends and family seeking early retirement in exchange for cash.

He later began working at an energy company under Momčilo Krajišnik,[3] but the pair were arrested in the mid-eighties, then charged and convicted of embezzlement and fraud. They had used company assets to build private homes for themselves in a ski resort town of Pale, near Sarajevo. Both served an eleven-month prison sentence. Several years after their release, they entered the political arena by establishing a para-government structure within Bosnia.

Besides Četniks, another paramilitary group was forming—the Serb Volunteer Guard, better known as Arkan's Tigers. They were led by Željko-"Arkan" Ražnatović,[4] a lifelong career criminal and one of Interpol's most wanted during the seventies and eighties. Arkan had several dozen convictions and outstanding warrants across Europe for burglaries, bank robberies, prison escapes, and attempted murder.

In the years leading up to war in Bosnia, Serbs also took over control of the Yugoslav People's Army by promoting only Serbs to the top ranks within the military and by planning to seize arsenals of weapons and artillery. Ratko Mladić[6] was one such career military officer. At the inception of Army of Serb Republic, he was appointed general.

This group of men, along with their subordinates, would later become better known as the "Butchers of Bosnia." With their moral compass askew, a highly trained terrorist organization with political and military leaders was on standby and ready to unleash atrocities on a grand scale.

When the United States and the European Community (now European Union) recognized Bosnia and Herzegovina as independent on April 7, 1992, within weeks, Ratko Mladić and his army besieged Sarajevo, the capital of Bosnia, by cutting off roads leading in and out of the city and by shutting off electricity and running water. Then they began shelling Sarajevo and other cities. At the same time, a Serb Republic (Republika Srpska) was established within Bosnia, and Radovan Karadžić was appointed President. Krajišnik was appointed speaker of the National Assembly of the Serb Republic.

Underground paramilitary groups dispatched and seized roughly half of Bosnian municipalities. Checkpoints were set up within cities, and overnight, the movement of Bosnian Muslims and Croats was interrupted. Major cities were cut off from one another and telephone communications disabled.

As the Serb leaders began joint operations against the Bosnian government, the Bosnian Muslims, and the Croats, the war began. As soon as conflicts erupted, in a rash attempt to stop the violence, the United Nations imposed an arms embargo on Bosnia while also sending in peacekeeping troops. But the arms embargo essentially left Bosnian Muslims defenseless against their aggressor, led by men and women, such as Slobodan Milošević,[1] Radovan Karadžić,[2] Ratko Mladić,[3] Momčilo Krajišnik,[4] Biljana Plavšić,[5] Željko - 'Arkan' Ražnatović,[6] and others.

In response, the Bosnian Army was formed in some cities by groups of civilians and members of the police organizing in attempt to provide territorial defense. The organization was poor, with no central command and limited access to weapons.

Meanwhile, the newly established Serb News Agency (SRNA) founded and anchored by Risto Djogo, began airing satirical programs aimed at

---

[1] Milošević, Slobodan (IT-02-54), United Nationals International Criminal Tribunal for the former Yugoslovia, accessed February 7, 2022. https://www.icty.org/en/case/slobodan_milosevic

[2] Karadžić (IT-95-5/18), United Nationals International Criminal Tribunal for the former Yugoslovia, accessed February 7, 2022. https://www.icty.org/en/case/karadzic

[3] Mladić (IT-09-92), United Nationals International Criminal Tribunal for the former Yugoslovia, accessed February 7, 2022. https://www.icty.org/en/case/mladic

[4] Krajišnik (IT-00-39), United Nationals International Criminal Tribunal for the former Yugoslovia, accessed February 7, 2022. https://www.icty.org/en/case/krajisnik

[5] Plavšić (IT-00-39 & 40/1), United Nationals International Criminal Tribunal for the former Yugoslovia, accessed February 7, 2022. https://www.icty.org/en/case/plavsic

[6] Ražnatović, Željko - 'Arkan' (IT-97-27), United Nationals International Criminal Tribunal for the former Yugoslovia, accessed February 7, 2022. https://www.icty.org/en/case/zeljko_raznatovic

mocking Islam and the way Muslims practiced their faith. I suddenly found myself staring at three chimpanzees prostrating on the floor as Djogo mockingly described the Muslim prayer practices to his viewers. Other nights, he cocked a gun on primetime news, describing the impending fate of Muslims. Djogo often compared the size of Bosnia to that of a Turkish mini-coffee cup. He displayed ripped-up maps of Bosnia and aired nationalist songs aimed at insulting the Bosnian President, Alija Izetbegović:

I don't like you Alija
Because you're a balija

Over the course of the war during primetime news, gaslighting on a national scale placated the critics and world's outrage with Karadžić on television, telling the world that Muslims bombed themselves to gain sympathy from the west. According to him, the media was fabricating stories of Serb brutality. There was no violence. "Muslims are leaving their homes voluntarily," Karadžić claimed, while Mladić instructed his troops not to shoot, but save their ammunition, and instead, behead the Bosnian Army soldiers.

What was dubbed by Serbs as a patriotic-defense war was later officially labeled a genocide by the International Criminal Tribunal for the Former Yugoslavia (ICTY). The so-called "patriots" who led jingo Serbs into war, were later collectively referred to as the "criminal enterprise" in ICTY indictment documents. The arms embargo on Bosnia was "an intervention which has enunciated, but then compromised principle at every turn. And which—by the proffering of ill-conceived so-called solutions—has served to incite, rather than ameliorate hostilities," later explained then Senator from Delaware, Joseph Biden at a July 30, 1993, Senate hearing, while proposing to lift the arms embargo to allow Bosnian Muslims to defend themselves.[7]

I understand the shadow politics well enough. What I don't understand at a personal level is the ferocity, ethnic hatred, and barbarism that was let

---

[7]   Joe Biden talks about aggression on Bosnia and warns of genocide, July 30, 1993. Clip of Senate Session, accessed February 7, 2022. https://www.c-span.org/video/?c4921451/user-clip-biden-1993-bosnian-crisis.

loose. Nor will I ever understand why 100,000 innocent Muslims in Bosnia lost their lives, nor why close to 800,000 of us were displaced all over the world, while millions of others suffered postwar trauma-related mental health issues and addictions.

Torture, rape, genocide, mass murder, and massacres were just some of broad violations of the Geneva convention for humane treatment of individuals in times of war perpetrated by the Serbs. The war in Bosnia was so unbelievably cruel and inhumane, the world had to sanitize what happened there by calling it "ethnic cleansing," sweeping it under the rug with the Dayton Peace Agreement. A more accurate description would have been "ethnic extermination" or just plain genocide, which, to the present day, some Serbs refuse to admit they conducted.

As a reward for this genocide, Serbs were granted the right to carve out integral parts of central Bosnia and call it the Serb Republic (the other part is the Federation of Bosnia and Herzegovina). What the Serbs were allowed to do would have been analogous to allowing Nazis to carve out a piece of Israel after WWII and call it the Nazi Republic. The formal establishment and recognition of the Serb Republic, with its roots in bloodshed, torture, rape, and mass executions was a codification of Serb victory by the western nations, and as such, a hard pill to swallow for a lot of Bosnian Muslims.

I got the first hint that something was amiss in our peaceful republic when I heard one of my classmates refer to another as "balija" one day at school. I had no idea what that meant, but it sounded like an insult. What made it even more confusing was up until that day, the two kids were good friends.

Later, I asked my dad what it meant.

"Which kids?" he asked.

"Vladimir and Emir," I asked. "Why?"

"Vladimir called Emir a balija?"

I nodded.

"Balija is a derogatory name for a Muslim. It's a slur, an insult."

"What's a Muslim, Dad?" I pressed on, even more confused.

"We're Muslim, honey. Emir is a Muslim name. Our family prays to God in a mosque. Vladimir is a Serb orthodox name. His family prays to God in a church. Until recently, these differences did not matter. But now they do, apparently." Then he quietly added, "Promise me that if anyone ever calls you balija, you will ignore them. Do not argue. Do not fight back. Do you understand? People are getting seriously hurt." Dad looked serious.

"I won't; I promise. But that's so stupid, Dad! Vladimir doesn't like Emir anymore just because they pray to God in different places?"

"These times are stupid, sweetheart. Please just do what I said."

"One more question. What kind of name is Igor?" I asked with a sense of urgency.

"Igor is also an Orthodox name," my father explained.

"I don't care. I still like him, even if he starts to hate me because I'm Muslim," I proclaimed.

Dad hugged me, then said with tears in his eyes, "Don't ever dislike someone just because their beliefs are different from yours. That's not a good enough reason. You can only dislike someone if they're not kind to you, but even then, wish them well."

My young mind was unable to comprehend the reasons for this sudden hostility and the national politics of division and hate sown across the country. Igor didn't understand either—his father was Orthodox and his mother Muslim—and our feelings for one another didn't change.

✦

As the situation escalated and war ravaged the country, some parts of the country were more dangerous than others.

Sarajevo, the capital of Bosnia, was put under siege for 1,425 days, the longest siege in the history of modern warfare. In those 1,425 days, bearded soldiers perched on top of hills directing heavy artillery, mortars, and sniper fire on the civilians below in an attempt to subdue them into capitulation. They cut off roads carrying food and supplies, cut off electricity and running water, then shelled the residents day and night. Men, women, children, and the elderly were targeted equally. In Sarajevo alone, between

1992 and 1996, 11,541 civilians lost their lives. Sarajevans didn't know if they would live one minute to the next.

Thus, the beautiful city that hosted the 1984 Winter Olympic Games became known as the City of Red Roses. No, not those kind of roses—not after the beautiful flower. Throughout the city, roads were pockmarked with mortar shell craters made bloody by the deaths of civilians who simply went to the market that day to buy food. Some happened to run outside for a minute to fill a bucket with drinking water. From above, these craters resembled roses, but in memory of the innocent lives lost, today those holes are filled with red resin.

The city of Banja Luka, where I lived, and surrounding areas were occupied by Serb militia from the start of war in 1992. As Muslims in Serb-occupied territory, we had no law to protect us. At any moment, those same bearded Serbs could break into our house, rape or murder us, and take anything they laid eyes on—jewelry, cash, food, art, anything. We were at their mercy.

As part of Serb's ethnic cleansing campaign, Muslim men of military age were taken from their homes and sent to concentration camps, where they were starved, beaten, tortured, and executed. They destroyed every Muslim religious artifact they could get hold of, and then they went after the mosques.

Banja Luka was home to sixteen mosques, each one between 300 and 400 years old, and each one blown up and leveled in 1993. Ferhadija mosque had great meaning to our family. Located downtown near the main square, close to where I grew up, it had been a World Heritage Site since World War II for its unique beauty and historical importance.

It was also a place dear to my heart. It was here that shortly after my birth, Imam Ibrahim Halilović led a prayer on behalf of my parents in celebration of my birth, asking God to grant me and my parents good health, protect us, and keep me on the right path. He prayed for me to be good to my parents and perfect in righteousness as I grew older. He blessed my name. This ceremony is as customary to Muslim families as a christening is to Christians. It could have been performed at any mosque, but it was deemed a special honor and privilege when performed at Ferhadija, which was considered the epicenter of Islam for Banja Luka natives, and the most beloved mosque.

Blowing it up wiped out centuries of rich fabric of history and culture. The night of the explosion stayed etched in my memory forever. On May 7, 1993, I was awakened by a loud explosion and rattling windows above my bed. Startled, I covered my head with a blanket to protect myself from shattering glass and quietly sobbed into my pillow. Moments later, Dad rushed into my room to see if I was okay.

"They must have just blown up Ferhadija. It sounded like it came from there."

"But why Ferhadija, Dad?" I sobbed as he hugged me.

"I don't know kiddo. I wish this madness would come to an end."

"It's like they just want to wipe us off the face of the earth, like we never existed." I couldn't stop sobbing.

Dad had nothing to say to that. He just hugged me closer.

No one got any sleep that night. Anyone brave enough to stand up to the militia were arrested and taken to concentration camps, where men were beaten, tortured, and starved, and women held as sex slaves and gang raped. Like the Jewish in Germany during World War II, Bosnian Muslims suffered mass executions during the war. The only difference was that Serbs did not use gas chambers. The atrociousness and brutality during the genocide years stretched the limits of human imagination to incomprehensible.

Ripping newborn babies from their crying mother's clutching arms. Babies who cried because they were hungry, because their mothers weren't lactating due to unfathomable stress with no formula to feed them. Shooting those babies. Simply because they were Muslim babies.

Some 200 men—who had spent months enduring beatings and torture at Trnopolje concentration camp near Prijedor—were being loaded onto buses. They were told they were being exchanged for Serb soldiers captured by the Bosnian Army. They were driven to Korićani Cliffs and ordered to exit the buses in small groups of three or four, then to kneel at the edge of the ravine. Serb militia would open fire on them as their lifeless bodies fell down into the abyss. Serbs would then throw hand grenades into the abyss—just in case anyone survived.

Boys as young as fourteen and fifteen—my age at the time—were being taken from their families, tortured, and then executed. While my male Muslim peers lost their lives, the children of fallen Serb fighters were sent to month-long vacations to the coast of Greece. Somehow, a month on the Mediterranean coast was supposed to make up for the fact that these children would now be fatherless, and the men's wives would be widows? A beach vacation could somehow buy their allegiance to the cause—the cause where their neighbors were being exterminated, while those of us who were lucky to survive, were being displaced all over God's green earth.

Suddenly, school names and street names in Banja Luka started getting renamed. Tito's Street was renamed to King Petar I Karadjordjevic—a Serbian King who sought to expand Serbia to neighboring territories in the early 1900s. Part of town called Mejdan got renamed to Obilicevo—a character elevated in Serb folklore, who fought the Turkish army.

As the war reached its peak, the worst massacre of modern-day post-WWII Europe took place in an otherwise quaint Bosnian town of Srebrenica. Even though the area was declared by United Nations as protected and safe from any hostilities or armed attacks, on July 11, 1995, Serb militia attacked the city, massacring over 8,000 civilians—women, children, the elderly, and disabled—over the course of several days, forcing parents to watch as soldiers raped and killed their children, leaving dead bodies on streets. The youngest victim of Srebrenica was a two-day-old baby named Fatima. Afterwards, the Serbs swept the streets with bulldozers, pushing the bodies into mass graves.

✦

Growing up in these times of horror aged me overnight. Instead of worrying about school and tests, I slept with one eye open, fearing the atrocities of war. Living in such fear and knowing the worst that humans were capable of robbed me of my childhood innocence, forcing a level of maturity on me that no child should be required to experience.

As for my parents, their harsh reality was trying to raise two teenage daughters in a country where we didn't know if we would survive to see the next day. Their worst nightmare was that they would wake up to the sound of Serb militia breaking into our house, taking turns gang-raping their daughters in front of them while they were held at gunpoint, powerless to protect us. Entire families fled in the middle of the night to avoid such a fate, sometimes without even saying goodbye to their loved ones. It was safer if fewer people knew of their departure.

Not all Serbs participated in the atrocities. Some were ashamed and didn't want anything to do with the war. They protected their Muslim and Catholic neighbors, often risking their own lives and endangering their whole families by hiding scores of men from capture in their homes. Our neighbors looked out for us. Even in the worst of times, there were good people.

✦

Like my grandmother's Prijedor neighbor, Milan.

Shortly after Mom and Ami moved to Prijedor, the Serb Četnik militia began rounding up all the Muslim men in our neighborhood. They were being taken to the front lines to advance battle lines and dig trenches for Serb soldiers. To them, Muslim men were disposable. When they came for Dad and took him away at gunpoint, I hid in Grandpa Namik's study, shaking in fear. I was terrified for my father. Would they torture and execute him? I was terrified for me. Would they find me and do unspeakable things? I was terrified for everyone I loved. Hours later, when it seemed like it was safe to come out from hiding, I tried to call Mom from the study phone. All I heard was a busy signal. (Later I learned that all Muslim phone lines were blocked.)

I was home alone, hiding and frightened, when word got out on the radio of the ethnic cleansing and massacres of the non-Serb population in Prijedor. That was where Mom and Ami were! I already knew that once the war had begun, Muslim homes in Prijedor had to be marked with white flags, and Muslims walking outside were obligated to wear white armbands. Apparently, things had escalated horribly. Serb militia were going house to house, raping women and children, murdering entire families, torching homes.

In a panic, I desperately tried to reach Mom on the phone and heard nothing but a busy signal. I dialed, got a busy signal, hung up. Dialed, busy signal, hung up. Dialed, busy signal, hung up. I did this over and over again for hours.

I was deeply distressed and in tears, imagining the worst—that they took Dad to a concentration camp to torture and kill him; that Mom and Ami were dead too; that I would never see anyone in my family again. I was truly terrified.

It finally came to me that maybe it was just Muslim phone lines that had been shut down. I remembered a Serb neighbor in Prijedor who had once made a promise to my grandmother that he would protect her and her family. It was his way of repaying an old family debt. His name was Milan. I searched through the phone book for his number, tearing pages as I went. I found it. It seemed that I had guessed right, that the Serbs had severed only Muslim phone lines. The phone rang through on the first try.

"Hello," came Milan's stern voice through the line.

"Hi, this is Annie, BB's daughter," I said in a shaky voice. "I apologize for calling you so late in the day, but I can't get hold of my mom or grandma, and I don't know if they're okay." I burst into tears at the relief of finally reaching an adult.

"Hey Annie. I'm not going to lie. Things are not good here right now. We can't talk on the phone. I was at your grandma's house earlier today, and everyone there is okay. I can't say the same for some of their neighbors, but I'm protecting your family and was planning on checking up on them again in a few minutes. You called me just in time."

Protecting a Muslim family during those times carried grave consequences, so I refrained from asking too many questions over the phone, as the Serb forces were known to listen in.

"Thank you so much, Mr. Milan. You have no idea how worried I've been all day. Please tell my family I love them." I was relieved to know my family had been alive earlier in the day.

"I will. Please call me back in about thirty minutes. I should be home by then and will give you another update."

"Thank you! Thank you so much!" I collapsed into the couch where I was sitting, all energy drained from me.

When I called back after thirty minutes, Milan confirmed my family was alive. "It will be a rough night, but I got in front of the soldiers who were passing by your family's house and told them that house was mine. They should be safe there tonight. Please call again in the morning."

Ami later told me about that night. Several older ladies from the neighborhood had gathered at Grandma's house to spend the night, hoping her two-story house was safer. Everyone slept in the upstairs hallway, hidden under an oversized dining table in case the house got bombed. All night they listened to neighbors across the street shrieking for help in terror, while my then-barely teenage sister Ami stuffed her sobs into a pillow, repeating incoherently, "We're going to die tonight. They're going to kill us all. God, please don't let us die."

With God's grace and Milan's protection, they made it through the night and through the rest of the war, though not without hardship and sacrifice. They rarely left the house, except to pick up humanitarian aid and food. Dad was released after several days with a severe back injury that almost left him paralyzed from the waist down, but he was alive.

Given the dangers and terrors of the war, Mom and Ami returned to Banja Luka, and Mom and Dad reconciled for the sake of the family.

In Banja Luka, we lived a life of daily terror and deprivation, hungry and afraid, not knowing if that day would be the one the Serb militia would storm our home. We lived on daily rations of beans, potatoes, macaroni, and rice, while our front door remained boarded up and reinforced with a metal bar. Power was out for days on end. Mom, Dad, Ami, and I spent our nights playing bridge under a flickering candlelight, MacGyvered out of a small jar of oil, shoelace, and a metal lid.

Finally, like many Muslim and Catholic families in Banja Luka, my parents decided to flee. I was sixteen and Ami thirteen, and we were kept in the dark until the eve of our departure. On a cold, snowy Tuesday night in

January 1995, our parents told us to pack a bag of essentials—toothbrushes, socks, warm jackets and a change of clothes. Late that night, after crying in protest at not being given a chance to say goodbye to my friends, I was allowed to secretly say goodbye to Igor and my parakeet Coco, whom I had to leave behind with our neighbor.

Igor was at a friend's house on the other side of town when he heard the news that my family would be leaving early the next morning. He borrowed a friend's motorcycle and rode it to my house without a license. To say goodbye properly, in person, he sped through frigid cold and fog, with snow covering a thick sheet of ice on the road.

I recall the somber moment in my cold, dark room with only a small candle flickering. The electricity was out again. His eyes didn't sparkle as they usually did. This time, they were filled with tears and sorrow. His lips barely moved when he asked if we should run away together, promising to keep me safe. He removed the gloves from his hands and ran his cold, shaky fingers across my cheeks to wipe away my tears while hugging me tightly and shivering—partly due to cold and partly in disbelief at suddenly being torn apart. He quietly sang the lyrics to "Don't Cry" into my ear. Since early childhood, we had both been big fans of Guns N' Roses.

I hated that moment. I hated being ripped away from everything I had held so dear to my heart, hated saying goodbye and not knowing if I'd ever again see Igor or friends I'd grown up with. The pain of that moment stayed with me forever. We both cried while saying goodbye and held onto each other tightly. I promised to write as soon as I could.

Dad paid a large sum of money to some Serbs on the take for us to be bussed out of Banja Luka to an undisclosed location where we were told we would be allowed to cross the border into Croatian territory.

Still not quite awake and waiting for the sun to rise on this cold, gloomy Wednesday, we showed up as instructed at a furniture showroom building on the outskirts of the city. Inside, a bearded, evil-looking soldier with a stone-cold face and dressed in camo, wearing a furry hat with a Četnik badge of a two-headed eagle pinned to the front of it—the symbol of Serb brutality—pushed my face into the cold wall of the interrogation room looking for cash or valuables. I might have been scared out of my wits had I not been utterly sad and resigned to whatever was about to happen to us.

Mom and Ami were next to me being searched by similar men in a similar way. Mom's stern look silently instructed me and Ami to stay quiet. Dad was taken to another room. All families went through the same search. We weren't allowed to take anything of value with us.

After the interrogation room, we were forcefully escorted into a crowded bus that took us to a peacekeeping zone controlled by the United Nations troops. This UN Zone was nothing more than a narrow strip of land secured by the UN troops between the Serb and Croatian enemy lines. The UN army had put up a military-size tent able to accommodate up to 200 people, meant to house refugees pouring into the camp from Banja Luka and surrounding cities. The camp was surrounded by a barbed wire fence and landmines.

Getting off the bus, I remember a sea of people just as lost and confused as we were being directed towards the tent. An industrial-sized air-heater was at the tent's entry, and an endless sea of bunk beds were set up inside. Inside the tent, it sounded like an overcrowded mall with constant chatter, even during late hours of the night. There seemed to be no privacy anywhere.

This was our new home.

We were taken to our bunk beds and given a pillow, a blanket, and a tarp. I was puzzled by the tarp at first, but it didn't take long to discover its purpose. That evening, as we were about to go to sleep, someone shouted to pull the tarp over our blankets to keep us dry from the water dripping from condensation on top of the tent. We slept in several layers of clothes in addition to our jackets and boots because even hell was frozen over that winter. I never knew how much I appreciated my warm bed at home until I shivered myself to sleep that night, hoping the next day would be better.

That next day I searched for a washroom but found, instead, a row of Porta Potties behind the tent. Behind each door, a thick sheet of ice-covered feces and urine. I shut the door in disgust, unsure if I hesitated because I was afraid of contracting some disease or because it was too cold to take my clothes off. In protest, I turned around and walked back to the tent, where I penned my first letter to Igor.

I was sixteen, couldn't use the toilet, couldn't shower, no longer had the comforts of my own home, my bed, or any privacy. I had been abruptly taken from the life I'd known, my school, my childhood friends, and my love. I was mad as I began writing.

My Dearest Igor,

I'm here in the refugee camp and felt compelled to let you know that we should have run away together. This place is absolutely terrible! No turning back now. I don't really know if and when I can actually mail this letter to you, but I will hold on to it until we're moved someplace else where I can send mail.

I don't want my first letter to you to be all doom and gloom, so here's something I like here. The food. We get these military MRE rations or Meals-Ready-to-Eat. It's a complete meal, with an entrée and a side dish, which you heat up by dipping the whole waterproof bag into warm water. They come in brown, vacuum-sealed plastic bags and every bag is a complete surprise. Some of them have ham, so I trade the ham with someone else or just eat whatever comes on the side. So far, my favorite entree is pasta with marinara sauce and my favorite dessert is the sugar cookie. It's compressed and hard as a brick. One could easily chip a tooth eating it, but it tastes good. You would laugh.

I miss you so much!
With all my love,
Annie

For a kid who grew up comfortably in an affluent family, I didn't complain much about my new living conditions. I was grateful to be alive, unharmed, and safe with my family, a privilege few Bosnian Muslims were granted those days.

There wasn't much to do in the UN Zone other than merely exist and pass time, talk to the other refugees, sit on our beds, and play cards all day. With temperatures often in the low 20s, we wore our winter jackets at all times. There was no place to shower. In full-on survival mode, I soon learned to not even think about such luxuries.

After several weeks, on a random Tuesday, a UN officer dressed in a light blue uniform shouted out names off a list. Our family's name and a few others were called and given fifteen minutes to gather our belongings. We were being moved to a refugee camp in Croatia. I learned later that we stayed in the UN Zone only until the Croatian government approved our transit visas. It would be in the more permanent camp in Croatia that we would wait for another country to approve our refugee visas.

Minutes later, about two dozen of us climbed on the back of a military truck with bench seats covered by a dark green tarp. There was no time to say goodbye to the other refugees we had met there. After several hours of a bumpy ride up and down Croatia's gravel backroads, avoiding enemy lines and minefields, that we found ourselves at a refugee camp named Gašinci near Osijek, Croatia.

With fully functional community bathrooms and running hot water, conditions here were slightly better than the tents in the UN Zone. I took a shower for the first time since we left Banja Luka. I would have thrown away the armpit-stench shirt I wore if I had another one to replace it with. Instead, I soaked it in soap and water and borrowed someone else's shirt until mine dried.

The refugee camp was surrounded by a barbed wire fence, and sanitary conditions, though better than those in the UN Zone, were not exactly top-notch. The food was what I imagine I would have received in a jail cell. But we were happy to be alive, and I met new friends with whom I kept in touch for many years. One of the first was Adem, a grungy-looking kid with the same taste in music as I had. His dirty blond hair down to his chin and blue eyes reminded me of my dearest Igor.

Within days, I ran into a girl I recognized from Banja Luka, Dženeta. As familiar faces in a sea of strangers, Dženeta and I quickly became inseparable. Together we met Mirsad, a good kid about a year older than we were. He was at camp by himself. Since he had no parents, our parents looked out for him. With such good new friends, my days at the refugee camp went by relatively quickly.

Together, we spent many nights sitting on a cold bench outside. The bench looked like a bus stop, with a slanted roof covered in graffiti. We made fun of each other and cracked jokes, shivering in the cold and laughing until dawn. None of us really knew how long we'd be there or where in the world any of us might end up, but we made the best of every day. We were homeless, yet those were some of the best times I had at that time in my life. I learned to savor every moment in life even to this day.

When not with my friends, I wrote letters to Igor almost daily, updating him on the refugee camp and my new friends. I never mailed any of the letters, though. Instead, I saved them in a journal until the war was over and post offices began to deliver mail to Bosnia again.

After five months in Gašinci, our family found a permanent home in San Jose, California through the International Rescue Committee refugee resettlement program, while Dženeta and her family were headed for St. Louis, Missouri. Adem and his family moved to Atlanta, Georgia, and Mirsad went to Minneapolis, Minnesota where he was reunited with his uncle. None of us had a say in where we would end up.

With a wary eagerness, we embarked on the next leg of our journey, happy to be leaving the squalor and uncertainty of the refugee camps, but not entirely sure what the United States had in store for us.

CHAPTER 3

A NEW LIFE
IN THE NEW WORLD

When I came to the United States in May 1995, I spoke very little English. Most of what I learned was from a few years of middle school English classes in Bosnia—and by listening to Guns N' Roses, the Doors, Aerosmith, the Cranberries, and the Beatles. Since I was the only one who could communicate in English even a little, my whole family relied on me to translate and fill out every form known to man—applications for Social Security cards, applications for ID cards, applications for welfare and food stamps, applications for jobs. Our Bosnian neighbors soon asked me to help them fill out applications as well. My English quickly improved, mostly because I had no choice. I was immersed in a new culture with little assistance and many people relying on me to help them navigate the language.

I imagine for some it would be a dream-come-true to live in California, but arriving in Silicon Valley as a sixteen-year-old refugee felt more like a bad dream in which I had been thrown out of an airplane without a parachute to crash-land in a foreign land and hit the ground running while making eggs and waffles for breakfast.

Newly-arrived refugee families were typically assigned a sponsor to help them acclimate to the new culture. Mom's older brother Sulejman, who had arrived in California from another refugee camp in Jordan just two months before us, was our sponsor. Mom's older sister Sadeta and younger brother Edhem, along with their families, were settling in Denmark, but within months, Aunt Sadeta and her family joined us in California, likely because Aunt Sadeta thought money grew on trees in America.

After Mom and Sulejman had a falling out following an incident with a sexual predator, which I will talk about later, Sulejman relocated with his family to Boise, Idaho, and we fell out of contact for a long time. Sadeta stayed in California, but because of her toxic personality, our family had less and less contact with her over time. Mom's mom was still in Bosnia, while both of Dad's parents had passed away. Dad's older brother Mahir and his wife and kids had stayed in Banja Luka. I never considered them family and don't have a single fond memory of them.

When we arrived in America, Uncle Sulejman and his wife Lida greeted us at the airport and brought us back to their two-bedroom apartment in San Jose. To save money on rent, Mom, Dad, Ami, and I were to share the two-bedroom apartment with Uncle Sulejman, Aunt Lida, and their two kids. They showed us to the kitchen where there was four of everything—four spoons, four forks, four knives, four plates, four bowls, four cups, and four glasses. There was one gallon of milk in the fridge, one carton of eggs, Wonder bread, several cans of food, and a few other essentials. We were clearly the interlopers here, one step away from being homeless. At least we had a roof over our heads.

Another Bosnian family living in the apartments told us about summer school and helped us sign up for the English as a Second Language (ESL) program.

ESL classes were an awkward experience. The classroom was overcrowded and consisted of a range of nationalities and age groups, all unable to understand each other. Students used hand gestures to communicate, while the teacher enunciated every word as if we were toddlers. I didn't have much trouble understanding what was being said, but I struggled to put words into cohesive sentences. The pronunciation of certain words was difficult, and I felt like a fool twisting my tongue around these, to me, strange sounds. I dreamed of magically waking up with the knowledge of perfect English.

The ESL teacher was very patient. Over and over again, she pointed to different pictures, pronouncing the words they represented and helping everyone read. I don't remember her name, but I do remember her as the sweet woman who helped me earn my first five dollars in America.

When the summer program was almost completed, our ESL teacher announced she was moving and needed volunteers to help her pack and clean her apartment. She said she could pay each person five dollars. I immediately raised my hand—five dollars seemed like a lot of money to a refugee kid living on welfare and food stamps.

She picked us up the following weekend since we had no transportation. This was the hardest five bucks I'd ever earned. Several of us packed boxes all day and carried them into a truck. Then we scrubbed the apartment clean, so our ESL teacher could get her security deposit back. She was so happy with our work, she offered to take everyone to a fast food place for dinner. Her treat!

I had seen fast food commercials on TV, and I looked forward with excitement to what seemed like the best burgers in the world. I ordered a big hamburger. Hungry after working all day, I sank my teeth into my burger before anyone else even had a chance to unwrap their food. I chewed, waiting for an amazing, mouth-watering miracle. Then I stopped chewing in disgust. I had never tasted anything so awful! To me, the hamburger tasted like a fried sponge. Even the community-pot food at the refugee camp had been better—at least we had real meat.

I was raised to be courteous, though, so I ate about half of the burger, but that's all I could handle. This sandwich gave me serious indigestion. I felt like a brick had lodged in my stomach. It felt wrong to throw away food, though, especially after having survived food shortages during the war in Bosnia. I carefully rewrapped the burger, explaining that I wanted to take half home for my sister. That was the last time I ever had a fast food hamburger.

In our first few months in California, I experienced many such moments of culture shock. One of the biggest was my first visit to a Costco. Big supermarkets weren't really a thing in Bosnia. We bought fresh produce daily from a farmers' market, and we shopped at mom-and-pop stores on every corner for our other groceries—milk, bread, snacks, cigarettes, and so on. We had one shopping mall in Banja Luka about the size of an average department store, with little boutiques, coffee shops, and bakeries.

When I entered Costco for the first time, my eyes went wide open. This one store could supply my whole city of Banja Luka with food, clothes, books, and lawn and garden equipment. Compared to the little shops in Bosnia, Costco was overwhelming with seemingly everything I could ever want stacked to the roof on floor-to-ceiling shelves and on the floor on wooden pallets.

"How do they even get all the way up there?" I thought to myself. It was only later that I put two and two together when I saw forklifts in action.

Everything in America was so large, especially the cars and roads. In Bosnia, the compact European cars could barely make it on the narrow two-way roads.

In retrospect, given my experience, I wouldn't take a recent refugee to Costco first thing. Maybe I would take them to a place the size of a gas station convenience store to slowly ease them into the American way of life.

We recovered from our awe at Costco quickly, however, when we found out how inexpensive cigarettes were there—eleven dollars a carton. We were a family of smokers. Just about everyone in Bosnia smoked, it seemed, and we knew only a few non-smokers. (We were shocked to find out how anti-smoking Americans were.) I had been smoking myself since I was twelve. Costco's cigarettes gave us something that created a bridge to our previous lives, to our culture in Bosnia, and we took full advantage. The Bosnian family next door let us borrow their Costco card anytime we wanted. From that point on, we became regulars, visiting at least once a week to raid the cigarette counter.

During those first few months in America, my mom and dad didn't have a job. Most of our days were spent at home or by the pool chain smoking and drinking coffee, eating watermelon, and baking in the warm California sun. We kids thought Tampico orange juice was a luxury, and we chugged it by the gallon.

Eating watermelon and smoking cigarettes to pass the time soon got old. Within a few months, Dad got restless. Back home in Bosnia, Dad was director of sales, a suit-and-tie kind of guy, who was a great provider. Before the war, our family never went without. In California, however, Dad was unemployable in his profession because he couldn't speak English. We needed welfare and food stamps to get by, which was not our way. Dad had always been honest and hardworking. Providing for his family had been a source of pride and the measure of personal achievement. Being unable to work or provide for his family and taking handouts from the government was humiliating for him. He got to the point where he said he'd rather clean toilets than sit idly at home.

One day I walked into the living room and found Dad sitting on the couch, clearly distraught.

"Dad, what's wrong? You okay?" I asked.

"I just want to jump off the balcony. I'm fed up, and I can't live like this anymore. I need to work!"

His statement hit me like a thousand bricks. I had never seen him like this before, and I wasn't sure how to respond. I asked again what was wrong.

Without really answering, he looked at me, then pointed to the phone book on the credenza on the other side of the room. "Go get that for me, please."

I was puzzled about how jumping off the balcony and the phone book were related but thought it best to go along with him. I quietly walked to the other end of the room and retrieved the thick book.

"Here you go Dad," I said, holding it out for him. "Why do you need it?"

He waved it off and told me to look through the directory for last names ending in "ich" or other forms that could be Bosnian.

"Okay, are we looking for other Bosnian families living nearby? Are you bored? Are you trying to meet new friends?"

"Call these numbers and ask them if they speak Bosnian," Dad said with determination. He looked like a man on a mission, and I wanted to help.

"Okay Dad. What do I do if they don't speak Bosnian?"

"You apologize, tell them you're sorry for bothering them and move on to the next number."

"Okay! And what if they do?"

"Then hand me the phone."

As odd as I thought that was, I did what he asked and called quite a few numbers. For most, no one picked up. I'd reach an answering machine, or they didn't speak Bosnian. When we were just about ready to give up, I found someone who spoke Bosnian! I handed Dad the phone.

"Hello, Sir. My name is Zahid. Thank you so much for taking my call," my father humbly said in Bosnian. "I am a refugee, and I'm looking for a job. I don't speak English, which is why I had my daughter call. I don't have a car, and I don't even know how to begin looking for employment here. We just got here a few months ago and don't know anyone. I don't know what to do. Do you know anyone who would hire me? I'm willing to do anything."

Suddenly, I was proud of my father's creativity—he was not the one to sit around and feel sorry for himself. This is why he was a sales director in Bosnia.

Bobby—the gentleman on the line—was caught off guard at the bold request, but soon recovered. Fortunately for Dad and our family, it turned out that Bobby was a general contractor whose business was taking off. He needed laborers. Bobby said he couldn't pay Dad much, but he was willing to give him a chance for a couple of days. He agreed to pick Dad up the next day at our apartment building, and just like that, Dad landed himself his first job in America!

Dad never forgot Bobby's willingness to take a chance on him. Later in life he often reflected on that day, observing, "When you're down, and it seems like there's no hope for tomorrow, a simple, random act of kindness from a complete stranger can change your entire outlook on life."

Maybe he really would have jumped off the balcony had he not found work. Fortunately, we'll never know.

Dad proved to be a hard worker, and Bobby kept him on full time. He was paid $50 for a twelve-hour shift, and he worked every day, including Saturdays and most Sundays. Never once did he complain about the long hours, that he was underpaid, or that he had had gone from a suit-and-tie job to hard labor. He was simply grateful for the opportunity and felt forever indebted to Bobby. They became lifelong friends. Dad's positive attitude in the face of this challenge served as a powerful lesson to me, one that I took to heart all my life.

✦

Between May and September of 1995, we had moved three times. From our first apartment in West San Jose where we stayed with Uncle Sulejman for several weeks, we moved to a slightly larger two-bedroom apartment in Mountain View, sharing it again with Uncle Sulejman and his family. The move to Mountain View came after our newly-met family friend Pervan insisted we move close to him so he could help our family out with transportation and other things, since Pervan had a car and we still did not.

Pervan was a middle-aged Bosnian man with partially gray hair and a receding hairline. He wore thick glasses, the kind that made his eyes appear small and beady behind the lenses. He was married with two kids. His daughter was only a year older than me but had already married an Arab man who made her wear a burka and rarely allowed her to visit her parents. I saw her once while we lived in Mountain View. Pervan's son was a few years younger than me and still lived at home.

Pervan consistently helped our family by chauffeuring us around. After several months of this, we had developed a certain level of trust in him. It only seemed natural for me to jump into his car one day when he offered to show me an American car wash. I had only seen them in movies and was excited to see one firsthand. It was an ordinary day, and I made small talk with Pervan on the way there about how much I missed my friend Dženeta from the refugee camp, and how I was hoping to find a job soon and save enough money to visit her in St. Louis.

As we pulled up to the car wash, out of the blue, Pervan offered to buy me a roundtrip plane ticket to St. Louis. This sounded a little strange to me. Pervan had his own family, so why was he offering all this help to us? I smiled and let him know I couldn't accept such an expensive gift, not after everything he had done for us already.

The car moved to the conveyor belt, and we entered the car wash. Spray nozzles immediately covered the front and back of the car and all four windows with white foam, completely encapsulating the car. Large rollers descended, accompanied by the loud whirring noise of the machinery. That's when, now that we were hidden away from the rest of the world, Pervan reached behind my head and pulled me closer to him, his lips puckered for a kiss. I froze, shocked that this older, unattractive man with jowls, bad breath, and two kids of his own thought he could just kiss me like that—and that I would even want to kiss him!

In a spontaneous reaction, I shoved the palm of my hand into his lower jaw a split second before his lips touched mine, sending his glasses flying. "What is wrong with you?" I yelled.

His glasses landed between his seat and the transmission and lodged there. As Pervan frantically dug for them, I moved as far away from him as I could, my shoulder blade pressing against the cold window. Afraid that no one could hear me over the noise, even if I screamed, I mentally prepared for whatever battle might ensue. I sure as hell wasn't about to let this pervert put his filthy hands on me without giving him a bloody lip or a black eye.

Either he realized his mistake or figured out we would be out of the car wash and in broad daylight in minutes, at which point I would have the opportunity to run from the car screaming. After retrieving his glasses and calmly putting them back on, Pervan placed both his hands on the steering wheel and pretended nothing happened.

With trepidation, I remained silently seated in the car, praying Pervan would take me home. I didn't know where we were, had no way of contacting my parents, or finding my way home on my own. Minutes later, we stopped at a red light. Pervan said quietly, "We're not going to tell anyone what happened back there."

"Can you please just take me home?" I insisted.

In the dreadful silence of the ride home, I realized why Pervan had been so eager to ingratiate himself with our family—he was a sexual predator. That had been a narrow escape.

Sickened with disgust and never one to stay quiet, as soon as we arrived at our apartment building, I dashed out of the car and ran home in tears. When my parents asked me what was wrong, I told them everything.

"That bastard!" Dad shouted, then left the apartment to talk to Pervan, I presumed. Mom comforted me in a loving embrace, wiping my tears as they streamed down my cheeks.

Within days, Mom and Dad packed our belongings and moved us from Mountain View back to San Jose. From that point on, we had no more contact with Uncle Sulejman either. In the days prior, Aunt Lida, eavesdropping on Ami's telephone conversation with one of her friends, overheard Ami call Uncle Sulejman an a-hole for not believing me and taking our side. Aunt Lida called Mom out on it. The whole family had a big falling-out, and we never reconciled from it.

✦

Mom, Dad, Ami, and I moved into a two-bedroom apartment in San Jose. I liked it there and felt safe. After months of sharing a room with my sister and two cousins, I had to share a room only with Ami. Several Bosnian families lived in the same apartment complex, and we quickly made friends with them. August was coming to an end, and I was starting my senior year at Prospect High School.

We were still without transportation, as were many of the other Bosnian families in the neighborhood. All of us Bosnian kids walked a couple of miles to and from school every day. As part of our after-school routine, we became regulars at a nearby grocery store. Penniless, we weren't there to shop. We were there for the grocery carts. We paired up, with one of us hopping into the grocery cart while the other pushed. Then we switched off until we arrived home. We didn't pay much attention to the signs warning that carts belong to the store and are not to be removed.

Before long, every Bosnian family in the neighborhood had their own cart parked in front of their apartment buildings instead of a car.

The grocery store soon caught on to us, however, and sent out a truck to drive around neighborhoods to collect the carts and return them to the store. We hated the drivers for taking our carts, as we thought of them as ours. We justified ourselves by telling each other we needed them more than the grocery stores did. The store had plenty of other carts, didn't they?

I imagine the drivers weren't too happy with us, either. They were only trying to do their job, and we were always trying to outsmart them. Instead of leaving carts on the street, we hid them behind apartment buildings and in bushes. We joked that Bosnian refugees across the United States could be thanked for pushing grocery stores to install sensors and locking wheels on their carts to prevent them from being taken out of the parking lot.

✦

Shortly after Dad landed his first job in America and my sister and I began school, Mom got bored at home alone. She was not the type of woman to sit around all day long, sipping coffee and socializing with other unemployed Bosnian women. She was as hardworking, strong, and independent as Dad, and she felt as if she wasn't contributing enough to the household, so she decided to look for work herself. Soon enough she found a new job as a housekeeper. As with Dad, this was a step down from her job in Bosnia.

In Bosnia, Mom was a mechanical engineer for a factory that made everything from windshield wipers to TVs. Mom talked about that job as if it had been the best thing ever, with eight weeks of paid vacation, guaranteed summer and winter bonuses, fully paid medical insurance with 100 percent coverage, and a year of fully paid maternity leave. Going from that to cleaning houses without benefits was quite a demotion, but like Dad, Mom didn't speak much English. Making money doing anything was better than sitting home doing nothing.

Meanwhile, Mom practiced her English skills, which led to several funny family stories we would tell over and over.

Mom and I always made the best of every situation, trying to show a friendly face to the world. One weekend, walking back to our apartment from the laundry room, we walked by a man who smiled at us. Mom smiled back in greeting, but instead of saying "Hi," she said "Bye."

Trying not to laugh, I asked her in Bosnian, "Mom, do you know how to say 'Hello' in English?"

She replied to me in Bosnian: "Yes, I do. 'Bye.' Right?"

Laughing, I explained that she had gotten her Hi's and Bye's mixed up. She joined in the laugher, and we both laughed hard. While still in tears, I asked Mom to pronounce the word strawberry, her most challenging tongue twister. After several failed attempts, we guffawed even louder, holding our bellies until we almost peed.

A positive attitude towards life makes everything easier. It certainly helped Mom with her new job cleaning houses. God bless those who clean other people's messy kitchens and baked-on grease, wipe pubic hairs and urine stains off dirty toilets, tidy up messy rooms, empty out garbage, vacuum an entire house and wipe off dust, all in a few short hours. House cleaners are everyday heroes no one ever talks about. It pains me to see how immigrants sometimes are portrayed as people who come to the United States to "steal American jobs." The jobs my parents took were jobs no one else wanted. I grew up witnessing firsthand a whole community of Bosnian refugees taking on the worst imaginable jobs, working hard to survive.

Mom never complained, but I could see the strain on her face some days. She would come home after a twelve-hour workday and scrub her hands clean in the bathroom for fifteen minutes straight. On days like that, she couldn't even look at food. I knew not to ask her any questions. But if it meant that her family wouldn't have to go without, she didn't even think about quitting, not even on the hard days. All I could do to help was to teach her English and make her laugh.

My parents didn't just talk about integrity, respect, hard work, taking advantage of every opportunity, and never, never giving up—they led by example. They showed Ami and me what each of those meant in practice. While they both worked extremely hard to give Ami and me the best life possible, neither of them ever asked for anything in return. They wanted Ami and me to focus on our education, so we wouldn't have to work the jobs they were working in America, so we could eventually go back home to Bosnia with our globally-recognized American diplomas. Dad always talked about living in America as a temporary thing. He wanted us to go back home after the war was over and the political situation hammered out. After his first solo visit to Bosnia four years later, he saw the devastation left by the war and changed his mind about returning.

When you're raised by parents like mine, it's not an option to become a failure and disappointment. The least I could do was live up to their expectations.

Lucky for me, school learning came naturally. Even as a young child, I had an unquenchable thirst for knowledge. Growing up, Mom often teased me about my never-ending why's and a million how's a day. Before the war, I competed with my classmates Meli, Sabina, Emina, and Sara, over who got better grades and more straight A's.

As a struggling refugee, I really wasn't an ordinary teenager with a normal life. The only normalcy open to me was the academic part of school. Especially once I conquered English, it was much easier to study and learn than to try to fit in with the Americans at school. They were obsessed with the newest trends and fashions, while I still wore the same old clothes I had brought from Bosnia.

Because I was still finding my way in a new country, I was the shy kid at Prospect High, though respectful and kind to anyone who went out of their way to talk to me. Other than these brief encounters, I was virtually invisible. I felt uncomfortable talking about the war and explaining where I had come from. As a result, I never initiated contact and hung out only with other Bosnian kids. While other kids went to pep rallies, school dances, and football games, I kept to myself. Other than being sent to the principal's office once for wearing an I'm Going Nucking Futs T-shirt, I sailed through senior year of high school unnoticed.

My parents wouldn't even let me think about skipping college to get a job after graduation. Everyone in my family had a higher education.

"No child of mine will be skipping college!" Dad ranted periodically. "Education is investing in yourself and your future. If you won't invest in yourself, why should anyone else?"

Dad also had a lot to say when the time came for me to pick a major in college. "Since you learned French in high school, and you speak English and Bosnian, you should study International Business in college. Languages are your thing; you learn quickly," Dad insisted, even though I only had one semester of French and could barely understand the basics.

"Ananas ne parle pas," I said to demonstrate my French-speaking skills.

"What? What does that mean?" he asked.

"Pineapple don't speak," I translated. "That's literally the only French I know. Besides, I really want to go to med school."

"No one in our family went to med school—it'll be too hard for you."

The man spoke. Therefore, it was settled. Back then, of course, I blindly followed Dad's wishes. It's how we were raised. So I chose International Business as my major because that's what Dad wanted.

Several mandatory economics classes later, I was failing college. I wasn't stupid, but there were basic things I didn't know, like what the stock market was.

"Stock market? What does that mean?" I asked during one of my classes.

"It's the stock exchange. It's when you own a share of the company you choose to invest in. Your assignment is to pick three stocks and pretend that you're investing a thousand dollars. Over the course of this class, you'll chart and track your progress. At the end of class, we'll see if your stocks made or lost money," the professor explained.

"We'll track what? And how do we track it?" I whispered to a student sitting next to me, who looked at me like I was an alien from outer space.

"In the newspapers," he replied.

"Argh." I was beyond frustrated, thinking to myself, "What does a refugee kid from Bosnia know about the U.S. stock market? Absolutely nothing! Nor do I care. Dad's the economics guy, not me! I give up."

Instead of trying to figure out the stock market and focusing on my assignments, I daydreamed about Igor. In about May 1996, the situation in the former Yugoslavia began stabilizing. The postal service and phone lines were operational again in Bosnia, making it possible to call home and mail all those letters I wrote. While I sent the letters immediately, it took me a few weeks to muster up the courage to call Igor. More than a year had passed since we had seen or talked to each other. I reached out to my friend Natasha to ask about him.

"I'm not going to lie to you; he's with someone. Also, he started hanging out with some really bad crowd after you left. We think he's using," Natasha's voice cracked over the phone.

"Using what? What are you talking about?"

"Heroin," she said. That shocked me.

Every kid reacted differently to traumas of war, loss, and separation from family members and childhood friends, developing their own coping mechanisms. Some fought to survive, and some sought to forget and drown out their pain and sorrows. One thing is true, everyone from my generation carried scars. I didn't want to judge Igor, but news of him using drugs broke my heart, not only because I never got over him, but also because he was a good kid and a friend. He came from a good home. He had a big heart and a beautiful soul.

I remember sitting on a bench on campus, scribbling into a notebook all the things I wanted to say to him when I finally called him and heard his voice. I wrote one thing, then ripped the paper out and threw it away. I wrote something else and threw that away too. I wanted to tell him that I loved him and that I had missed him more than I could ever put into words, but I didn't know how to. What do I say after so much time had passed? I literally couldn't put it into words.

When I finally called him and heard his voice for the first time in forever, we both silently waited for the other person to say something first. I never told him I still loved him. He never said it to me either. We didn't have to. Our love was still very much there, though stifled by the distance of two continents, the entire Atlantic Ocean, and the fact that he had a new girl.

"She's nothing like you," he tried to explain. "I missed you, and I was lonely after you left. She was there, but I don't really care about her." He made long pauses between sentences as he emphasized words, like he had been feeling guilty.

I couldn't really hold his honesty against him. "I missed you too. I wrote you letters but couldn't send them until recently. I hope you get them soon.' I changed the subject. "I started college. I'm not doing so well in school, though. I don't like any of my classes."

"Why don't you like them? You should take advantage of the opportunities you're given. If you don't like what you're doing, try something different. I want you to be happy."

Although my heart was metaphorically separated from my body and residing on another continent over 6,000 miles away, I promised Igor I would do better at school. He promised me he'd kick his drug habit and get clean.

*

Most of my college homework required work typed on a computer and printed out. We didn't have a personal computer at home, and I didn't want to ask my parents for one because we didn't have enough money. Instead, I used the college library computers, which meant longer hours at school and less time to study at home. My parents recognized the struggle and one day took me shopping for a new PC.

My first computer came with America Online dial-up and set my parents back $1,600. I still don't know how they were able to afford it, but when we first brought it home, it made me feel like an astronaut with a spaceship computer.

I unboxed the bulky monitor and PC, then scampered around my bedroom, hooking up cables, connecting the keyboard and mouse, excited to launch my spaceship. The first thing I heard was the sound of AOL dial-up modem attempting to connect to the Internet through a phone line: "Pssssh-hhhtweeekkkk-shhhhweeeeekkhhkkshhh. Welcome!" These were the early sounds of a successful connection to the Internet.

I was the only Bosnian kid I knew, besides Ami, who experienced the first days of Internet. She sat next to me in awe the whole time. Within days, I discovered the online world. The only thing separating me and the online world was my school work and whenever one of my family members picked up the phone to make a call. That automatically disconnected me from the Internet, prompting another dial-up call to AOL. From that day forward, I became a tech geek.

My favorite thing to do online was frequent an old-school Internet Relay Chat program where I later discovered a chat room called Bosnia. This was before fancy social media apps like Facebook Messenger, Skype, Viber, or WhatsApp allowed kids to quickly find one another and video chat regardless of the distances separating them. The closest thing we had in the mid-nineties were chatrooms, which you logged into and typed your messages back and forth. This technology enabled kids like me to connect with others in real time, particularly long-lost friends from Bosnia, who were, by then, scattered around the globe.

As my computer skills in Internet chat rooms improved, my college grades rapidly declined. Back then, due to my parent's low income, the only way I could afford college tuition was through a financial aid program. I needed to keep at least a "C" average to stay in the program, but my average was lower than that. Mom and Dad didn't know my grades were slipping to the point I was sure to lose my financial aid. I didn't have the heart to disappoint them after everything they had done for Ami and me.

I decided to take Igor's advice. While I disliked all my classes related to International Business, I thoroughly enjoyed technology classes. I spoke to a guidance counselor, and she recommended I major in Computer Science instead.

Switching majors was not particularly hard, but convincing my dad was quite an undertaking. Dad was adamant about staying the course and getting a degree in business. After all, he was a businessman, so I should be one too (a businessperson, at least). He knew one could earn a steady income with a business degree, whereas Computer Science was a completely unknown field for him. Dad wasn't convinced I would be able to make a decent living majoring in Computer Science. Mom supported any decision I made, as long as it made me happy. It took some negotiating, but eventually Dad gave me his blessing.

Dad had been right about one thing though. I was good at languages, and computer programming was nothing if not language based. In fact, for me, computer languages—C++, Java, Visual Basic—were a lot easier to learn than French or the stock market indexes. I was a natural when it came to writing software code, calculating statistical equations, and solving difficult calculus and math problems. My grades quickly soared from there.

With something to prove to my dad and all the Bosnian gossip ladies who said a Computer Science degree would not get me far in life, I fast-tracked my studies, quickly earning an associate degree in Computer Science as well as the credits to transfer to a four-year university. It took me eighteen months.

At twenty years old and fresh out of college, I was ready to enter the corporate world full time. It's not that I was in a rush to have the responsibility of a job; it was more that I wanted to start making my own money and help my parents out financially. I knew my parents would never accept money from me, so I approached Mom with a proposition. "Ami and I want to start shopping at the mall and wear nicer clothes, like other kids our ages. We no longer consider ourselves impoverished and want our clothes to reflect that. Shopping for clothes at Goodwill is definitely not cool. If I made my own money, you would no longer have to worry about spending so much money on us."

Mom agreed, but said, "Under one condition, that you will continue your education and get a bachelor's degree."

I gave Mom my word that I would.

Sadly, I broke that word, and it may have been the only promise to my mom I didn't keep. The year I graduated from the associate program, Ami and I planned a visit to Bosnia, the first one since we left. I was accepted into a four-year program and shortly after that, Ami and I had headed to Bosnia. By the time we had returned, the deadline to register for classes had passed. I made the same mistake twice, with spring and fall registration. In the break before the next registration, I landed my first full-time job and never went back to school, something I always regretted.

✦

Oh, and that trip to Bosnia led to Ami and me both getting married.

I had met Alen online in one of the Bosnia internet chat groups. He lived in Sarajevo, and we spent countless hours chatting online and joking around. We became great friends. When Ami and I travelled to Bosnia for the first time after the war, we visited family in Sarajevo for a few days, making plans to meet up with Alen. We arrived to several feet of snow, a thick sheet of ice, and temperatures in the low 20s.

Knowing I would be accompanied by my sister, Alen decided to bring someone to the meetup—his best buddy Hamza. At first, Hamza and Ami were not particularly fond of one another. Hamza was convinced that Ami was a spoiled brat from California who couldn't handle a little bit of Bosnian winter. Meanwhile, Ami the daredevil found Hamza too boring when he ordered fruity strawberry juice at the bar when everyone else was getting liquor.

While the two bickered, Alen and I were having a grand time, so much so that when it was time to leave Sarajevo, I asked him and Hamza to travel to Banja Luka with us so we could spend more time together. Hamza and Ami eventually buried the hatchet, and to everyone's surprise, began dating.

When our party of four arrived at Banja Luka, word got out quickly that I was in town. Of the many people who called that evening to set up time to hang out, I only wanted to see one person—Igor. We had remained friends since that first time I had called him from the United States and kept in touch over the years, but we hadn't seen each other since I had left about five years before. Igor was always with a new girlfriend, and this time was no exception. Our friendship, though, remained unchanged. When he found out I was in Banja Luka, he demanded to see me.

We met for dinner that same night—Igor, his girlfriend, Alen and I. I wasn't sure what to expect. I wanted to see him for old times' sake, even if just as friends. Igor and I never needed words to communicate. We could simply look into each other's eyes and every feeling, every memory we shared from the past came rushing back in a heartbeat, even our first kiss by the river. We knew we secretly still harbored feelings for one another, yet out of respect to our companions that evening, not once did either of us bring up the past. We stuck to lighter topics and caught up. I knew he had gotten clean, but it felt good to see him in person doing well and to know that he was all right, even if he wasn't with me. I just wanted him to be happy. His new girlfriend seemed nice, but clearly didn't know about Igor and me. Neither did Alen, for that matter.

As the evening came to an end, Igor's girlfriend and Alen exchanged pleasantries. Igor used the opportunity to grab my jacket off the chair and hold it up for me to put on. Giving me one last hug before we parted, he discreetly whispered into my ear, "I wish it was me taking you home tonight."

"Me too!" I whispered back, as Alen's hand reached for my elbow to ask if I was ready to leave.

That night, when I went to bed, I thought about Igor all night, as I had many previous nights since I had left Bosnia. A big part of me wanted nothing more than to call him in the middle of the night, ask him to meet me somewhere alone, and rekindle the flame that was clearly still burning. I knew he would do anything for me. Another part of me (admittedly smaller) thought about his girlfriend. I didn't want to be the cause of anyone's heartbreak. Tossing and turning in bed as the first rays of dawn's sunlight creeped into the room, I decided it was best to leave things as they were. The next day, I began dating Alen.

Alen and I stayed in touch through the chatroom, and Ami and I returned to Bosnia six months later during summer break. We stayed for three months, spending our entire summer with Alen and Hamza. I didn't plan on getting married that summer—not without my parent's blessing or knowledge. Deep in my heart, I felt it was always supposed to be me and Igor, but he seemed happy with someone else. Marrying Alen never felt right—but I did it anyway. Self-sabotage was my go-to trauma response.

Five days before Ami and I left for California, Hamza, Ami, Alen and I eloped. We tied the knot in a small ceremony at City Hall in my hometown of Banja Luka. We didn't have a fancy wedding ceremony. We didn't even have wedding dresses, barely a ring and a witness. Dad would later be heartbroken when he found out, robbed of the opportunity to walk his daughters down the aisle.

When we returned to States, Alen began acting irrationally. Jealous and controlling, he demanded I stop going out with friends and spend all my free time chatting online and on the phone with him. That brought about conflict and arguments, expensive ones considering our telephone bill was more than $500 every month. I quickly realized marrying him was a grave mistake and asked for a divorce or an annulment. He refused to sign the papers. I didn't have the funds at the time to hire an attorney to pursue the divorce legally, so I decided to carry on with my life like I was no longer married until he agreed to release me from the marriage. That would come several years later. Until then, I stopped calling him, and he eventually stopped harassing me. Other than immediate family and a few close friends, out of embarrassment, I didn't tell anyone I was married.

Meanwhile, Ami and Hamza's love blossomed, and they continued to rack up the telephone bill until they were reunited again. I gained a brother-in-law, and that made me happy.

CHAPTER 4

THE WORKING LIFE

By the early 2000s, Mom and Dad were both employed at the same manufacturing company. Dad was still a laborer, working for the company's facilities group. Mom became a quality control inspector for the printed circuit boards department. As my parents' English had improved, so had their salaries. By then, they owned a three-bedroom condo in the heart of Silicon Valley. Mom sold some stock from her company's employee stock purchase program and used the money to buy brand new cars for Ami and me. We even had health benefits through their employer and were living comfortably as middle-class almost-Americans. We were still legal aliens, on our way to becoming naturalized citizens a year later. Our Medicare, welfare, and food stamps days were long behind us.

I was still on my break from college and looking for a job. Getting hired without any previous work experience proved to be a bigger challenge than I thought it would be. The companies I applied to were all looking for someone with experience. How does a kid fresh out of college gain experience if no one wants to hire them? Luckily for me, Dad was a good worker and had made friends with some higher-ups where he worked. Someone helped pull a few strings to arrange an interview for me with one of the managers on the Help Desk, and I was hired to an entry-level position.

My first job was to sort documents alphabetically in a filing cabinet. Not exactly high-level work, but I was determined to make a name for myself. Within two weeks of starting, one of the night-shift employees abruptly resigned, which created an opening for an IT Help Desk agent. I saw this as my chance. Without hesitation, I boldly walked up to my supervisor and said, "I want to help out! I want to be considered for the Help Desk position, and I'm more than capable of handling the added responsibilities given my background in computer science."

He hesitated but opted to give a newbie a chance. Instead of risking being short-staffed, he said, "I'll be interviewing for his replacement, but we can try it out for two weeks." Then he warned me, "It will be temporary, just until we find someone else."

"Yes, sir. I understand," I replied, while thinking to myself, Yes! My proverbial foot is in the proverbial door. My supervisor didn't know that this refugee kid from Bosnia was not about to let a good opportunity slide by. I worked hard and stayed long hours. I took the time to address every issue and develop personal relationships. I had the quickest issue resolution times of anyone else on the desk. Before long, my supervisor was so impressed, he turned my two-week assignment into a permanent Help Desk position. I even got a pay raise.

Small victories in corporate America made me hungry for more. I learned as much as I could about the job. Volunteering to help others and late nights at the office led to other promotions—first to team lead, then to supervisor, and eventually to manager. Becoming a manager was surreal. I was the youngest person there, and I was everyone's boss! I had always been mature for my age, but this was a great honor and privilege—and responsibility.

With a better title came a better paycheck, as well as more responsibilities. My boss began sending me out on travel assignments, weeklong trips to different cities. This refugee-kid from Bosnia did not turn anything down. I wanted to see as much of the world as possible, and I eagerly took on every opportunity for a company-paid flight, hotel, rental car, and meals.

✦

I travelled for work a lot, but I travelled for pleasure, too, usually accompanied by Ami.

In the summer of 2001, I had been travelling more and more for work and burning out a bit. I needed a break, so I asked Ami out of the blue one day if she was up for a trip on my dime. She was unemployed at the time, and I had a good income with few expenses, since I was still living with our parents.

Ami wanted New York City. "Let's go to The Big Apple! Can you imagine? Times Square, Manhattan, what do you think?"

"Meh, I don't know, Ami. Lots of walking in a big city doesn't sound like a relaxing vacation to me. I was thinking more like a beach. What about Hawaii? Sounds of the ocean, warm sand in our toes, lying out in the sun all day."

"Hawaii sounds good too. I mean, you're paying, so it's your call."

I just wanted to be lazy and not worry about work, deadlines, or projects. All I wanted to worry about was keeping a steady supply of sunblock. Just thinking about it brought serenity, reminding me of the month-long summer vacations we took as children with Mom and Dad on the Adriatic Sea. We were carefree then. The juice of the fresh peaches dripped down our arms as we ate them, and we would laugh while washing off in the warm waters of the Adriatic. We chose Hawaii. For two Bosnian refugees in their early twenties, a week on a beach in Waikiki would be a dream come true.

When we arrived at the airport, we received a warm welcome from the local tour guides in charge of our transport to the hotel. They seemed surprisingly happy, laid-back, and in no particular rush to get anywhere. As they gave us fresh Hawaiian leis, beautiful white and pink flowers strung together to be worn around our necks, one of the friendly tour guides exclaimed, "Alooooha! Welcome cousins! We are all family here. If this is your first time in Hawaii, this lei symbolizes love, peace, friendship, and the spirit of Aloha."

Hawaii abounded with hospitality, and I instantly knew I would fall in love with the tropical paradise. Listening to the locals talk about different meanings of Aloha brought a smile to my face—hello and goodbye, peace, kindness, love, compassion, living in harmony, sending and receiving positive energy. It reminded me of the Bosnian rahatluk as a way of life—the art of enjoyment and delectation, where nothing was ever rushed, and we took the time to enjoy life in all its simple pleasures. In Hawaii, Aloha was all around us and made me feel good. From the minute we landed in Honolulu, we were transformed by a new world and the warm, welcoming nature of the islanders.

Our first few days were exhilarating. We spent the days at the beach, and strolled through the Waikiki shopping district at night. The air in Waikiki smelled of fresh, salty ocean water and heavenly scented plumeria. It was my first time seeing these elegant flowers, which grew on trees adorned by large dark-green, veiny leaves. They were everywhere and came in delicate colors—white, yellow and shades of pink. Ladies wore plumeria flowers in their hair.

Everything was exotic in Hawaii. Different varieties of banana plants decorated the streets with their oversized leaves. The sweet scent of jasmine flowers filled the air. Large banyan trees in the nearby park astonished us with their thick long roots descending from the branches to the ground. Extremely agile, fluorescent-green geckos, with red stripes across their heads like war paint, jumped from one root to another, taking residence in its shelter. Ami and I had never seen anything like it.

We stayed at the Outrigger Reef on the Beach, an open, airy, and relaxing oceanfront resort with stunning views of the sunset and gentle Hawaiian music reverberating through the lobby. A beachfront restaurant, Shorebird, offered stunning views of Waikiki beach while we ate, as well as the Pacific Ocean and Diamond Head, the crater of an extinct volcano and the crown jewel of Waikiki. Shorebird became our favorite spot for breakfast, lunch, and dinner, as we tried out the different dishes on the menu.

Halfway through the vacation, Ami and I were sitting at dinner, eating teriyaki burgers, and discussing our food. We found it a rather odd pairing of meat and grilled pineapple, topped off with sweet teriyaki sauce, which we were trying for the first time. This was a far reach from our typical Bosnian cuisine. Our taste buds were not used to the tropical flavors, but the food was delectable. Fresh pineapple, locally grown on the island, was perfectly ripe, juicy, and sweet—just as those peaches we ate on hot summer days we spent on the Adriatic coast. Our first visit to Hawaii was perfect.

That same night, a group of loud young men took over the restaurant's bar. Surrounded by laid-back vacationers and islanders enjoying a nice, quiet meal, these six or seven guys were drinking and laughing, their voices reverberating throughout the room. No one really complained as they just seemed to be having fun. We tried to ignore them while we finished our meal, when out of nowhere, a waiter approached our table, carrying two glasses with drinks we had not ordered. He pointed to the group at the bar as the source of our libations. We thanked the waiter and sent the drinks back, letting them know that Ami was married. Several minutes later, the braver of the loud boys made their way to our table.

Louie introduced himself first and sat next to me, without asking permission. I found his boldness and confidence intriguing. We exchanged jokes as if we had known each other for years. He explained that they were U.S. Navy sailors and were staying at our hotel for a few days after being deployed at sea for the larger part of the year. They were in the final stretch of deployment, heading home to their families in San Diego.

The jokes kept coming and our nice, quiet dinner turned into a party. We called them the Navy boys, and they called us the Bosnian chicks. Hours went by quickly. It was getting late when Ami excused herself to call Hamza. Louie wanted to continue hanging out.

"If you're up for it, we can take a drive up to Diamond Head. I rented a Mustang."

I asked Ami if she cared if I went with Louie.

"You guys have fun." She smiled at me, then turned to Louie. "Bring her back at a decent hour."

"Well then, sister approves!" I said. "And how often do I get a chance to see a volcano? Sounds fun! Let's do it."

The group disbanded, and Louie and I made our way to the front lobby. The valet delivered the Mustang, a white convertible. I had never ridden in a convertible before. After we hopped inside the car, he lowered the top and turned up the music on the radio—the high-energy trance, "Sandstorm" by Darude. It all seemed so surreal and Hollywood-like. I was awed that it was all happening to me. As he sped through the city, I felt both a rush of adrenaline and fear of getting pulled over by the police. When we hit a bump in the road, we went airborne. I raised my arms as if I was on a rollercoaster. My first ride in a convertible was nothing short of exhilarating.

Once we arrived at the crater, we saw that the gate to the visitor center was closed. Since we couldn't get in, Louie parked the car just outside the gate, and we got out to revel in the view. I felt like a girl in a movie out on an evening filled with laughter, a thrill ride to the crater, with the two of us alone, overlooking the beautiful moonlit shores of Hawaii, breathing in the sweet scent of plumerias on the gentle breeze. It was the most romantic experience I had to that point. I felt an undeniable urge to kiss him.

Cue in the lone park ranger on duty, who interrupted our dreamy moment to tell us we weren't allowed to park outside the gate after closing. Louie apologized, then started a conversation with the guard, something about aliens. The ranger stood his ground, though, and we soon realized he wasn't going to leave us alone. Disappointed, we decided to call it a night and head back to the hotel. At the hotel, we said our goodnights, making no plans to see each other again.

✦

The next day, Ami and I spent the day at the beach, coming back to our room in the afternoon to shower and prepare for the sunset dinner cruise we were both looking forward to. I was sitting on the floor in front of a floor-to-ceiling mirror on the closet door applying makeup when someone knocked on our door. Ami and I looked at each other puzzled, not expecting anyone. Who could our mysterious knocker be?

I looked through the peephole and to my surprise, saw Louie standing on the other side of the door with a friend and a grin on his face. I panicked! I ran back where Ami was sitting and whispered. "Oh my God, Ami, it's him. It's him! It's Louie! He has a friend with him! What should we do? What should we do?" As much as I enjoyed my time with Louie the night before, I hadn't expected him to come looking for me the next day and wasn't ready for it.

"Well, I'm pretty sure they already heard us talking, so you should probably open the door and see what they want," Ami said matter-of-factly. "Also, try not to look so freaked out."

"Okaaaay, but we don't have time to hang out. We have to go. Right?"

"Yeah, but you don't want to be rude. He seems like a decent guy, and judging from the looks of it, he might have a thing for you, since he's out there standing in front of our door." Ami winked.

I gave in and opened the door.

"Bosnian Chicks!" Louie said laughing.

"Hey, what's up Louie? Mark? What are you guys doing here?"

"Oh, we just came over to hang out. Is that okay?" Mark said casually, making his way inside our room.

"That's fine, come on in. But you guys can't stay long. We have to leave soon. We have this dinner cruise thing we booked a few days ago and can't be late, or they'll leave without us."

"Okay, no worries. Can we hang out with you until you leave? We brought Jack and Coke," Louie said, grinning. He made his way to the sink and poured out half a bottle of Coke, then refilled the bottle with Jack Daniels.

I burst out laughing. "You guys are unbelievable. Are you hanging out at Shorebird again tonight?"

"Yeah, we'll be there. You should come by after your dinner thing or what-ever. What time is it going to be over?"

"I don't know when we'll be back. They said the cruise lasts until ten, but I'm not sure when the shuttle bus will bring us back to the hotel," Ami explained. "We can try to swing by if it's not too late."

"It doesn't matter how late, we'll be there." Louie hugged me as he handed me the Jack and Coke bottle.

"No thanks, I'm good. I'm not much of a drinker, Louie, but we'll try to make it. We can't promise anything, though."

Our dinner cruise was enjoyable, but other than the brochure-worthy sunset, it wasn't very eventful. Surrounded mostly by couples holding hands and a group of elderly tourists, Ami and I began feeling seasick shortly after dinner and looked forward to docking and getting back on dry land. At the hotel, we opted for an early night and got ready for bed. I drifted away to sleep thinking of Louie and wondering if he was thinking of me too.

A loud knock on our door got me out of bed first thing the next morning. It seemed that Mr. Louie had been counting on our joining the party, and we had disappointed him.

"Bosnian chicks! How come you didn't show up last night?" he asked.

"We got pretty tired and seasick, sorry," I replied, still rubbing the sleep from my eyes.

"We waited for you, but it's cool. Hey, do you guys want to go to the beach with us today?" He looked directly at me this time, challenging me to dare say no. "It's our last day here. We ship out tonight."

"Let's do it. We're going to eat some breakfast first, and we'll meet you there," I agreed.

"All right, see you downstairs. I'll save you guys a good spot in the shade. Don't bail like last night."

When we got to the beach, he already had a couple of towels laid out on the sand for us. We put our bags next to his neatly folded clothes and started the sunblock routine. Louie needed some help with sunblock for his back, and I was happy to oblige. I found his self-confidence playful and charming. How could I say no?

After rubbing sunblock on each other's backs, we took my floaty and ran towards the water, while Ami stayed behind to catch a tan. Louie and I both hung onto the floaty, as he took me really far into the ocean. The thought of sharks swimming underneath us set off panic alarms in my head, while Louie laughed it off, teasing me.

"I'm scared being this far away from the shore. What if a shark swims up and attacks us? They're all around, you know!" I told him in all seriousness.

His face went serious for a moment. Then he propped himself out of the water to lean into me. He gently kissed me, then whispered, "I'll punch the shark in the face for you."

He seemed sweet. I knew I was getting caught up in the romance of this charming sailor and the beauty of Hawaii, though I knew that that evening Louie and I would go our separate ways, never to see each other again. We were just two strangers caught up in an incredibly sweet romantic moment. I was still squealing about the shark whenever his leg brushed up against mine, and after a while, we headed back towards the beach.

That afternoon, our group retreated to our separate rooms to shower off the saltwater and sand. I was getting ready to say goodbye to Louie when he knocked on our door, this time carrying bags, I saw through the peephole.

After I opened the door, he leaned into me and said, "You smell good. What perfume are you wearing?"

"It's one of my favorites, J'adore by Christian Dior." I smiled at him. "It's French for 'I adore you.'"

"I'll have to remember that," Louie said playfully, flashing his big smile.

As the sun began to set that evening, our time together came to an end, and we said our goodbyes. I didn't think he would be able to call from the ship, so I gave him my email address to keep in touch until he reached San Diego.

Ami and I still had a few more days in Hawaii, but when Louie left, he took a piece of my heart with him. I checked my email several times a day to see if he had written. He hadn't, and I was disappointed at the thought of never hearing from him again. To my surprise, his friend Mark emailed a few days later to check on us. He mentioned that Louie was keeping his yellow shirt under his pillow, the one that smelled of my perfume from the last time we were together. This brought a big smile to my face.

❖

Ami and I were scheduled to fly home on September 11, 2001. I had always been afraid of flying, so when Mom called that morning at 5:00 a.m. Hawaii time and got me out of bed, my first thought was she just wanted to wish us a safe trip. I was still half asleep when I picked up the phone, and Mom seemed shaken. I wondered if everything was okay with her and Dad. Then she told me to turn on the news. I stumbled out of bed to find the remote control in the dark. I turned on the television to horrifying images of the twin towers of the World Trade Center in flames. News reporters were talking about hijacked planes crashing into the building.

Half asleep and unable to fully comprehend what happened exactly, I panicked. "Mom, you know I'm afraid of flying. Why did you have to show me this?"

"Honey don't be scared. I wanted to let you know that the U.S. had been under a terrorist attack. The government has grounded all air travel. I don't think you'll be able to come home today."

"What do you mean 'grounded all air travel,' Mom? Our flight is in a couple of hours. How are we going to get home?"

"Your flight is probably cancelled. No one is flying. You'll have to call the airline and find out." Mom spoke somberly while at the same time trying to calm me down.

I remember shock and tears rolling down my face, as I listened to Mom finish what seemed to be the longest sentence in the world. Time stood still. I was scared and confused like the rest of the nation that day. I was sad for all the people who had tragically lost their lives, and I had no idea how we would get home. We had no way of getting back to the mainland. Terrifying visions from the war we thought we had left behind in Bosnia came rushing back.

Thousands of what-if scenarios raced through my mind in a flash. I needed to wake up Ami, but I had to compose myself first because I didn't want her to be scared. With Mom still on the phone, I woke Ami up and told her what was going on. We both hugged each other and cried as we watched images on television in shock and disbelief. Some time passed before we peeled our eyes away from the television and made our way downstairs to the front desk to ask them if we could extend our stay a few days. Before leaving the room, I called my boss to let him know we were stuck in Hawaii for the time being. He reassured me not to worry about work, to take care of myself and Ami, and that he and his wife were praying for our safe return home.

We got into an elevator with a happy-looking American couple from Wisconsin who had arrived the day before. They didn't seem too concerned about the Twin Towers or the fate of those who were still unaccounted for. Their lack of empathy made me mad.

Downstairs, a big screen television was set up in the bell desk area and people had gathered around it, staring in disbelief at the news coming from the other side of the country. People hugged each other. Some cried. Stupefied, Ami and I made our way to the front desk to ask if we could stay until we would be able to arrange another flight back home. The Outrigger staff showed us their true Hawaiian hospitality by allowing us to keep the same room. They even reduced their rates in half for the additional nights.

There was nothing more we could do except go back to our room and wait for whatever was to come next. We didn't feel like going to the beach anymore. With the whole country in mourning, our vacation was officially over.

It took another three days before were able to board a plane home after waiting for several hours in the newly established TSA screening line. On board the plane, the atmosphere was tense. Everyone felt uneasy flying that day. When we touched ground at San Jose International Airport, every passenger on the plane cheered and applauded in relief. Ami and I couldn't wait to deplane and run to hug our parents. I'd never been so happy in my life to see them.

I tried writing to Louie shortly after returning home. I even looked for him when I visited San Diego many months later. By then, he had already moved to Seattle, and we lost all contact. But the memory of that week was one of those nuggets I pull out whenever I need a lift.

CHAPTER 5

HUSBAND MATERIAL

In 2002, the company was expanding, and it had acquired another company headquartered in Huntsville, Alabama. I was in charge of merging our two Help Desks and was sent to Huntsville for five weeks. I was scheduled to stay at a furnished apartment rather than the usual hotel.

It didn't take me long to realize that Huntsville, Alabama was only a three-hour drive from Powder Springs, Georgia, where Adem, my friend from the refugee camp, now lived with his girlfriend and their new baby. We had kept in touch over the years and were up-to-date on each other's lives. I knew about the new friends Adem made over the years. I felt as if they were my friends by default, since he frequently talked about their hangouts and escapades.

I called Adem. "Guess what? I'm going to Huntsville, Alabama for a month for work. Isn't that a three-hour drive from where you live?"

He could barely contain his excitement. "Yeah, Huntsville is really close. Are you coming out to see us? That would be fantastic! You could stay with us over the weekend."

"Are you sure about that? You guys just had a baby. I don't want to impose, but I definitely want to come and see you. I could get a hotel room."

"Are you freaking kidding me? You're staying with us! End of story. And you'll finally be able to meet Filip! It's going to be awesome!"

I had heard so many stories about Filip. It felt like I knew him already. He was from Sarajevo. He and Adem met in high school and had been best friends ever since.

"I can't wait to meet Filip! I'll call you when I get to Alabama! I can't wait to see you guys!"

✦

I flew out to Huntsville on a damp, humid, and hot summer day and checked into the apartment I was about to call home for the next several weeks. I was happy to find the place had everything: a fully equipped kitchen, separate living and dining rooms, a comfortable bed, and an inside washer and dryer. I unpacked my bags and settled in for the night.

The following morning I put on a sleeveless pale-pink silk blouse and black ankle-length dress pants to make a good first impression on my new team.

It was my first time in the South, and I cranked up the car's air conditioner to full blast, but I was still sweating. I rolled down the window to see if that would help, but the air felt more like a hot damp cloth slapping me in the face. Back up went the window. As I pulled into the office parking lot, my skin was sticky, even though I had just taken a shower thirty minutes earlier. I gave thanks for our mild California climate.

Walking briskly through the lobby, I felt eager to get into the air-conditioned building and the team's office when I was nearly yanked off my feet. I twisted around on the security guard, who now held me by the arm and seemed well past retirement age.

He squeezed my arm. "Miss, y'all have a sweater, Miss? Your shoulders must be covered, or I can't let y'all into the building."

He spoke slowly with a thick Southern accent. Because I wasn't yet sure how the word "y'all" was used, I assumed there were people behind me also wearing sleeveless blouses and turned around to look for a fellow partner-in-crime. Much to my surprise, everyone behind me was male. Not a single one of "them-all" wore anything that even remotely exposed their shoulders. I realized he was addressing only me.

"Umm, no Sir! Why would anyone want to wear a sweater in this heat?" I replied.

"It's in the company dress code, Miss."

Considering that I literally just flew out to Alabama from our company's headquarters in California to train these guys on our corporate processes and didn't remember anything in our dress code mandating covered shoulders, I politely replied I was going inside regardless.

The old man wasn't budging, insisting I go back to my hotel room and change. I asked him if he wanted to call my boss to explain why I would be over an hour late for my first day in Alabama while I scuttled back to my hotel room to get a sweater in 95-degree heat and 97 percent humidity.

He finally backed off and let me into the building while pointing a finger at me like I had just been told proper. "Tomorrow, y'all bring a sweater Miss!"

"Will do, sir! Y'all's bringing a sweater tomorrow; you can count on it."

I was raised to not be rude to my elders, but I couldn't help myself. Once I was out of the old man's range of hearing, I uttered a few choice Bosnian curses.

The remainder of my first week in Alabama was uneventful. I spent my time answering questions about policies and procedures while anxiously awaiting the Friday afternoon road trip to reunite with Adem and meet his new family in Georgia.

✦

Before leaving the office on Friday, I printed out directions to Adem's house. As I sat in the car, excited for the upcoming weekend, I turned up the radio to eighties rock music to keep me company on my three-hour journey.

I was excited to see Adem's family and meet his famous friend Filip in person. At the time, Adem was my only refugee friend who had progressed out of his parents' home, having his own rented two-bedroom apartment. He was only a year older than me, and I was exceptionally proud of him for stepping up when he found out his girlfriend, Kendra, was pregnant, and they decided to be a family. Their daughter Addie was a delight and a blessing.

When I got to Adem's apartment, Kendra and he were excitedly waiting for me. They ordered pizza, and we got caught up on life's most recent events as we ate. I was playing with baby Addie when Adem suggested we pick up

Filip so I could meet him. The plan was for the four of us to hang out and play video games that night.

On the way, Adem told me that Filip's car had broken down and warned me about Filip's mom. "Don't be surprised if she comes out of the house and acts rude. She can be a little crazy sometimes."

"Oh, please! Moms love me. I'm not worried about that at all. I just really can't wait to finally meet this friend of yours I've heard so much about."

"Oh, you'll meet him. He's pretty funny. He usually ends up spending the night. I hope you don't mind if he stays. It should be really fun."

"The more, the merrier, right?" I said cheerily.

"That's my girl!"

It was getting dark outside by the time we pulled up to Filip's house. Adem went to get him. Kendra was in the front passenger seat while baby Addie and I were playing peek-a-boo in the back seat. Adem and Filip walked out of the house and towards the car. As they approached, Adem opened the back door and said, "Annie, meet my friend Filip. Filip, meet my friend Annie from the refugee camp. And Annie, scooch over, Filip's sitting in the back with you."

Filip was somewhat of a giant. At six-feet, four-inches tall, his broad shoulders took up half of the back seat. With strong arms and bear paw hands to match those double-wide shoulders, Filip looked dangerously cute. His thick, wavy dark-brown hair hung down to his jaw line, and he had gorgeous blue-gray eyes.

"Hey, what's up?" he said in a deep, casual voice. Then he turned to the front and said, "What's up Kendra?"

"Hey you. I've heard so many stories about you. I feel like I know you already," I said, trying to sound cute and friendly.

"I know. I've heard all your refugee camp stories too. Adem talks about it all the time. I feel like I was there with you guys." He laughed.

Adem's Altima was pretty crowded. I was squeezed tightly between the car seat and Filip the Giant, but I didn't mind sharing a tight space with someone who seemed like a really nice guy. Since he was best friends with one of my dear friends, there was a warm familiarity between us from the start, and I secretly began crushing on him from the moment we locked eyes.

Back at Adem's apartment, the guys opened a bottle of Hennessey and set up the Nintendo Mario Cart while Kendra took Addie to bed. I was never much of a drinker or very good at video games, but it was exciting to spend time with Adem and his family, have some fun, and get to know Filip better. We raced in pairs, guys versus girls, and the girls were winning. The guys were competitive and getting wound up about losing, laughing off their frustration while pledging to even out the score. "Yeah, yeah, beginner's luck! We'll get you next time." I laughed so hard, my belly hurt.

There was a lot of friendly banter, teasing, and tongue-in-cheek humor that evening. Before we knew it, it was 4:00 a.m., the Hennessey bottle was almost empty, and everyone was getting tired. Adem and Kendra brought out a couple of blankets and pillows before saying goodnight and retreating to their bedroom. Alone in the living room, Filip took off his shirt and neatly placed it over the chair before shutting off the lights and laying down on the floor, saying, "You can have the couch. I'll sleep on the floor. Just throw me a couple of those couch pillows please."

Check out Mr. Awesome over there! I thought to myself.

"Hello, Annie! Can you throw me a pillow, please?" Filip said a little louder this time, trying to get my attention.

As much as I tried to deny it, my crush on Filip was going into overdrive. He settled in on the floor several feet away from the couch while I tucked myself snuggly into a blanket, thinking of something clever to say to no avail. I wanted to keep the conversation going after we said goodnight, but I struggled for words.

After a moment of silence, Filip whispered, "You comfortable over there?"

"Umm, yeah, I'm good. Are you?"

"Oh yeah, I love this floor. It's amazing. You have no idea."

I burst out laughing at his sarcasm. By now, I badly wanted to tell him to just come and lay next to me, but I was slightly embarrassed and could feel my heart racing fast inside my chest. Oh, what the heck, I thought to myself, then blurted out, "We could share the couch, I suppose."

"Nah, that would be awkward. We just met."

"You're right. Okay, I'm going to sleep," I said, as I turned to the other side. "Good night."

After a moment of silence, Filip whispered again, "I'm not going to touch you. I swear to God."

Filip's late-night shenanigans were making me giggle. By now, I was curious if he was as much of a gentleman as I thought he was, and I continued teasing him. "Do you want to switch places?"

"Oh no, I'm cool. I'm just kidding. Sweet dreams."

At that point, I was no longer able to resist him and offered up half of the couch. "Okay, listen. Come up here! You can lie next to me, but that's it, you understand?" I waved my finger in front of him.

"It's okay. I'm already asleep. I'm fine, really!"

"I know you want to," I said.

"Ugh."

I heard him get up and walk towards the couch. I scooted over towards the back to make room for him. Filip lay next to me on his back, interlocking his fingers tightly across his chest. At first, I lay on my side, with my head against his upper arm, awkwardly trying to keep my arms to myself. I felt uneasy, and I could tell he was uncomfortable too while keeping to his side of some imaginary boundary line.

"This feels weird," I finally said. "You mind if I just hug you?"

"Yeah, come here," he said as he placed his arm under my head. "Oh my God! This feels so much better."

I snuggled up to him and listened to his heartbeat while drifting off to sleep feeling safe in Filip's arms. Lying next to a man without worry that he would take advantage of me made me appreciate him.

The next morning, we woke up to Adem and Kendra giving us a curious eye while they made coffee.

+

We had breakfast at Adem's before heading out. There was a fair in town that weekend, and we all decided to take Addie.

Filip and Adem took turns carrying Addie on their shoulders while she squealed with joy. There was something indescribably adorable in seeing Filip, who didn't have any kids of his own, act so responsibly with Addie. He seemed skilled and attentive, making Addie laugh the whole time. She couldn't pronounce Filip's name and called him Uncle Fi. Their bond was cute, but even more so, I found it incredibly attractive seeing this giant man care for a tiny little human.

"You're so amazing with Addie, Filip. It's very cool to see the three of you make that kid so happy," I said.

"Thanks. I really want to start a family of my own. So this is like practice I guess." Filip chuckled, but then he got serious again. "I see how happy the three of them are together, and I want that too."

"You're still young. I'm sure that will happen for you. I admire what Adem and Kendra are doing. My friends and I are still going out and having fun when we're not working. I travel a lot, trying to see the world. No one in my group of friends has really thought about having kids yet. But I guess it would be cool someday. They look happy. You have to find the right person who wants the same things, I suppose."

"Yeah, I know. Don't get me wrong. I have fun too. But you know, after a while, you get tired of going out all the time, clubbing, drinking, hooking up. It gets old sometimes."

"I know what you mean. I feel the same way. I don't drink or hook up, but I've been going out with my friends for a couple of years now, and yeah, it's getting old. I want to find someone to settle down with, travel and have fun together. Then have babies."

"You're smart,"—he paused—"and also very beautiful. You have a great job. I'm sure settling down won't be a big problem for you when you're ready."

"Aw, thanks Filip. You're very sweet! You're making me blush." I gently pushed his arm. "Even though I'm not thinking about kids right now, I do have a name picked out for my son if I have a boy."

"Really?" Filip quickly lifted his eyes to look into mine. "How so?"

"I want my son to be named Namik, after my grandpa, who died on my birthday."

"Wait, how did your grandpa die on your birthday? How old were you?"

"I was eight. He was in perfect health the night before. We laughed, he hugged and kissed me goodnight, and we went to sleep. He had a massive heart attack around 5:00 a.m. and never woke up. He said he'd get me a gift when he got his retirement check but didn't live to see that day. I made a promise to myself I would name my son after him. Over the years, I discovered the Perseid meteor showers. Every year, they peak on my birthday, and you can see shooting stars in the sky at night. So every year, on clear nights I lie outside and look at the skies. I like to think that's my grandpa showering me with shooting stars as gifts. He always gave me the best presents."

"Wow, that's interesting. You'll have to tell me more when we're alone," Filip said, pointing to Adem and Kendra walking toward us.

They had picked up some hot dogs for us. We ate and headed back to the apartment to play another round of video games. That night, we stayed up late again laughing. After another near-empty bottle of Hennessy, by 3:00 a.m., Adem and Kendra retired for the night, leaving Filip and me alone on the balcony smoking cigarettes. I think we both just wanted to be alone together for a bit.

Standing by the balcony railing and looking out into the grassy area below, I was telling Filip about how chilly California nights can get. Georgia air was so sticky and humid. What looked like a thick layer of fog was covering the grass while street lights threw shadows on nearby trees.

"Are you chilly?" Filip asked.

It seemed like an excuse to hug me, and I instantly felt butterflies in my stomach at the thought of us cuddling again.

"I am a little chilly, yeah," I said, playing along.

"I'll get you a blanket."

He disappeared briefly into the dark living room only to reemerge with a blanket, which he wrapped snuggly around my shoulders and pulled me closer to him. With my back pressed against his chest, his arms wrapped around my belly, he asked, "Does that feel better?"

"Why, yes. That feels really good. Thank you," I said as I turned around, now facing him.

I rested my head against his chest and took a deep breath, thinking about how good he smelled as he rubbed my back.

"What cologne are you wearing? It smells really nice."

He ran his fingers across my hair and replied, "I don't really know. I grabbed the first thing I found in Adem's cabinet."

"Oh, nice! Seems like you were planning this, even put on cologne for me Mr. Fi," I gently put my hands on his face, then said, "Your face feels really soft too."

I was dying for him to kiss me and in anticipation leaned in closer. "It's this shaving cream," he said, at which moment our lips came together.

He wrapped his arms around me a little tighter, pulling my body closer to his. As he released me, I said, "That was a very romantic first kiss."

"Definitely something we can tell our kids about," he smiled.

A tingling feeling coursed through my body, as if hundreds of butterflies were fluttering in my stomach. I couldn't let myself fall for this guy so quickly, I told myself, but who was I kidding? I didn't want our moment to end.

"Are we sharing the couch again tonight?" I asked.

"Yeah! Why? You want to go inside?"

"Yeah! And I want to hear more about that shaving cream. Like, what brand do you use?" I giggled.

"You think you're funny, huh? I was just talking about shaving cream. I had no idea you were going to kiss me."

"I kissed you? You must be mistaken. I'm pretty sure you kissed me."

I loved how easy it was to talk to him and how much we teased each other. As we went to bed, he kissed me gently on the forehead and said, "We should go to sleep. You have to drive back to Alabama tomorrow. Get some rest before the baby wakes everyone up."

Alabama! I couldn't believe it was Sunday morning already, and I was about to leave in a couple of hours. I had four more weeks of work in Alabama, though. As we drifted off to sleep, I was already planning another weekend in Georgia with Filip.

CHAPTER 6

CARPE DIEM

After I returned to Alabama, Filip called that evening to make sure I had arrived safely. I found it charming. From that point on, we spoke on the phone every night for hours until we both fell asleep. Filip seemed like a true gentleman—caring, genuine, and sweet, and he knew how to make a girl laugh. I knew I was falling hard for him. I also knew going back to California would be hard. Daydreaming about Filip at work made my day fly by. The stresses of a fast-paced job melted away when I heard his voice on the other end of the phone. I found his jokes and his teasing irresistible, and by the time I returned to California, he was all I could think about.

We kept in touch daily, but I suspected the chances of Filip coming out to visit me in California were slim-to-none. He made it clear that he wasn't making a lot of money, and he had to pick up extra shifts at work just to save enough money to replace his broken-down car. I knew Filip lived paycheck-to-paycheck and was helping out his parents with their finances.

I wasn't interested in his income. I simply liked him for the way he made me feel.

A few months into our long-distance relationship, I couldn't have been prouder of him when he called one day shouting out his exciting news. "Guess what? Guess what? I just bought a new truck. A used Nissan! It's green! Also, I was thinking of applying for a new job! One of my friends can hook me up. He said delivering medical supplies pays better money than what I'm making here. With this new truck, I can make larger deliveries, and if it all works out, I can start saving money for an airplane ticket to California!"

"Honey, are you serious? I'm so proud of you. I would love it if you could come. And not to take away from your good news, but I've got good news too."

"What is it?"

"It's not for sure yet, but I may have to come to Alabama again soon."

"What? When? Really? That's great!"

"Don't get your hopes up just yet! It has to be confirmed." I didn't want him to be disappointed if the trip didn't come through.

"How long do you think you'll be able to stay?" he asked.

"I'm not sure yet. My boss said something about a furnished apartment again, so probably a couple of weeks!"

"Look at you, Queen Bee! High rolling, making big money and all!"

"Let's just wait and see what happens. There may be another girl from India staying in the apartment with me this time. I need to train her while I'm out there."

"Okay, keep me posted. It would be so awesome to see you again."

"Really? Are you saying you miss me, dear?" I continued coyly.

"You know I think about you every single day," Filip replied. "It's been a while since we've seen each other. I'm missing you a lot. Can't wait to hug you again."

"I know. I miss you a lot too. I'm not a really big fan of being away from home for such long periods of time, but being with you when I'm out there makes the whole trip worth it. I love you."

"Love you too! Let me know as soon as they book your trip. I'm so excited to see you again!"

✦

Within a month, I was on my way to another five weeks in Alabama. I flew out a few days early to settle in, but my co-worker roommate wasn't arriving from India for another few weeks. With his new truck, Filip was mobile, and we made plans to meet in Alabama for the weekend.

We talked about exploring Huntsville together. By then, Filip was my shelter from the storm and my safe haven. Each weekend, Filip made the three-hour drive, and we spent every weekend together while I was in Alabama.

I had always dreamed about that kind of great love, extraordinary stories of men and what they would do for women they adore. I was fascinated by the story of the Mughal Emperor, Shah Jahan, who was so devastated after losing his wife Mumtaz, that he dedicated himself to building a monument unlike any other in the world to honor her life and love. I never expected the Taj Mahal from Filip, but in the throes of new love, I felt he would do for me anything within his means, just as I was willing to do anything for him.

As the end of my trip approached, before we said goodbye to each other, Filip promised to visit me in California soon. His words made me so happy I began rambling on about different places in the Bay Area I wanted to take him.

"We could take Highway 280 north and drive up to San Francisco. There's a cool house right off the freeway and it looks just like the Flintstone house. I can't wait for you to see it. When we get to San Francisco, we could take 19th Avenue towards the Golden Gate Bridge and drive past all those cute, colorful San Francisco houses. Do you remember the Full House TV show? I can show you where they lived. When we drive over the Golden Gate, there's an exit to a vista point where we can stop. From there, we'll drive to Sausalito, which is an adorable town on the Bay with breathtaking views of San Francisco, Oakland, and the Bay Area. We can walk to the marina and look at the boats docked at piers. Then we'll go to one of those cozy coffee shops and have ourselves a nice, warm cup of coffee and some pastries. After that, I want to take you back to San Francisco and drive to Lombard Street. They have this beautiful, cute, curvy little road lined with flowers. From there, we have got to go to Fisherman's Wharf, because I want to show you the street performers and the Bushman—who literally jumps out of the bushes scaring people! I wonder if you'd get scared if he jumped in front of you. Also, there's people there with their whole body spray-painted in silver paint, including their face! At the end of the day, we could drive up to Twin Peaks and look at the city together as the sun goes down. That would be romantic. Oh Filip! I can't wait!" I was talking a mile a minute. I could hardly catch my breath.

Filip smiled and said, "Sounds like you've been thinking about this for a while now."

"Well, yeah! Aren't you curious to see where I live? To meet my family, my friends?"

"Of course. I can't wait to meet your family and friends. I always wanted to visit California. I can't wait to see those cool places you're talking about."

✦

The end to this Alabama trip was filled with anticipation of Filip's upcoming visit. We were getting serious. My family and friends got to hear all about Filip, and everyone was excited to meet him in person. While I still occasionally went out with friends to clubs and bars, the whole club scene was starting to feel old. It no longer felt right going out every night as I did before I met Filip. I wasn't interested in meeting anyone else. Things between us were going well and I didn't want to give Filip any reason to doubt my love. It was already hard enough being far away from each other.

Filip, too, seemed as if he would rather spend most of his nights on the phone with me than go out with his friends. Other than hanging out at Adem's and having a couple of beers, Filip cut down on his visits to clubs and bars to once or twice a month. Then they stopped altogether after an incident that didn't seem like a big deal at the time, but in retrospect, was a bit of a red flag. Instead, at the time, it actually brought us closer together and solidified our relationship.

It was late spring of 2002 and an otherwise ordinary Sunday with Mom in the kitchen making food, Dad in the living room doing a crossword puzzle, and Ami and I getting ready for the swimming pool. Just as we were about to leave, Adem called to let me know that Filip had been arrested the night before.

"Me, Filip, and few other guys went to a bar to have a few beers. Filip had too much to drink. Some guy at the bar made fun of his accent, and Filip got into a brawl with him. Bouncers stepped in and asked both men to leave.

And you know Annie that Filip's not the type who stands on the sidelines taking disrespect and walking away. He approached the guy outside to tell him he shouldn't be making fun of someone's accent. The situation escalated quickly, one thing led to another, and Filip ended up punching him, which landed the guy flat on his back on a table. Security called the police. They showed up almost immediately and took Filip away. He spent the night in jail, but his parents bailed him out."

I called Filip right away.

He picked up immediately and said, "Well, I'm all right, but I do have a court date in two weeks. They said I will have to pay a $5,000 fine or go to jail. Since I don't have $5,000, I guess I'll have to do my time."

"What? Are you serious? You can't go to jail. I have some money saved up, not the whole $5,000, but I'll get the rest. When do you have to have it?"

Filip burst out laughing.

"What's so funny Filip?" I said, confused and annoyed at the same time.

"I'm just kidding. I do have to go to court, but I don't have to pay $5,000. The guy I punched said he was drunk and told the police he won't press charges. But it's cute how you're all like, 'I have some money.'"

"How did you think I was going to react?"

"Well, I honestly thought you'd say something like 'See ya when you get out of jail.'"

"You know me better than that. Oh my God, you had me worried sick! That wasn't funny. Don't ever do that to me again!"

He grew serious. "I love you, and I just want you to know that really means a lot to me that you'd do that. I didn't think I'd be saying this to you so soon, but the fact you would do that for me without any hesitation makes me think you're the one for me. I seriously want to spend the rest of my life with you. I want to start a family and have babies with you."

A range of emotions went through me from wanting to punch his arm for scaring me to wanting to bury myself in his arms for all the sweet things he said afterwards. I didn't know whether to laugh or cry.

"Baby, I love you too. I want all those things as well! But I'm mad at you for scaring me like that! I'm going to kick your butt when I see you, just so you know!"

He just laughed.

I wouldn't have to wait long. Several weeks after Filip's arrest, he called to ask me to take a week off from work so we could spend some time together when he visited.

+

Our family was facing challenges of our own around this time. Mom and Dad were on the verge of splitting up, and Ami had returned to Bosnia to wait with her husband Hamza for his visa to United States. Ami had been married to Hamza for about two years by then, the exact same length of time I had been married to Alen, since we were married the same day.

Yes, I was still married to Alen, since he hadn't agreed to a divorce, and I hadn't pushed it. I never kept Alen a secret from Filip, though, and told him the whole story early on. Filip didn't care. He knew how I felt about him.

I missed Ami very much, but I wanted her to be happy and follow her heart. I wanted the same for my mother and father, but that seemed to mean they'd be going their separate ways, the prospect of which just made me sad.

+

Life had brought Mom and Dad their ups and downs. When I was a young child in Bosnia, Dad had had an affair, and Mom and Dad separated. Before Mom had a chance to fully process Dad's infidelity, though, the war broke out in Bosnia, Mom and Dad got back together, and the whole family went into survival mode. Fleeing the country and assimilating to new culture had brought Mom and Dad closer together for the good of the family, but she never truly forgave him.

Now that Mom and Dad were settled in the United States, somewhat financially secure, and facing an empty nest, Mom was ready to move on. She began putting her own happiness first and stopped making sacrifices for Dad, even though by then Dad had become the best version of himself and a good husband to her. He was devoted, worked hard to provide for his family, and was a good man. For her own reasons, Mom wouldn't—or couldn't—get over his past betrayal. I believed there were times when Mom flat-out couldn't stand being in Dad's presence.

Mom was making good money, and for the first time in her life, she could afford to live by herself. While seeing my parents split up after everything they had been through and survived together made me sad, I couldn't blame Mom for putting her needs first. Having raised her kids, she had every right to follow her own heart and destiny.

Dad didn't take the news well. He felt it was unfair to upend their lives after he sacrificed so much for the family. To him, this was a time for the two of them to finally relax and enjoy life together. He appreciated Mom for sticking by him through his wild years and wanted to grow old with her. He was so mad at Mom that he once said, "If Mom leaves me, I'll marry the first whore I come across." It was painful to watch them grow apart.

When Mom stopped sharing a bed with Dad, he booked a flight to Germany and took off for several weeks without telling anyone how to reach him, where he would be staying, or even why he had chosen Germany. I was naturally worried for his safety and hurt by his actions. It took me years to understand that running away was Dad's way of coping with the loss. Back then, I wanted him to stay and try harder, to fight for Mom. I believe Mom wanted him to fight for her too. Instead, he went to visit a childhood friend in Germany. With Ami in Bosnia and Dad gone, it was just me and Mom back home in the States. Our family was falling apart.

✦

With all this happening, I was beyond happy Filip was flying to visit. I needed a friendly face and an escape from it all. I couldn't wait for him to tease me. I couldn't wait to laugh at his jokes, relax in his arms, and just live a little. I couldn't wait to feel safe again. I looked forward to introducing Filip to Mom and felt sad that Dad and Ami wouldn't be there to meet my amazing boyfriend.

Filip flew out on June 28, 2002 and planned to stay until July 7. He and Mom really hit it off. Mom loved that he always made me laugh. With disdain, Mom told Filip about Alen and the many fights we had gotten into for hours on the phone. She added how delighted she was to see my eyes light up with happiness every time I talked about Filip. Filip praised Mom's home-made cooking, which made her like him even more.

Filip also met my best friend Jasmina and her boyfriend Hari that week-end. Hari was a great cook, and we had a good time over dinner and drinks. It made me happy to see Filip enjoy himself in the company of those I loved the most.

We spent the first two nights at home, then drove to Lake Tahoe and Las Vegas for a few days. On our first day in Lake Tahoe, we lounged by the shore laughing all day, before retiring to the hotel room for the night. Tired from the five-hour road trip and crisp, fresh mountain air, we went to bed early. I was still on cloud nine waking up next to Filip the next day, but I soon realized that for me, the ten days together were not going to be enough. I didn't ever want him to leave.

As we lay in bed cuddling the next morning, I looked out the window toward pine-tree covered mountains in the distance when it hit me that Filip would be going back to Georgia too soon. All of a sudden a great sadness swept over me. Out of nowhere, I began to cry, tears rolling down my cheeks.

Alarmed Filip sat up. "Babe, babe, what's wrong? Why are you crying? Did I do something wrong?"

"Nothing. No. I kind of don't want to talk about it." I tried to compose myself.

"No, you have to tell me! What's going on? Are you breaking up with me or something?"

"No, silly. That's not it. I'm crying because you're leaving in a few days, and that makes me sad." I broke down sobbing again.

Filip hugged me tightly. "Well, I am leaving. For right now, yeah! But I don't want to go. And I'm coming back. It's hard with my parents back there, and I don't have a job out here. I need some time to figure things out, but I want to be with you too."

I felt better immediately. I understood his predicament intellectually, as well as the challenge ahead of us, but the heart wants what it wants. Filip gave me faith that we would somehow find a way to be together. In the mean-time, we both had to be patient.

CHAPTER 7

PATIENCE AND A CONDO

Waiting is the worst. Some days would have me thinking if I could just hibernate until Filip comes back, but I'm not the kind of person who fritters her life away without purpose or meaning. I like to keep busy, and in times of anticipation, I turn to work, friends, hobbies, and self-improvement.

I was a few months shy of twenty-four with a steady job, several years of employment history, and a car payment. I had excellent credit and a savings account with some money in it. I often wondered where we'd live if Filip moved to California. Not with my mom. It was time for me to live on my own, I decided, regardless of what Filip decided to do.

With so many start-up companies in the Bay Area in the early 2000s, the real estate market in Silicon Valley was booming. Home prices were high, but mortgage loans were easy to obtain. Mostly out of boredom at work one day, but also out of curiosity, I went on one of those websites that ask your income and debt and automatically calculate an estimate for the loan amount you could qualify for. Decently sized one-bedroom condos in the same complex where my parents lived were in a reasonable price range. I decided to get pre-qualified for a loan and find a real estate agent.

It didn't take long before a condominium I liked came on the market. It needed some work, but nothing major—new carpet and a fresh coat of paint. It had one bedroom and one bathroom and was on the second floor with a small, cute balcony overlooking the courtyard and a man-made pond. The pond had a water feature, and when I closed my eyes, I drifted into a relaxed state of mind. Tall pine trees surrounding the balcony provided ample shade while allowing the perfect amount of light to shimmer into the living room. Combine these with an assigned carport spot, and I was sold. I especially loved how close it was to my parents' home. I could have a place of my own and still be within walking distance of my family, something I had always dreamed about.

Without thinking another moment, I asked my agent to submit an offer. I didn't want to get my hopes up too high, so aside from my parents, no one else knew of my plans in case the deal fell through.

To my great surprise, the agent called back within a couple of hours to share the good news. "Your offer was accepted!"

I rushed to his office to get the paperwork started. I was ecstatic and couldn't wait to finally tell Filip about it.

He'll be super proud of me! I thought, as I dialed his number.

Filip's first reaction after I told him was, "Why did you do that?"

That's not what I was expecting. "What do you mean, 'why' silly? I'm buying a condo! Holy crap, I'm buying a condo!" I squealed with joy as reality began to sink in.

"Yeah, but why didn't you tell me about it?" Filip pressed.

"I wasn't sure it was really going to happen, and I didn't want to get my hopes up. I mean like, I'm just a kid from Bosnia, you know? I never imagined in my life I could own a condo in California and still can't even believe this is real!"

"Yeah, I know. I just wish you'd told me!" he said moodily.

"Aren't you going to congratulate me?"

"Yeah, yeah! Congratulations, big shot!" he said sarcastically.

I was not about to let Filip ruin my glorious moment. "Thanks, how very generous of you." I didn't try to hide my own sarcasm.

Despite Filip's lack of enthusiasm, I went ahead with the purchase.

With a thirty-day close of escrow, the clock had already started ticking. Week one—order a home inspection and start the loan process. Week two—

remove contingencies and submit more loan documents. Week three—review the title report.

Things were moving at the speed of light.

Filip and I still managed to squeeze in at least an hour on the phone every day. For me, those conversations were fit in-between work and calls to the bank, the home inspector, the real estate agent, Mom, my sister, and Dad. I was so busy time flew quickly for me. Meanwhile, time was dragging for Filip, who was still trying to figure everything out on his end. Could he really move to California? What would his parents do without him? What would he do without them?

I met Filip's parents, Olga and Mateo, during one of my Alabama business trips. They seemed like nice people who struggled financially. Over time, I grew friendly with them. Olga called periodically to catch up, and this soon turned into a weekly phone call. I felt as if I had already become a part of their family.

Olga was a very large and dauntingly loud woman, with a full set of thick dark hair that looked to me like it could use a trim. She smoked like a chimney and was missing all her teeth, which was ironic since she had worked as a dental assistant in Bosnia. At family events, she dictated orders at her children, who marched like little toy soldiers without objection. She was always the loudest one at the dinner table. I could see why Adem felt intimidated by her. I respected her authority to such a degree that I never once addressed her informally.

Mateo, on the other hand, was a sweet, hardworking man and the polar opposite of Olga. Around the same age as my dad, he was a rugged-looking man, hardened by life, who had fought in the Bosnian war defending the city of Sarajevo, though he never talked about it. He had big broad shoulders like Filip, silver balding hair, and piercing blue eyes. He appeared tough, but with his family, he was tender and affectionate. He always called Olga "Kitty," even when she barked orders at him. That affection spilled over toward me. Mateo called me his sweet daughter-in-law long before Filip and I had even discussed marriage.

Filip loved and respected both of his parents tremendously. I understood why Filip struggled with the idea of leaving.

Filip decided to confide in his father and ask for advice (or his blessing). He told his dad he wasn't sure what to do. On one hand, he felt obligated to stay close to his parents in Atlanta and help out. On the other, he saw a future with me and didn't think it was fair that I leave a good-paying job to be with him. After listening intently, Mateo looked Filip square in the eyes and asked, "Son, do you love her?"

"I do love her," Filip answered.

"Does she love you?"

"She does, Dad." Filip smiled as he thought of me.

"Then you should go be with her," Mateo concluded.

"But Dad, what about you and Mom? What about my sister?"

"Don't worry about us, son! We'll be fine. If you really love her, and she really loves you, you should go and be with her. Love is what matters."

Mateo himself had moved from his family's home in a small village in Serbia to the big city of Sarajevo, so he understood. His father's blessing meant the world to Filip, and soon thereafter, Filip and I began planning our life together.

When Filip called to tell me, my heart raced with excitement. We didn't have the logistics of his move worked out yet, but the decision had been made and the rest would fall into place. I promised to ask my dad to help Filip get a job at the same company where all of us worked. My life was starting to unfold beautifully.

On October 3, 2002, I finalized the purchase of my condo and became a proud first-time homeowner at the age of twenty-four. I felt on top of the world that day, driving to the Title Company to sign the escrow documents. With every page I signed, I stared for a moment at my signature, admiring my grown-up name on my grown-up documents, recognizing the significance of the moment. I felt a sense of pride and incredible accomplishment. None of my friends owned any real estate. I was the first one! I—a refugee kid from Bosnia—had just purchased a condo in one of the most expensive markets in the world! All by myself. Hard work really did pay off. I was inspired to work even harder.

Following the signing, I met with my agent at my new condo to receive my very own first set of keys. After a final walk-through, the agent congratulated me and left. Overwhelmed with joy, I lay down on the floor of my empty living room making snow angels on the carpet, planning the next steps. Before Filip arrived, I wanted to replace the dingy old carpets and paint the walls. But I wanted to wait for Filip to pick out the furniture. This was really happening!

From that point on, Dad and I made many trips to home improvement stores and spent every spare minute of our time remodeling. We had the new off-white Berber carpeting put in, and we painted the walls of every room a bright eggshell-white, as well as the trim, the hallway doors, and kitchen and bathroom cabinets. Within a few weeks, the place was sparkling, and the entire place smelled fresh and clean, ready for new memories to be made. The unit was small, but now it felt homey and beautiful.

By the time it was move-in ready, Filip had picked a moving date, and I got a one-way ticket to Atlanta. We would drive across the country together. It was an adventure I had been looking forward to for a while, but more than anything, I was excited to start a brand-new chapter in my life with Filip. There were so many new beginnings—I was a new homeowner; my boyfriend was moving to California; I would be living with him for the first time. I was becoming a real adult! The possibilities were endless; life seemed amazing.

The time in Atlanta was bittersweet. Filip was sad to say goodbye to his family while I was excited about starting a life with him. For two days before we left, we stayed at his parents' house to give Filip time to pack. He didn't have much to move really. He had a DVD player, ten seasons of Friends on DVD, and a black zip-up binder with close to a hundred music CDs. I loved his CDs and looked forward to listening to them in the car.

Before we left, Olga insisted on purchasing a housewarming gift for us. We needed everything from spoons to furniture, but Filip's family was on a tight budget. Off to Walmart we went to choose a microwave and coffee maker. To me, it was the thought that mattered. We chose the least expensive microwave oven and coffee maker on the shelf, both white to match the freshly painted kitchen cabinets.

As we walked the aisles of Walmart, an oversized tan entertainment center caught my eye and Filip's too. "This would look great on the living room wall, Filip," I said. "If we had a TV large enough for it."

"If we had a TV period!" Filip laughed. Then he said, "You know what, Babe? I like it. Who cares? Let's get it." His eyes lit up as he grabbed the tag. We had plenty of room in the truck.

We spent the night before we left hanging out with Filip's family, watching Bosnian comedy TV series and laughing. The next day, however, was more somber. Filip's sister and mom cried while Mateo stood by stoically. He hugged me, smiled, and said, "My sweet daughter-in-law."

As Filip and I settled into the car, Olga shouted, "Take good care of him and call us all the time. Filip is not much of a talker, but I know I can count on you to call every day. And come back to visit often."

"We will," I promised, as Filip backed out of the driveway. We waved goodbye from the car, and we were on our way.

As we got on highway I-20 West out of Atlanta, I was excited, nervous, and happy all at once. When I get like that, though, it affects my bladder, and I have to stop for bathroom breaks way more than usual, sometimes more than once an hour. Not good for road trips. We weren't on the road for twenty minutes when I asked Filip to pull over. Ten minutes after that first pitstop, I was squirming in my seat ready to stop again!

"Are you okay? At this pace, it'll take us two weeks to get to California." Filip was on a mission to get to California in record time.

"I'm so sorry. Maybe I have a urinary tract infection or something. Let me pick up some cranberry juice." I was too embarrassed to tell Filip the truth, so I faked an illness.

"Okay, just hurry up please. I want to get back on the road."

After two more pitstops in the next sixty miles, I calmed down, and the rest of the day was smooth driving. Filip was a champion. Even when I offered to relieve him so he could rest, he pressed on. Filip drove close to

1,000 miles on day one. After being in the car for over fifteen hours, we called it a day and checked into a hotel for the night.

We got back on the road early the next morning, only stopping for gas and food. Filip drove another 1,000 miles that day, and again we spent fifteen hours in the car listening to music, laughing, and having a good time. I couldn't help but think that if we could spend two days cooped up in a car like this and still have a good time, we were meant to be together.

By 10:00 p.m. on day two of our drive, we had reached California's state line. With only a few hundred miles left to go, I asked Filip to stop and spend the night at the hotel so we could arrive fresh the next day. But Filip was determined, insisting it was better to save that money for furniture. He pressed on for another several hours. In total, he drove 2,400 miles door-to-door in about two-and-a-half days.

We pulled into the condo parking lot around 4:00 a.m. I called Mom to let her know we had arrived. She was happy that we got home safely, but irked we drove so late without rest. We planned to stay with my parents until our condo was ready.

We walked straight to the bedroom, and nosedived into bed next to Ami and Hamza, who had arrived from Bosnia a few months before. With my parents in the next room and my grandmother in the room over, my parents' three-bedroom condo was at full occupancy.

We slept in, and when we woke up, Mom made coffee and breakfast for the family. After we fueled up, Filip and Hamza retrieved the futon from my old bedroom and carried it on their backs to our new place. Following behind, Ami and I lugged the pillows and blankets. They plopped the mattress on the living room floor, we propped the pillows against the wall, and flipped a plastic laundry basket upside down as a temporary coffee table. Hamza also helped Filip carry the entertainment center we brought from Georgia and helped assemble it.

Hamza and Filip bonded over assembling furniture together while Ami and I lay on the futon mattress teasing them. It took a couple of hours to put together the massive structure. Then, Ami and Hamza left, only to return an hour later carrying a very large box between the two of them. As a housewarming gift, they bought us a new TV. Not only was I beyond happy to have Ami back from Bosnia after nine long months, but now the four of us had a new place to hang out. Once we hooked up the TV, we lay down like sardines on the futon to rest. Filip popped in his Friends DVD and as the theme song came on, my heart fluttered with excitement. This was our new home.

Since Filip and I weren't quite standing on our own two feet, Mom insisted on helping to pay for our furniture. Over the next couple of days, we visited a number of furniture stores and settled on a comfortable beige, faux-suede couch and loveseat with a matching recliner. Mom also insisted on buying a bed for us, suggesting a California king. "It will come in handy when the two of you decide to have a baby," she said with a smile.

We didn't want Mom spending all that money, but she wouldn't hear of anything else. Our new furniture was scheduled for delivery the day before Filip was to start a new job with Dad.

We picked up other necessities—dishes, cups, glasses, silverware, pots, and pans, and suddenly we were adults with our own place—that had a nice ring to it. With two car payments, a mortgage, and utility bills, money was a little tight, but with budgeting and wise spending, we could make it work.

Even though Mom and Dad were officially split up by this time, they remained on good terms. After I moved out, they put their three-bed-room condo up for sale. Mom rented a smaller, one-bedroom condo in our building. Ami and Hamza rented in the same complex one building over, and Dad found a place about a ten-minute drive away. While we no longer fostered dreams of going home to Bosnia together, we all lived close enough to each other to be a family. I'm grateful for those happy memories. It was a blessed time in our lives.

CHAPTER 8

FAITH AND FIGHTS

I was raised to believe in God. People talk about God as if there is "my God" and "your God," and only my God counts. That's not how I grew up. When I was a child, I was taught that there is only one God for everyone, though there are different beliefs about how to worship. I was further taught to love my own faith and beliefs and respect those of everyone else as well.

As it was explained to me by my elders, Islam means peace and being Muslim means finding peace within yourself. My elders often greeted one another with the Arabic saying as-salaam-alaykum, meaning "peace be upon you."

We are Bosnian Muslims, and as Europeans, we have different customs from Arab Muslims. We were not obligated to go to mosque, for example, and Ami and I were not expected to wear a hijab to cover our hair. To my knowledge, no women in my family wore these garments. I grew up with the essence of Islam.

In Bosnia, there is a mix of cultures and religions, but you'd be hard-pressed to tell one from the other. We all dressed the same, and Muslims and Christians lived side by side, celebrating different holidays with gusto and camaraderie. My family visited our Christian friends for Easter and Christmas, while our Christian friends visited us for Ramadan and Kur-ban Bayram (also called Eid el Adha or the Feast of the Sacrifice), two major Islamic holidays equivalent in importance to Easter and Christmas. The holidays were times of joy and feasting, regardless of faith. Families, friends, and neighbors came together in harmony.

Ramadan is a month of fasting where Muslims refrain from consuming food, drinking liquids, indulging in sexual pleasures, holding impure thoughts, and smoking between sunup and sundown. In our community, children were encouraged to fast, but were not obligated to. It was mostly elders who observed the practice, as working parents were also excused from the obligation as well.

Women cooked food and desserts for iftar, the first meal eaten at sundown to break the fast. Whether they had been fasting themselves or not, preparing the iftar meal was an honor and privilege. Feeding those who had been hungry all day was considered a good deed, and as such, only the best, most nutritious meals were served. Those who fasted also earned good deeds by honoring one of the five pillars of the Islamic faith.

During the month of Ramadan, every day is a feast with a delicious five-course meal, including walnut-rich baklava for dessert. At sundown, we kids cheerfully ran outside waiting for the lights on our neighborhood mosque to light up, signaling an end to that day's fast. As soon as the lights came on, we ran home to tell our elders it was time for them to break their fast. We raced to see which kid first yelled "it's time" at their front door. As we ran through the streets, the aroma of homemade meals filled the air. The chatter of friends and family sitting down to these lavish dinners are among my favorite childhood memories of Ramadan, and I will always miss that about Bosnia. Nowhere in the world have I come across communities as tightly knit as those in Bosnia.

Ramadan Bayram marked the end of a month of fasting. It was followed by a three-day celebration, which meant even more great food and desserts, and a special treat for us kids. During those three days, folks of all religions wore their Sunday best and visited family and neighbors. It was customary for children to wish a happy and blessed Bayram to the hosts, followed by a traditional kiss on the hand to show respect. In return, the elders gave kids gifts of cash and invited visitors into their home to share a meal. For us, Bayram was like Thanksgiving, with guests unbuttoning their pants after overindulging in food while the kids eagerly counted their money.

Considered the holier of the two holidays, Kurban Bayram is called the Feast of Sacrifice because it honors Abraham's willingness to sacrifice his son Isaac on Moriah as an act of obedience to God's will. At the last minute, however, God provides Abraham a goat to sacrifice instead. (In the Qur'an, Abraham is Ibrahim, Isaac is Ishmael, and Moriah is Mount Arafat.)

Both of my grandmothers shared these stories with us kids. We listened with great fascination as they taught us about Islam, its similarities to Christianity as well as its differences.

When I thought about having children of my own, I envisioned raising them in the same spirit I was raised. Filip was raised Catholic, but he and I agreed to raise our children to celebrate all the holidays of our two families and would not push one religion over the other. Instead, we'd teach them about Islam and Catholicism so that when they grew up, they would equally love and respect both faiths.

✦

Once we settled into the condo and our new life together, we started trying for a baby, and it didn't take long. She must have wanted us as much as we wanted her. We're pretty sure our little baby bean was conceived on the Fourth of July because a few weeks later, I felt queasy and exhausted. A magical white stick confirmed a positive pregnancy, and Filip and I jumped for joy on that glorious Saturday morning shortly before my twenty-fifth birthday.

At our first sonogram appointment, my heart was pounding from excitement. Then I saw her, a little kidney bean-shaped dot in black and white on the screen in front of us. Tears of joy streamed down my face. At six weeks, this particular appointment was supposed to confirm a viable pregnancy and ensure the baby was in the right place inside the uterus. I certainly didn't expect to hear a heartbeat, but when the rapid "whoosh, whoosh, whoosh" came on, I was profoundly humbled.

From that moment, everything changed for me. Once I knew I was creating new life inside my body, my life took on new meaning. It was no longer just me and Filip. It was baby first, then me and Filip.

That meant eating healthy and kicking bad habits. Until then I had smoked a pack of cigarettes a day, but I quit cold turkey. Poisoning myself with smoke and nicotine was bad enough; poisoning my baby was unacceptable.

This took some adjustment on everyone's part. Not only did I say no smoking in our place, I asked my parents and Ami and her husband not to smoke in their places either since we constantly visited back and forth.

Mom's initial reaction was not as I had hoped or expected. "This is my house. You don't live here. Why do I have to smoke outside at my own house?"

"Mom, think about it. Do you really think I can bring a newborn baby into a smoke-filled house?"

She backpedaled almost instantly. "Oh my God, you're right. No more smoking here either. We can smoke on the balcony."

It had been a while since we had a baby in our family, and I was the first one in my group of friends to have a child, so there was no one I could really rely on for advice. I was eager to learn everything there was to know about pregnancy, and what to expect when the baby arrived. I visited bookstores weekly for the latest in pregnancy books. I learned about a baby's development during each week of pregnancy and got a sneak peek at how my body would be changing. I read online columns with pregnancy advice and was reminded of my childhood dreams of delivering babies.

I read that I would start to see a baby bump by the end of the first trimester, but other than morning sickness and profound fatigue, I didn't notice visible changes to my body for a while. However, I could sleep anywhere and anytime. I was sound asleep by 8:00 p.m. every evening, getting a full eleven hours of sleep each night. I took power naps in the car during work breaks and slept even more at home during hour-long lunch breaks.

Early pregnancy had other strange effects. I couldn't stand most smells, including the scent of Filip's cologne, which I had loved before. I couldn't rest my head on Filip's chest without getting nauseated. I couldn't wear my own favorite perfume, J'adore, which I had to replace with a low-key antiperspirant. And just about any kind of food made me gag. Most days, all I could manage to eat was toast and Baby Bell cheese melted in the microwave.

Luckily, the fatigue and morning sickness went away as soon I entered the second trimester. Because the baby bump had yet to appear, my clothes still fit. I felt good enough to go out again.

An opportunity came when the famous Bosnian pop star Dino Merlin announced a concert in the Bay Area. Mom was a huge fan of his nostalgic, whimsical love songs, accompanied by Beach Boys type music. Filip had several Dino Merlin CDs in his collection, and we knew his songs by heart. Dino was a legend in Bosnia, and every Bosnian I knew was eager to see him perform live. On the day of the concert, Mom, Ami, Hamza, Filip, and I drove together to Palo Alto's Edge nightclub where Dino would be performing.

The Bosnian community from California and beyond turned out in droves. Several dear friends whom I hadn't seen in a long time came to the concert, as well as my cousins Enes and Enver, Aunt Sadeta's sons. Mom was happy to see them and catch up before the show. I introduced Filip to everyone and boasted about how happy we were to be expecting our first child.

When the show began, people flocked to the front. Dino riled up the crowd with old classics and got just about everyone singing, hugging, and dancing. We were all having a great time. Halfway through the show, the band announced a thirty-minute break, saying they were happy to be there among so many smiling faces and looked forward to the second half of the show.

As soon as music stopped, much of the crowd headed outside to smoke. Since I no longer indulged, I decided to forgo the chilly California evening and secondhand smoke, opting to stay inside and catch up with other friends who stayed back. Mom and Ami stayed inside with my cousins and friend Sanela. Filip, Hamza, and a few others went outside.

While we chatted, waiting for the concert to start up again, the Palo Alto Police Department and Fire Marshalls unexpectedly showed up, apparently in answer to complaints that the noise was too loud and the crowd too large. As a result, Fire Marshalls blocked the entryway, preventing anyone from going in or out. They were counting ticket stubs to determine how many people were attending.

Filip motioned at me through the window to come out. I shook my head and tried to explain with hand gestures and facial expressions that the Fire Marshalls wouldn't let anyone leave. Filip had been drinking pretty heavily, and I couldn't seem to get him to understand. He grew increasingly more animated, then turned agitated. I didn't know what else to do.

About forty-five minutes later, when people started coming back inside, Filip stomped up to me, visibly angry and already yelling. "I was waving at you. Why didn't you come out?"

"They weren't letting anyone in or out," I explained, thinking it was no big deal. I had been having fun with my friends.

"So you just leave me outside like that?" Filip raised his voice in front of everyone.

Embarrassed, I tried to pull him aside. I had just been telling everyone what a wonderful person Filip was. "I didn't leave you out there, Filip. I told you. I couldn't get out. Big difference."

"You think I'm stupid?" he said, shaking my hand from his arm. "You think I'm stupid? I know you just didn't want to come out with me. I'm your husband. You made me look foolish. Do you think I'm stupid?" Filip was waving his hands in the air, which got the attention of others in our party.

"Listen, Filip! Maybe that's what it looked like, but I swear to you that's not what happened. I really don't want to argue with you in front of everyone. Maybe we should just go home."

This just upset him even more. His face was getting redder, and he was gesticulating wildly. I remembered what Adem had told me about the night Filip got arrested in Georgia, and I grew scared.

Mom, Ami, and Hamza walked over to us and asked Filip to calm down. My cousins, who are both about six-foot-four, stepped to either side of me, my own security detail. The venue's actual security guards joined us to make sure I was okay. I told everyone Filip and I were fine, that he just had a little too much to drink. I didn't want to cause a scene and asked our group to help me get Filip to the car, so I could take him home. What had started as a fantastically fun night had taken a nasty turn.

With the wisdom of age and therapy, I now know that I was not the one making a scene that evening, Filip was. I just wanted to get home as quickly as possible to avoid further embarrassment. By removing him from the situation, though, I was also preventing him from facing consequences for his actions.

This was our first big fight. I suppose every couple has them, but to me it came as a shock and surprise. I hadn't seen this side of Filip before. I guess I had thought that now that he was with me, he had left all that behind him in Georgia.

I didn't say much on our way home since I didn't want to provoke him further. I thought it was best to get him to bed and let him sleep off the booze and whatever was causing his anger. I would figure out what to do in the morning.

We got home and went straight to bed. It wasn't long before Filip was snoring while I tossed and turned all night. As I lay in bed, I wondered why he acted that way and in front of everyone I knew. If he was upset, why couldn't he just talk to me about it like an adult? I had never seen him that drunk—or that angry. That wasn't my Filip. I was angry myself, as well as disappointed, sad, confused—and pregnant! What had I gotten myself into?

I got very little sleep that night and when morning arrived, I was even angrier. I needed some time to think about this, and for that to happen, Filip had to leave, at least for a while.

When I told Filip of my decision, he pushed back. "Where am I supposed to go? I have no one here." He said it as an accusation, as if I had dragged him away from everything he held dear and was holding him prisoner.

"I don't know Filip. Figure it out. I need some space from you right now."

"Okay, wow! I move here for you and now you need space? Wow, that's just great!"

"Do you remember last night? Yelling at me? In front of my family? In front of all my friends? Do you remember people trying to get you into the car, Filip? Any of those things ring a bell to you? What did I do to deserve that?"

"Yeah, I do. I remember. And I'm sorry; these things happen. What more do you want?" Filip shrugged without an ounce of sincerity.

"Are you? Are you really sorry? Or are you just saying that because I asked you to leave?"

"Leave where? It's not like I have a mom and dad here to run back to."

"Out of my place, Filip. I want you to leave my place. Now. Get out. Get a hotel room or something. I don't know, and I don't care." I held the front door open for him.

"Your place," he sneered. "Now it's your place? How long did that take to hold over my head?"

This, too, was a Filip I hadn't seen before. Filip the victim, everyone and everything out to get him. What could have been settled with a sincere apology and a simple promise not to act that way anymore was now spiraling out of control.

"If you really want to go there, Filip, I did buy this place by myself before you moved here. So yes, it is mine, technically. But you know what, if you're not leaving, I am. I can't even look at you right now." I marched towards the closet to gather my clothes.

"What? You can't leave." Filip seemed confused by my sudden change of heart.

I draped the clothes over my arm, grabbed my toothbrush and few other belongings, and walked out the door. "Watch me!" I slammed the door behind me and marched down the hallway to Mom's apartment.

Mom opened the door and knew instantly why I was there with a pile of clothes still on hangers folded over my arm and tears streaming down my face. She gave me a big, long hug. "Everything's going to be okay. All couples fight. You two will get through this."

"The way he talked to me, Mom, last night and this morning. Like it's my fault he moved here. I don't understand. If he didn't want to live here, he shouldn't have come. That's no reason to yell at me and embarrass me in front of my family and friends." I couldn't stop crying.

"Try to calm down first. You guys will sort this out." Mom let me out of her hug and went to the kitchen to pour chicken noodle soup into a bowl. "Have some soup. It will make you feel better."

I tried some of the soup, but I didn't really feel that much better.

Two minutes later, my cell phone rang. It was Filip. I let it go to voice mail. The phone rang again. I didn't pick up. He called several more times without leaving a message, after which Mom's phone rang. She looked at me sympathetically, and said she didn't want to be rude, so she picked up. I heard Filip's voice asking to talk to me. I shook my head, refused to take the phone Mom held out to me.

Seconds after Mom hung up, we heard loud knocking on the door. I assumed it was Filip. I asked Mom to ignore him, but she was getting tired of being in the middle and opened the front door. "Listen, Annie's really upset with you right now," she said. "And given your behavior last night, she has every reason to be. You need to respect her wishes and give her some space, please. Try calling back later. She'll talk to you when she's ready. But right now, it's best if you leave."

That actually worked. He didn't sound too happy about it, but he left.

After Filip left, I put my stuff away, and Mom and I watched a movie. Later, Mom went into the kitchen to make us lunch. Her food always made me feel better, and she knew it. Several hours went by before Filip called Mom again to ask if I would talk to him. It was just as we sat down to eat a late lunch. I heard him ask Mom for advice on what he should do, and Mom telling him I'd be spending the night at her place. Mom suggested Filip get some rest too, and tomorrow would surely be a better day.

On Monday morning, everyone returned to work. Filip didn't call all day, which gave me enough room to cool off. On more of an even keel, I went to Mom's place after work. After some time had passed, Filip must have realized I wasn't coming home. He called my phone. I didn't pick up. Within minutes, someone was knocking on the door.

As soon as Mom swung the door open, Filip announced, "I came here to ask her to come home."

"Listen, if she wants to talk to you, you're welcome inside," Mom replied.

I walked to the door with my arms crossed, ready to hear what he had to say.

"Come home, please. I feel really bad about what happened," Filip turned to me, this time sounding sincere.

"Then why'd you do it?" I was still hurting from the way he had acted and spoke to me.

"I don't know what came over me. I was drunk. I wasn't thinking straight. I'm sorry." For the first time since our fight, this felt like an actual heartfelt apology.

"What you did—" I paused, trying to find the right words. "—in front of all my friends, embarrassed me."

"I know. I was being stupid. It will never happen again. I promise." Filip took my hand to reassure me.

"Yeah, you were! If you don't know how to drink, you shouldn't drink at all." I pulled my hand back. I wasn't ready for physical contact just yet.

"I know! You're right! I don't know my limits. Can you please come home?"

"I think I'm going to stay here another night."

"But we're having a baby. You have to come home, please?"

"Filip, no. I need more time. Maybe tomorrow, but not tonight."

At this Filip grew frustrated, some of his sincerity melting away as he returned to our place. Mom leaned in for a hug. She understood.

I kept my word. The following day, I gathered my toothbrush and clothes, and went home. Filip seemed happy to see me, but I was holding a deeper hurt by his behavior.

"We need to talk," I said. I had prepared a little speech. I spoke firmly, looking him straight in the eye. "I didn't leave you. I needed some space. I needed some quiet time away from you to think without fighting with you. What you did was wrong, and I hear what you're saying. You had too much to drink and you didn't know what you're doing, but that doesn't excuse your behavior. I don't like how you acted toward me. That hurt my feelings. You should know your limits when you drink, and you might think about totally stopping if you can't do that."

"I know, I know. I love you, and you're absolutely right. I'm really sorry about everything, and I promise it won't happen again." Filip sounded sincere, loving, and caring—finally. "I'll do better next time. I promise."

"Please do! I don't want to go through this again. This was tough on me. You made me cry."

He took me in his big, strong arms into a warm, loving hug. "I love you so much. I was miserable without you. I didn't know what to do." He kissed my cheek.

"I was sad, too, Filip, and I love you too. Let's not fight anymore."

"I agree, my love."

We had made up, as if nothing had ever happened. We were happy to be in each other's arms again. Filip's fingers ran through my hair. I tickled his nose with my hair, which I knew he didn't really like. He laughed.

We were us again and quickly settled back into our day-to-day routine. I had faith that Filip would make good on his promise. After all, as he had pointed out, we were having a baby.

✦

The next few weeks flew by as doctor's visits became more regular, and we prepared for our baby's arrival. Neither of us knew how to be a parent, so we were naturally nervous about the prospect. But we were also certain of one thing—both Filip and I couldn't wait to meet our little bean.

Shortly after entering the second trimester, I began to feel flutters inside my belly, like little bubbles. Little bean was learning how to stretch and swim. At first, those flutters felt like butterfly tickles, but soon they grew strong enough for Filip to feel them. The first time he felt the baby kick, his face lit up with joy and he leaned into my belly, shouting with excitement. "Hey! What's up? I'm your dad." We both burst into laughter.

From that point on, we spent our evenings on the couch after work, waiting for the next kick, talking to my belly, and playing music to our baby. Filip and I were the kind of people who couldn't wait—couldn't wait until our next ultrasound appointment, couldn't wait to find out the sex of our baby, couldn't wait to meet him or her, and couldn't wait to hold our child in our arms.

Halfway through the pregnancy, we scheduled the ultrasound appointment where we would find out if our baby was a boy or a girl. Filip and I went together, hand in hand, enthusiastic to see our child on the ultrasound monitor.

The majority of men I know want their firstborn child to be a boy to ensure the family name is passed on to the next generation. Not Filip. Filip had fond memories of Addie, Adem, and Kendra's baby girl and hoped for a baby girl of his own. He dreamed of carrying her on his shoulders and spoiling her like a princess. Every time he talked about having a girl, how he would take her to fairs and hold her hand on roller coaster rides, I fell more deeply in love with him. The way he talked about our growing family made his eyes sparkle with happiness and joy.

I, on the other hand, simply prayed for a healthy and happy baby. Whether our child was a boy or a girl, I knew I would love the baby with my whole heart and soul and would try my best to give him or her a good life.

As eager as we were to find out if we were having a boy or a girl, it seemed that our baby bean did not want to reveal itself yet. The baby stubbornly sat in a yoga position with legs crossed, and our doctor couldn't determine the sex. We saw ten fingers and ten cute little toes and were grateful the baby was developing on track, but the sex remained elusive.

The ultrasound tech had me jumping through hoops to get the baby to move. "Okay, try rolling on your side," she instructed. When that didn't work, she tried another tack. "Try lying on your back. Maybe that will get the baby to move."

I did everything she said, hoping to get some results, but no luck. Then she asked me to stand up, walk around, and hop back on the table. The baby stubbornly held the same position. We must have spent a good twenty minutes in that room with the tech wiggling the ultrasound wand on my belly to tickle the baby while I held my breath. Nothing. Just as we were about to accept that we might not learn our baby's sex at this appointment after all, I turned once more to the side, exhaling in disappointment.

Just as I did that, the tech's face lit up. "Wait a minute, don't move! I see something. I can't say with a 100 percent certainty, but I think you guys are having a wonderful, healthy little girl. Congratulations!"

"Really, it's a girl!?" Filip laughed excitedly. He turned to me. "I told you!"

The joy in his eyes was as bright as the sun. Everything he had been dreaming about was coming true. He laid his arms on my body as I lay on the examination table. "We're having a girl! Thank you so much!"

Happy tears trickled down my face. I pictured everything Filip was dreaming, and then some. A beautiful little girl with light brown hair, pigtails, and the most adorable big, blue eyes sitting on top of her daddy's shoulders, laughing and giggling. Our family picnicking together in the park and going to fairs and festivals. Our little girl smiling on a merry-go-round and a Ferris wheel, her face bright with fun. I thought about the future and how wonderful it would be for her to have a sibling one day, maybe a baby brother, who would be her best friend, like Ami was to me.

As soon as we got out of the doctor's office, we sat on a bench in front of the doctor's office for an hour, making phone call after phone call to dozens of people congratulating us and sharing our joy. Our little bean was the first grandchild on both sides of the family. We wanted to let the whole world know we were having a baby girl. She was only halfway to being born but was already loved by so many people, near and far. We were beyond blessed as we thanked the Heavens for the promise of the bright future that lay ahead of us.

CHAPTER 9

THE GIFT OF LIFE

After we made up from that awful fight on the night of the concert, things were great between us for a while. I lived what many women would consider a dream life—happily in love with a man who greeted me with arms wide open at the end of a long day, who made me laugh as he shouted into my belly while he spoke to our unborn child, and who gladly went back to the grocery store to pick up the right kind of feta cheese to satisfy my pregnancy cravings. In many respects, Filip was an angel.

Sure, he had his dissatisfactions, but who doesn't? He didn't like that we lived so far away from his parents and was vocal about missing them. He also missed his sister and his friends, Adem and Kendra. He didn't talk about it much, but I think he was put out that I had a better job than he did and owned the condo on my own.

And though I pushed it as far back into my mind as I could, the possibility of a repeat of that awful night loomed over everything.

✦

It all came to a head when his mother, Olga, suddenly fell gravely ill and went into the hospital. She was hospitalized immediately. That's when we got the call from Filip's family.

The doctors saw something on her scans that looked troublesome and scheduled an explorative surgery. The unexpected news came as a shock.

The thought of her being healthy one minute and finding out she might only have a few months to live the next shook me and Filip to the core.

Naturally, Olga was worried. "I was looking forward to holding my first grandchild. Now I may not even live long enough to see the day she's born," she said to me.

I tried to console her, hoping my words didn't ring hollow. "Don't give up hope. We don't know what this is. And whatever it is, I'm sure there are treatments. We're here to help you fight this thing!"

"I have no hope!" Olga lamented. "They gave me a day to prepare for this surgery. A day. Can you believe that?"

Filip jumped in. "You will get through this, Mom." Filip looked at me, and we both shared the same thought.

"Don't worry Olga," I said. "We'll get Filip on the next plane out of here."

Filip hung up the phone, buried his face in his hands, and cried. I had never seen him that upset.

That evening, we got Filip on an early morning flight after shelling out a pretty penny for the last-minute ticket. The flight would allow him to arrive at the hospital around the time Olga was scheduled to come out of surgery.

I drove him to the airport early the next day. We were both scared with uncertainty. Filip was torn between leaving me behind, pregnant and alone, and being there for his family. With my family nearby to look out for me until his return, I insisted he go.

Filip said goodbye at the airport, still unsure about his decision. I drove home, hoping to catch a few more hours of sleep. Just as I dozed off, the phone woke me up again. The ID indicated it was Mateo. I picked up immediately. "Hi, Mateo. What's the news?"

"Sweet daughter-in-law, Olga's out of surgery and everything is fine," he said, giddy with relief. "The good news is that she'll make a full recovery."

"Thank God! I'm so relieved!" I exhaled deeply. "Filip will be so happy. I've never seen him so upset."

"He can relax now. We all can. She's well. The surgery went well too. Thank you both for being so supportive. I don't know what we would do without you."

"You are very welcome. That's what families are for. Please tell Olga I wish I could be there, and I wish her a fast recovery."

"I sure will, my sweet daughter-in-law."

Good news offered major relief. I was too excited to go back to bed and couldn't wait for Filip's plane to land. I wanted to share the good news, so he could stop worrying. He must have been terrified. Olga was only forty-seven. Losing such a young parent would have been devastating.

When Filip's plane landed, Mateo was there to greet him and tell him the good news. They drove straight to the hospital, and the family rejoiced.

Two days later, Olga was released. When they called me from the car on the way home, everyone was in good spirits and laughing, even Olga.

Filip had left home in a hurry and had planned to stay in Atlanta for at least a week. Now that his Mom was headed home, he decided to use the rest of his time in Atlanta to catch up with family and friends. Before hanging up, Filip said he was going out with Adem that night.

I had no problem with the two best friends catching up. He missed his Georgia friends, and I wanted him to be happy.

I logged into our bank account the next day to pay bills and saw a $255 charge to Meehan's Bar and Grill. I thought this was an error, or worse, fraud. Who spent that much at a bar? I called Filip to let him know of the suspicious charges on the debit card.

"We went out last night; I told you," Filip replied.

"Okay, love, $255 seems a little excessive." I tried to remain calm, but we had just spent a small fortune on Filip's flight and had a baby on the way. We didn't have much to spare. I expected Filip to have more common sense.

"I took Adem out. We had some appetizers and a couple of beers."

"That seems like a lot for appetizers and a few beers." I was honestly confused and just trying to understand.

"The waitress brought us some shots too. They were like $11 apiece. I had no idea they were so expensive."

"How many did you guys have Filip? I'm not mad. It just seems like a lot of money. You went there to see your sick mom and now you're partying with your buddy. We have a baby on the way." I was hoping he'd at least admit that hadn't been his best idea ever.

"I get it!" Filip fired back instead. "I can't spend time with my friends. This is about me coming out here. I knew I shouldn't have come." This was typical Filip. When he was backed into a corner, he turned the tables and lashed out.

"Did I say you shouldn't have gone? I love Olga, too, and I'm the one who bought the tickets. I'm talking about the bar tab. We don't have much to spare, Filip." I was near to crying I was so frustrated. "I can't talk to you right now. I have to go. Bye." I hung up.

Within seconds, Filip called back. "So that's it? You're just going to hang up on me like that? I expect more respect than that."

He was fuming, but now so was I. That's not how you treat your partner, the mother of your child. I had supported Filip and his family and expected to be heard. If Filip wanted a silent partner, a wallflower who didn't question her man, he was with the wrong woman. He should support my strength, admire it. That strength is what had gotten us this far. Instead, it enraged him.

"Yes," I said as calmly as I could. "And I will do it again, because I am done with this conversation." I hung up for the second time and shut off the phone.

I spent the next two hours in tears. Later that evening, I turned my phone back on to several messages from Filip, all of which I decided to ignore. When he called again around 8:00 p.m., I picked up, and we ended up fighting over the phone for over an hour. While I was on the phone with Filip, my other line rang and Olga's number came up.

"Why is your mom calling my other line? Aren't you home?" I asked Filip.

"I'm in my old room. I don't know why my mom is calling you." He seemed just as puzzled as I was.

I put Filip on hold. "Hey, what's up? I'm on the other line with Filip. I thought he was at home."

"Yeah, he is home. It's just that he's been on the phone for a while, and I wasn't sure who he was talking to. I'm glad it's you. Okay, I'll leave you two alone. Bye now." And she hung up.

I never got a chance to ask who she thought Filip had been talking to. When I went back to Filip's line, that made us chuckle together and put the fight behind us. I chalked up that fight to stress about Olga's health scare and decided to let it go. Again.

When Filip arrived home, I was happy to see him.

✦

Time flew by with Olga recovering from surgery and Filip and I getting ready for our baby's arrival. We had decided to name her Amaya.

Between two baby showers, we had most of what we needed. This presented a problem, however. After assembling the crib, the baby swing, and the diaper changing station, we found our one-bedroom condo way too small. We would barely have room for the three of us, let alone Filip's family when they came to visit when the baby was born.

We decided to look for a bigger place for our growing family and list the condo for sale. We hoped to rent half of a duplex with a fenced-in backyard and a swing set where our baby girl could play and grow. We came by a charming place, not too far from where we lived. It felt perfect, so the condo went on the market, and we put a deposit on the duplex.

The real-estate market was booming. An offer on the condo came through within days, the sale date just two weeks before Amaya was due. Ami, Hamza, Mom, and Dad all pitched in and helped with the move. For the first time since we immigrated to the United States, we had our own washer and dryer in the garage. The thought of not having to lug baskets to a laundry room was liberating.

We had settled into our new home just days before Amaya's due date. On the day she was due, I held my breath in anticipation all day, waiting anxiously for the first signs of labor. At the end of the day, after not having felt even the slightest of contractions, I broke down in tears. I couldn't bear waiting another second to finally meet my little girl and hold her in my arms.

The following day, I decided to keep busy by sorting through a few unpacked boxes. As I wobbled around the house, sporting an oversized belly, my eye caught something scurrying in the nooks and crannies. I looked more closely, afraid of what I would see. But I was right. Cockroaches! I hate cockroaches. Close to panic, I scuttled to the phone to call our new landlord. He didn't ask any questions, acting as if he had been expecting the call. He told me he'd send over an exterminator and disconnected the call.

Within hours a man wearing a Terminix uniform arrived. As he sprayed along the baseboards and in the cracks and crevices, the nasty little creatures crawled out of their hiding spots and went everywhere. It was like a horror movie. The sight of cockroaches crawling on the floors and walls petrified me. I waddled to my car and sped off to Mom's place. I was not about to go into labor in that roach-infested house doused in insecticide, and I was definitely not going to bring my newborn child back there.

On the way to Mom's, I called Filip in tears. He attempted to calm me down without much success.

"The only way I can calm down, Filip, is if I never have to set foot into that nasty, awful house ever again. I'm not going back there! You have no idea. They were everywhere. They were crawling on our baby's things. Ugh."

"How about I meet you at your mom's after work? We can figure out what to do," Filip replied in a soothing voice.

"Okay. All right. But if figuring it out means going back to that nasty house, you're going by yourself."

When Filip got home from work, we agreed to stay with Ami and Hamza for a couple of days until we figured out our next steps. I was already two days past the due date.

That night, I woke up a little after 2:00 a.m. with strong and consistent labor pains. Thinking this could be it, I woke up Filip, so he could get ready while I took a shower. But as soon as I got into the shower, the pain stopped! A false alarm. Disappointed and frustrated, we waited another forty-five minutes and went back to bed.

After a rough night with little sleep, Filip, Ami, and Hamza insisted on staying home with me instead of going to work. I felt it unnecessary, as there were no signs of labor, and convinced them to go to work, promising I'd call if anything changed.

Mom had been checking in with me first thing in the morning for any updates. When she heard about our night, she called in to work to take the day off to stay with me. I couldn't convince her otherwise. Since Ami and Mom lived in the same complex, I took a walk over to Mom's place in hopes of getting labor started. She made us breakfast, and we enjoyed a quiet morning together.

Sometime around noon that day, as I waddled to the bathroom, I felt a warm gush of liquid stream down my legs. I wasn't sure if that was my water breaking, so I put in a call to my doctor's office. They suggested I go to the hospital to get checked out. Excited, Mom and I alerted Filip, Ami, and Hamza, and I called Dad.

We weren't in any rush. Mom lived across the street from the hospital, and I wasn't in pain, so we waited for everyone to get home before going to the hospital together. When I suggested walking there, my family looked at me aghast, then ushered me into the car, drove over two parking lot speed bumps and across the street to hospital's admittance area.

The labor and delivery staff had been waiting for us. They checked me in when we arrived and let us know I'd be staying. This baby's birth was happening, finally! Everyone was in good spirits, joking and laughing, until the labor pains kicked in full force.

Suddenly, my pain went from a tolerable six to fifty-six on a zero to ten scale. I doubled over, my entire body cramping into a contraction for what seemed like an eternity. Then the spasms relaxed briefly, I caught my breath, and they started again. This went on for several hours and made me want to vomit and pass out with each wave. Finally, I caved and requested an epidural injection. I felt a deep appreciation for my mom and centuries of women before me who had gone through this kind of pain without relief.

Nurses moved me to a birthing room, at which point, I had lost the feeling of pain in my stomach and lower back, as well as the use of my legs due to the epidural injection. Worn out and exhausted, I dozed off. A little before 11:00 p.m., the doctors returned and advised it would be several hours before delivery. I dozed off again. Not twenty minutes had gone by when I was hit by an intense pressure, as if my bottom were about to fall off.

I called for the nurse again.

She said, "The doctor just checked you. You haven't progressed enough. Try to go back to sleep."

"No, you need to call the doctor! Now! I feel like everything is about to fall out of me."

The nurse gave in and called for a doctor. Sure enough, as soon as I was examined again, half dozen nurses and assistants poured into the room, clearing out family members to make room for trays, unwrapping sterile instruments, and preparing for delivery. Mom and Filip stayed in the room with me.

I didn't want my firstborn child to be born on April Fool's Day, but my dear Amaya had a mind of her own. Precisely twelve minutes after midnight on April 1, our little bundle of joy made her magical appearance. As they handed her to me, my entire body was quivering and shaking uncontrollably. The doctors say that's a normal reaction to adrenaline and hormonal changes after delivery.

I was crying and laughing at the same time as I set my eyes on our beautiful little miracle for the first time. They placed her on my chest, and I whispered, "Hello, Mommy's gorgeous little bean. It's so good to meet you. Welcome to the world, beautiful."

Her eyes were closed, but as soon as she heard my voice, she tried to open them. Bright lights in the room bothered her, and she quickly closed them tightly. I pulled her closer to my face, our foreheads almost touching, and I put my hand over her eyes, to block the light from bothering her. Amaya opened her eyes again, this time allowing me to see those adorable deep blues and looked straight at me. We stared at each other for a couple of seconds, sharing a magical moment before she closed her eyes again.

No feeling in the world can describe the joy of becoming a new parent. Filip draped his big frame over both of us, as if shielding us from the outside world, hugging both Amaya and me at the same time while whispering to her, "Hi baby!" Then he turned to me and said, "Isn't she beautiful?"

"Would you like to hold your daughter, Filip?" I asked him.

"She's so small, I'm afraid I'll break her." Filip held up his large hands.

"You won't break her, silly," I said, handing her to Filip.

"She looks like a loaf of bread, all wrapped up snug in this blanket." He laughed as he took Amaya in his arms for the very first time, holding her as gently as he could.

The moment Filip took Amaya in his arms, several nurses shouted at the same time that she looked just like him: "A female version of her daddy," one said.

✦

As I recovered, Mom and Ami stayed up late into the night getting acquainted with Amaya. Filip, Hamza, and Dad left the hospital to rest up in preparation for packing our stuff for another move. Unbeknownst to me, while I was in labor, Mom had reached out to her old landlord in the same building where I had owned my condo and made arrangements with him to rent her old one-bedroom apartment to us. Filip signed the lease in the morning and with the help of my family, moved all our stuff while I was in the hospital.

By the time Amaya and I were released from the hospital, everyone pitched in to move, unpack, rewash baby clothes and decorate the living room with balloons, ribbons, and pink Welcome Baby banners. Filip got me a lovely bouquet of roses, and I felt like the luckiest woman in the world to have an army of a support system to get everything done. I imagine no one got more than a few hours of sleep.

✦

On our first day with the new baby in the new apartment, Ami and Hamza came to visit, both with mischievous smiles. Clearly, something was up. I prodded them for clues.

They hesitated, but finally they announced that after a year of trying, they had just found out that Ami was pregnant.

"I'm going to be an aunt?" I screamed out. "Oh my God! Congratulations, you guys!" I got up carefully from my rocking chair to give them both a hug.

"Thanks!" Ami said. "We still can't believe it! But please don't say anything to anyone yet. We want to wait a few weeks."

"Of course! Oh my God, you guys are going to be parents too!" Tears of joy ran down my face because I know how much they both wanted a baby.

✦

To say that Amaya's first week on this Earth was exciting and eventful would be an understatement. Filip's family flew into town to stay with us for a week to meet their first grandchild. With nine adults and a newborn baby crammed into a small apartment, our living room was packed with people and filled with lots of laughter. The only guests we could have were my best friends Jasmina and Hari, but they were more like family. All other friends had to wait to visit.

The only private mommy-and-daughter time we had was while breastfeeding. It was a learning experience for both of us, and the beginning was slow and painful. Amaya latching on made my toes curl in pain, but I was determined to give my baby the best nutrition I possibly could.

Mothers' bodies are miraculous. As a woman, I'd been biologically engineered to produce the most ideal combination of vitamins, proteins, carbs, and fat—a super-cocktail of antibodies, hormones, amino-acids and living organisms to help my baby fight off infections and develop her body and brain. I was also burning all kinds of extra calories, which helped me return to my pre-pregnancy weight quickly. I felt like Supermom! Breastfeeding was convenient, quick, and free. We didn't have to buy formula, the food was readily available, and zero prep time was required.

Filip took some time off work to help out around the house while I recovered, and until his family left. The week flew by quickly and then Mateo, Olga, and Filip's sister Tina headed back to Atlanta.

That afternoon was the very first time that Amaya, Filip, and I were finally alone with no visitors. I fed Amaya and put her to sleep in her crib in our bedroom. As I quietly closed the door behind me, I found Filip sitting outside on the balcony, smoking a cigarette. He looked at me lovingly and smiled, "Come sit with me, love. I want to have a cigarette with the mother of my child."

"Ugh, you know that if I have that cigarette now, I'm going to start smoking again." Before the pregnancy, it was how we used to relax after a long week at work.

"Just one. I really want to have a cigarette with you."

We both deserved a break after the whirlwind of a week we just had. I took a cigarette out of the pack that Filip was holding out for me and sat in his lap as he lit it up for me. That first hit of nicotine after months of being smoke-free made me lightheaded and dizzy. Then after a bit it had a calming effect. Filip and I hugged, smoking our cigarettes in silence.

✦

Now that we had some time to breathe, it hit us. Everything had changed. We were parents now. Everything that came before this moment was irrelevant. From there on out, we had a tiny little human we were responsible for. This little person, sleeping peacefully in her crib in our bedroom, was the most important person in the world to us.

CHAPTER 10

A MOSTLY BLISSFUL TIME

Amaya was an easy baby. More than anything, she loved being held—and I loved holding her. She slept peacefully on my chest while I rocked her for hours, watching her sleep, gently rubbing the back of her head. Amaya had a soothing effect on me. After feeding, she dozed off into a deep slumber, snuggled comfortably in my arms. An overwhelming sense of calmness and bliss would come over me each and every time. Seeing her content made me relaxed and sleepy, my body completely loose, my mind carefree. I would get lost in those moments of utter happiness and could never understand moms who leave their crying infants in cribs until they learn to soothe themselves. The thought of Amaya crying made me shudder. Why would I ever leave my beautiful, innocent newborn child to cry herself to sleep if all I had to do was pick her up and soothe her? All she wanted was love and a dry diaper. I enjoyed every second of our time together, quietly humming the words to Guns N' Roses "Sweet Child O' Mine" while rocking her to sleep.

When she was awake, her big eyes watched me constantly. She soaked in everything happening around her. When she heard a sound, she snapped her head up to investigate. Every once in a while, she arched her tiny curled-up body as if trying to make herself appear bigger. Her ten perfect little fingers and ten perfect little toes sprawled out as she let out a big yawn like a tired old man.

At two weeks old, she smiled at me for the first time. It was more of a reflexive smile in the middle of a dream, but a smile, nonetheless. A sense of incredible joy came over me. There was no better feeling in this world than seeing my child smiling.

After we became parents, Filip was incredibly loving and sweet with Amaya and me. Our relationship was thriving. He was attentive and caring. He never shirked his share of childcare, and often jumped in to help with Amaya's diaper changes in the middle of the night, or to care for her while I showered and ate. He was thoughtful and considerate, and I adored that about him. It didn't matter to me that we weren't married yet. We were a family.

But Filip had a few surprises up his sleeve.

On the morning of my twenty-sixth birthday, he got up first and made me coffee, which was not the norm. Filip sat on the couch next to me, restless, acting slightly off-kilter and awkward. He handed me a cup of coffee, then carefully moved the coffee table out of the way and got down on one knee. As he took my hand into his, he pulled out an eighteen-karat gold engagement ring, embedded with two rows of diamonds and stumbled through his words. "You gave me a family—something I always dreamed of. Will you be my wife?"

It was a simple and loving proposal, so I responded with a simple, "Yes," after which we hugged and then grabbed our phones to call our parents.

I often had had qualms about not starting our family the traditional way— by getting married first, then having a baby. I regretted jumping into marriage with Alen when I was younger and not considering the impact of that decision. While still on maternity leave, I had extra time and a chance to set things straight. This was my chance to redeem myself and do right by Filip and Amaya. I filed for a divorce from Alen.

By then, Alen had moved on too. He was happy in another relationship, and he no longer wanted to stand in my way. And so, my first marriage ended in an uncontested divorce.

Filip and I could start planning our wedding.

✦

Six weeks of maternity leave flew by in the blink of an eye. Going back to work was rough. My career was important financially, but secretly I dreamed of being a stay-at-home mom. Considering I made more money than Filip and

Amaya's medical insurance came through my employer, staying home was not really an option.

Finding good childcare so I could return to work wasn't easy, though. Leaving our sweet girl in a daycare center overcrowded with other babies where she would not receive a sufficient amount of care and attention was a non-starter. Hiring a full-time nanny was not in our budget. I would have preferred leaving her with family, but everyone worked full time.

A Bosnian woman named Shayla, who was unemployed at the time, offered to babysit Amaya part time for us at home at an affordable rate. She was a friend of a friend and seemed like a decent woman, so Filip and I decided to give her a try. I invited her to spend a couple of hours with us the weekend before I was scheduled to return to work, both to give Amaya a chance to get used to Shayla and to give Shayla time to learn our routine.

To put off formula-feeding for as long as possible, I was pumping breast-milk to freeze for Amaya to drink while I was at work. That meant waking up at 4:00 a.m. every morning and subjecting myself to thirty minutes of excru-ciating pain as the pump extracted enough milk to fill a four-ounce bottle. However, the sacrifice was worth the payoff if it meant my daughter got the best nutrition possible.

Shayla thought she knew better, though, and insisted on supplementing the breastmilk with formula. When I called her out on it, she said, "I just don't think she's getting enough food."

"Are we talking about the baby who is in the ninety-fifth percentile for height and weight? There's a week's supply of milk in the freezer. She does not need formula."

"I think she does," Shayla insisted.

"And I think we're done here." I showed her the door while explaining that we would no longer be needing her services.

This was a rash decision, perhaps, but I wasn't going to have other people make decisions for my baby. We'd have to figure out something else, like we always did.

That's when Mom stepped up. She arranged to work ten hours on Fridays, Saturdays, Sundays, and Mondays, which gave her Tuesdays, Wednesdays, and Thursdays to take care of Amaya. Meanwhile, I arranged to work from home on Mondays and Fridays. Between Mom and me, we had the whole workweek covered and Amaya was in safe hands.

Mom was truly wonderful with Amaya. She adored her first grandbaby and spoiled her every chance she got. She sang lullabies, played peek-a-boo, read nursery rhymes, and made Amaya laugh. If Filip and I had to be away from our child, there was no better person in the world to care for her than Mom. There wasn't anything Mom wouldn't do for Amaya. Not only was she the best babysitter in the world, she came free-of-charge, and because she was better organized than I, she used Amaya's nap time to cook for us! A double bonus.

We fell into a routine, and before we knew it, Ami's and Hamza's time was coming. We started counting down the days until we'd get to meet another little miracle.

✦

Life can be a roller-coaster ride. In one moment, our family was feeling on top of the world with happiness and joy at Amaya's arrival and Ami's news that she was expecting a child of her own. But Ami's first trimester was not going well. She had a rough time with morning sickness, nausea, and vomiting, which landed her in an emergency room on several occasions, severely dehydrated and requiring IV fluids and glucose.

By the time she was seven months along, both Ami's and Hamza's companies downsized, and they were let go. One partner out of a job can be unnerving when expecting a first child, let alone both. With mounting hospital bills, the worry was magnified tenfold. Luckily, Dad jumped to the rescue, helping Ami and Hamza get hired managing a small residential apartment complex with thirty rental units. In exchange for a free one-bedroom apartment, they were in charge of maintaining the grounds, marketing available apartment units, and cleaning up.

This meant they had to move immediately, even though they had a few more months left on their lease of a two-bedroom condo. Instead of paying penalties to break out of their lease, Filip and I offered to take over their condo. We needed the extra space, and the rent was only $200 more per month. That meant Filip and I were moving for the fourth time in eighteen months.

With so much moving, packing, and unpacking for all of us, the last two months of Ami's pregnancy went by quickly. After months of waiting, we finally got the long-anticipated call that Ami was in labor. Hamza was rushing her to the hospital as I left work in a hurry to meet them there. In fact, the whole family made it there in record time, and within minutes, Mom, Dad, Filip, and I congregated around Ami's bed, offering ice chips and foot rubs.

After hours of labor, at around two hours past midnight on December 5, 2004, baby Amra was born. Hamza, Mom, and I were in the room to witness this incredible moment and welcome beautiful baby Amra to the world, and what a beauty she was. Tears of joy ran down my face as I hugged my sister tightly and welcomed her to motherhood. I knew Ami would make a great mom, and I knew Amaya would have a best friend for life in her new cousin.

I ran out to the waiting room where Filip and Dad were waiting with Amaya in anticipation of happy news. I congratulated my dad on becoming a grandpa for the second time and Filip on becoming an uncle for the first time. We celebrated while hugging and kissing each other.

It was my turn to return the favor by going all-out decorating Ami's place with Welcome Baby signs. Mom and I snatched the keys to their apartment from Hamza and went to work. With white and pink ribbons, streamers and balloons, we made their one-bedroom apartment postcard perfect. When Ami came home from the hospital, we muffled our yells into a quiet "Surprise!" to keep our sleeping beauty Amra from waking up. Ami was touched—and happy to be home.

+

Around this time, Filip was making his fair share of hospital visits as well. He had a work-related injury and went out on disability. Without work to keep him occupied all day, Filip turned into a grumpy old man. I attributed his constant agitation to the pain of the injury. Everything began to bother him—

my friends coming over too often, my sister and her family spending too much time at our house, my mom living too close. The list only grew.

The only thing that seemed to brighten up his day and put a smile on his face was playing video games and spending time with Amaya, so Filip decided to watch Amaya full time until he was cleared to return to work. This would end up taking more than three years. One good thing, though, was that Filip staying at home allowed Mom to go back to a Monday through Friday work schedule. I had missed seeing Mom on the weekends.

✦

With all the health issues, hospital visits, and constantly moving around, we needed a celebration badly, so Filip and I began planning our wedding. I did most of the planning and ran things past Filip, a process that worked well for us. Neither of us were interested in spending a small fortune on an elaborate wedding. We opted for a small, family-only ceremony at City Hall instead.

We paid for Filip's family to fly out to California. Ami was our Matron of Honor, and Hamza our Best Man. Though Olga and Mateo could only stay for a few days due to work, Tina was taking a break from school and decided to stay for the whole summer.

Our wedding took place on September 2, 2005. For a refugee kid from Bosnia, this was a significant day.

My wedding dress was a romantic, off-the-shoulder, sleeveless neckline ball gown with floral appliques and a royal train. I dressed at Mom's place, and, with family by my side, walked downstairs where the limousine, which was parked in front of our building, was waiting. My gorgeously tall and handsome Filip stood by the limo driver, who held the door for me while Filip held out his hand to help me inside.

Filip wore a light grey tuxedo with peak lapel, a matching grey vest, and a white dress shirt. Filip's tux hugged the natural shape of his big, broad shoulders, and his light blue tie accentuated the color of his eyes, bringing out their warmth. Everything looked stunning on him, down to his polished black shoes, which matched the color of his hair. I felt like a princess that day in my wedding dress standing next to the man I loved. While everyone was looking at me, the only person I saw was the father of my beautiful baby girl, who was about to become my husband.

Our simple and elegant wedding ceremony was wonderful—although in the middle of saying our vows I became overwhelmed with a sense of joy and pride and began crying uncontrollably. Sobbing and laughing at the same time—and apologizing profusely for crying while repeating my vows—I said "I do" to Filip. I loved him with my whole heart and was proud to become his wife. Afterward, everyone teased me for being the family niveler, which I could not deny. I even cried at commercials.

The first thing we did as a married couple was to hop back inside the limo, which whisked us away for a ride around town while the family went back home to prepare for the reception. Our driver suggested a picturesque ride through Saratoga Hills with breathtaking 180-degree views of the Bay Area.

As we left City Hall, Filip popped open a bottle of champagne, toasting to a long-lasting marriage with a smile. "May we always be happy together!" he said cheerfully raising his glass.

"Hear, hear!" I smiled back at my gorgeous husband. "I love you!"

"I love you too! Always and forever!"

The driver pulled up at a vista point where we parked and had the driver take pictures before he took us back to the condo.

Reunited with family after a romantic limo ride, we packed three cars and drove together to the reception hall. As a surprise wedding gift, Ami and Hamza had bought a karaoke machine, hooked it up, and passed around a microphone from one family member to another for everyone to say a few words in tribute.

Tina had written a touching song, which she sang beautifully, bringing everyone to tears. Hamza and Ami sang a parody of a Bosnian song about a village man getting married, twisting the words to apply to Filip and me. By the time they were done, everyone was laughing.

After the toasts, Filip and I had our first dance as a married couple, holding our sweet daughter between us while sharing a perfect moment. Then a full-on karaoke party broke out, and we all had a wonderful time.

Two days later, we took Filip's parents to the airport for their return to Atlanta, then went home to pack for our Hawaii honeymoon.

Since Ami and I had been to Honolulu in 2001, I had always thought it would be the most romantic place for a honeymoon. Both Ami and I had wanted to go back there ever since, while Filip, Mom, Tina, and Hamza had never been there. We all agreed that Hawaii was the place to go. Our honeymoon turned into a big family vacation.

While we were putting the trip together, Filip teased me by saying things like, "Who drags their whole family on their honeymoon?"

There was only one answer to that. "People who have a baby first, then get married, and need a babysitter. Don't worry. We'll have fun, family and all. Hawaii is awesome!"

The five-hour flight turned into a continuation of our wedding reception, with everyone joking and talking, switching seats every thirty minutes, and passing food, drinks and snacks up and down the aisle.

After we checked into our hotel rooms, the first order of business was to meet downstairs at the Shorebird Bar and Grill for a meal and cocktails. I was looking forward to a local favorite, called lava flow, made from slushy cream of coconut, with pineapple and strawberries. While we waited for our food, we sipped on our drinks and watched the ocean's clear turquoise water swell into waves and crash onto beautiful yellow sands of Waikiki shore.

Over the next several days, Filip and I got to spend quite a bit of alone time honeymooning, as Mom and Tina took turns watching Amaya. We booked a romantic sunset dinner cruise and stood on the deck of the catamaran ship as we toasted each other while watching the sun set over the Waikiki beach. Later that same evening, we took a long, romantic stroll on the beach by ourselves. A day later, we rented a car and drove through the busy highways of Honolulu up to North Shore, where we explored a normally quiet part of the island, which only comes alive in December when it hosts the world's top surfing competitions.

It was a great trip! Neither of us had considered leaving Amaya at home. Bringing her and family along worked out perfectly. We had our precious cargo with us but could still venture out on our own. And we had fun with family on the beach too. Filip and Hamza dug a knee-deep hole in the sand for Amaya and Amra to play in and filled it up with water—their own private pool. While the girls played in the sand, Filip and Hamza entertained the beachgoers that day by wearing the straw hula skirts and coconut tops Mom got for Amaya and Amra. Everyone laughed at their antics.

+

Shortly after returning from Hawaii, I began longing for another child. Amaya was eighteen months old, and that seemed like a good age gap. At twenty-eight months apart, Ami and I had always been very close. Filip and Tina, who were five years apart, didn't seem as close.

Still unemployed, Filip was not thrilled with the idea at first. It took some persuading, but eventually Filip conceded, and we began trying.

I had another week-long trip to Huntsville coming up in early January. This would have been my first business trip since giving birth to Amaya, and I couldn't imagine being separated from my little girl. A week away seemed like an eternity. I suggested to Filip that the three of us fly together to Atlanta on the preceding Friday night, rent a car, spend the weekend with Filip's family, then drive together to Huntsville where I could work during the week while Filip and Amaya explored the city. At the end of the week, we would all drive back to Atlanta to spend another weekend with Filip's family and fly back home on Sunday afternoon. It seemed like a great way to catch up with his family.

I felt queasy as soon as we landed in Atlanta, but I figured I caught a bug on the plane. I labored through the weekend visit with Filip's folks and the work week in Huntsville, but by Friday, the nausea had gotten worse. Was I pregnant already? I decided to wait it out without saying anything to anyone.

After we packed our bags to return to San Jose, I asked Filip to take me to a grocery store to buy a pregnancy test. Excited at the possibility of another baby, we rushed through the aisles, paid for the test, and drove back to

Filip's parents' house, exhilarated. With Filip impatiently sitting next to me at the edge of the bathtub, I took the test, and within seconds, it flashed a positive result. We both squealed with joy, trying hard to keep our voices down.

It was fitting we tell his family first, considering we found out at their house. Like a couple of high schoolers sneaking around the school hallways, we held hands as we walked together to the living room.

"So, we have something to tell you guys," Filip started, with a boyish grin.

"What is it? Is everything okay?" Olga sounded worried.

"Everything is fine! It's really good news," I said.

"What? What? Sweet daughter-in-law, tell us."

"Annie's pregnant again!" Filip jumped in, a big smile on his face.

"Oh my God! Seriously?" Tina yelled out.

"Wait? What? You've been here this whole time, and you didn't tell us?" Olga scolded but in a happy way.

"We literally just found out two minutes ago!" I said.

"My sweet daughter-in-law!" Mateo hugged me. "Does that mean we are the first to find out?"

"Yep, you guys are the first to know!"

"Wow! I cannot believe it, congratulations!" Olga yelled.

"No wonder you looked a little pale, Annie. Congratulations guys!" Tina winked at me as she gave me a hug.

Mateo held Filip's eyes meaningfully, then patted him on the back and said, "My dearest son! I'm so proud of you! Congratulations to you both. We're honored and happy you told us first."

We went around the room, everyone hugging and kissing, while Amaya stared at the commotion with her big blue eyes, not sure what to make of the silly adults around her. It was a perfect ending to a great weekend with Filip's family.

✦

When we arrived in San Jose, Ami and Hamza were waiting at the airport, while Mom waited for us at home, watching Amra and cooking. We couldn't wait to tell everyone. As we walked in the front door, I hugged Mom and blurted out, "It looks like you're about to become a grandma for the third time!"

"Welcome home! Wait, what? You're kidding?" Mom replied.

"Really? You're pregnant again?" Ami joined in a hug.

"Yes, she is. Let's hope for a boy this time!" Filip said.

Hamza gave him a congratulatory pat on the back.

"Wow, congratulations! When did you guys find out?" Ami asked.

"Just this morning, right before we left Atlanta. I was late a few days and decided to take a test and what do you know? We told Olga, Mateo, and Tina before we left and couldn't wait to tell you."

"Oh, I'm so glad you got to be there to tell your parents in person," Mom said to Filip.

"I know. That worked out. You should have seen the look on their faces! They were so surprised!"

"I bet! That's wonderful. Congratulations to you both!" Hamza hugged me.

✦

That day, our entire family was full of joy, overcome with elation and overwhelming happiness, with so much to look forward to, but the joy was short-lived. Within days, Hamza was diagnosed with a life-threatening disease and would soon begin an aggressive course of treatment.

As Hamza's medical treatment kicked into high gear, I noticed that Ami didn't look so well either. She was pale and complained of nausea and exhaustion. I suggested she take a pregnancy test, but she insisted she wasn't pregnant; it was the stress of Hamza's disease. Between Mom and me, we eventually convinced her to take the test and to everyone's surprise, it was positive! We were due only days apart! This baby was a miracle and a blessing in disguise, as he would be the last of my parents' grandkids.

✦

Though the baby was a blessing, things did not get easier for Ami and Hamza. For the next several months, they spent most of their days in the hospital. Perhaps the only good, among all the bad, was the fact that our family could always count on one another in times of need.

Hamza and Ami temporarily moved in with us. Filip stayed home with Amaya and Amra while I worked, and Hamza and Ami shuttled back and forth to the hospital.

Soon, Hamza's hair began to come out in handfuls. Seeing swaths of hair on his pillow each morning took a toll on him. None of us could imagine how he must have felt, and it was heartbreaking watching him deteriorate so quickly. Tired of feeling powerless to help, one evening Filip whispered to me, "Grab the electric head shaver and follow me to the bathroom please."

I did as he requested.

"What's up? What are we doing?" I asked.

"Help me shave my hair off. If I do it, maybe he will too. It has to make him feel better, right? I don't know how else to help. What do you think?"

"I think that's a great idea! It's breaking my heart to see him pull his hair out and slump into his chair every time."

"I know! Me too! I'm going to do it." The shaver buzzed away as he cut off his thick hair. I helped him get the spots he missed, and soon he was as bald as an army recruit.

We decided to turn it into a big production and throw a little humor in the mix. When the bald-headed Filip came out of the bathroom into the living room where Hamza and Ami were watching TV, I called out, "Woohoo! Hey guys, check out Filip! He looks like a freakin' mob boss! Hot damn!"

"Wow, Filip! You do look like a mob boss! You look great!" Ami smiled, and just like that, Hamza felt encouraged to shave his head too.

As Hamza got sicker and sicker from his treatments, and Ami got sicker and sicker from morning sickness, we cherished the simple pleasures and treasured every good day, as they were few and far between. Every little thing helped, even if it was simply to project some positive energy. Every smile counted. Small joyous moments were celebrated as successes.

One day, Mom barged into the house with an oversized juicer, several large bags of green leafy vegetables, five-pound bags of carrots, and beets and apples. In an instant, she turned my kitchen into a juice bar, determined to pump nutrients into everyone. She made bottles of red and green detox juice she called her "little soldiers" sitting on the countertop, lined up and ready to battle maladies.

After three long months of battling his disease, going in and out of the hospital with any number of complications, Hamza finally reached his final week of treatment. His test results were improving. Ami was also feeling better; her morning sickness was subsiding.

Hamza had to go through one more major surgery. This procedure was rare and complicated, typically lasting around twelve hours. On the day of the surgery, we waited countless hours for an update. Finally, we got word that Hamza was moved to a recovery room. The surgeon came out with an update for Ami.

"The surgery was very successful. His recovery will be tough, but he's expected to make a full one. He's in the recovery room. You can visit him as soon as he wakes up."

"He's going to be okay? Are you sure?"

"Yes, he's going to be okay," the surgeon replied.

"Thank you, Doctor! Thank you so much!" Ami jumped with joy and relief.

After he woke up, Hamza was in a lot of pain, but for the first time in months, he was in good spirits and a smile had returned to his face. We hadn't seen him joke around since he was diagnosed, yet he was spitting out jokes like a first-rate comedian and making everyone laugh. When he laughed, though, his incision hurt, but he was having too much fun after months of misery to stop telling jokes. He'd put his hand over the incision and say, "I'm okay! I'm okay!" Ami would give him a look of wifely concern, indicating he needed to take it easy and rest, at which point he would simply wink at her and smile.

Our mischievous husbands even managed to get in trouble once or twice during Hamza's weeklong hospital recovery. Beginning to feel better, Hamza asked Filip to take him out for a walk in a wheelchair one day, practically yanking out the hospital equipment that was still attached in a rush to get out. When Ami and I returned to the hospital, we assumed that Filip had taken Hamza to the bathroom, but only after a good forty-five minutes did they show up, giggling like schoolboys, Hamza still attached to his IV drip apparatus, the drip lines all tangled with the monitoring cables.

As Hamza was slowly nursed back to health, laughter and joy had returned to our life. We were blessed to have each other in a time of need.

CHAPTER 11

TROUBLE IN PARADISE

I dreamed of becoming the kind of parent who gives her kids everything I missed as a teenager due to the war—from the basics, such as a stable home with running water and electricity, a good education, and family and friends who lived nearby, to the finer things, such as attending cultural events and traveling the world. My dream was to be an amazing mom because I was raised by an amazing mom.

My mother always put her kids first. At 5'4" and 130 pounds, Mom may have been small in stature, but she moved mountains for us with strength, grace, and elegance. During the war, when it came to choosing between putting food on the table or selling furniture from the house, she sold the furniture to feed her children. Without flinching, she uprooted her life and relocated to another continent to keep her kids safe from war. Without ever losing her joie de vivre, Mom went from an office job to cleaning toilets, so her children could graduate from school. Even after we became independent adults, she never hesitated to jump in and help by switching her work schedule to babysit, offering cash to Ami and Hamza when they lost their jobs, or buying a juicer and showing up with a bagful of healthy food to nurse those she loved back to health. She showed up without fail, no questions asked. She treated Filip and Hamza like the sons she never had.

Mom was the most reliable person I knew. We joked that she should wear a Wonder Woman star on her forehead and a Superwoman cape on her back, but she would put both super heroines to shame. She took care of business and took care of everyone. That's the kind of mom I have always tried to be.

✦

As soon as Hamza felt better after his surgery, and a healthy pink replaced the deathly grey in his face, he and Ami arranged to visit Bosnia for a few weeks. He missed his family and wanted to see his parents. His appetite had returned, and so had Ami's. It was good for the two of them to get away for a while and recover, eat hardy Bosnian food, and regain their strength.

After such a rough patch, Filip and I needed a break too. For a couple of months while Ami and Hamza stayed with us, we had no privacy, and we were run-down, emotionally and physically, from stresses that come with having a family member battle a life-threatening disease.

✦

Following Ami and Hamza's departure, Filip and I were able to focus on ourselves and Amaya, unwind and relax, and enjoy the simple pleasures of life. My baby belly was starting to show, and our second baby was beginning to kick and jab. Every so often, a tiny foot slid across my belly, protruding like a little alien. Excited, I would pull up my shirt for Filip and Amaya to see. Filip liked to play peek-a-boo with the baby's foot, poking it and pushing it back inside my belly to make it disappear, then waiting for the foot to reemerge. It made Amaya giggle every time. She had her own gentle way of bonding with my belly. She would press her lips into my bellybutton and sing to the baby, cradling the sides of my belly with her little hands. Her voice was delicate and soothing. I had no doubt she would make a great sister.

My cravings with the second pregnancy were different from those of my first. With Amaya, I craved ice cream and chocolate. With the second, I craved pickles. (Is it odd that today each of my kids love the same things I craved while they grew in my belly?) According to an old wives' tale, if a woman craves sweets during pregnancy, it means she's carrying a girl. If she craves non-sweets, she's carrying a boy. That was a good sign since we wanted one of each. This pregnancy felt different from the one with Amaya—

it just felt like a boy. We would soon know for sure, as another ultrasound was coming up. Filip and Amaya tagged along for the visit.

During the exam, Amaya grew upset. She must have thought the doctor was hurting her mommy, and she began to cry.

Filip picked her up in his arms and directed her attention to the screen. "Look, it's the baby!"

I took her hand and tried to explain what was happening. "That's your baby brother or sister. It's inside Mommy's belly, and the doctors need a special camera to see the baby. They just want to take a quick picture. Don't you want to see what the baby looks like?"

"My baby?" she said in her sweet baby voice.

"Yes, this is your baby right here on the screen honey."

The doctor joined in, turning to Amaya. "Look, your baby is waving at you! Say hi to the baby."

"Hi baby! My baby!" Amaya wiped her tears and smiled brightly.

"Yes love, it's your baby!" I was overwhelmed with emotion.

As the doctor prepared to reveal the baby's sex, I couldn't help noticing the baby's legs were spread wide apart as if to leave no doubt that he was, indeed, a boy.

"Would you like to find out if your baby is a boy or a girl?" the doctor asked.

"I think it's pretty obvious it's a boy, right?" I asked.

"Yes, a healthy boy."

Filip jumped out of his chair and yelled, "What? We're having a boy? Oh my god, I'll have a son." He was jumping up and down with Amaya still in his arms, her chubby cheeks bouncing.

"Yeah honey, it's a boy! Amaya, you're going to have a baby brother!" I said.

"Baby butter!" Amaya's pigtails flopped on her father's arms.

When we came out of the doctor's office, we immediately took to our phones to share our big news while Amaya happily chased the ducks around the pond. That she would have a brother to look out for her, and he would have a big sister to give him advice as they grew up and made me happy.

✦

I always had grand plans for our family's future, so when I found out that a house next door to Filip's parents in Georgia was up for sale, my imagination ran wild. Olga told us about it one day, somewhat half-jokingly, suggesting we buy it now and someday move into it. The house was very similar to theirs, and without even looking at the pictures of the inside, I knew the ranch-style brick house was spacious with a big yard and an oversized deck connected to an above-ground pool. It was listed for a steal, especially compared to the cost of California homes.

It was a big decision. While we weren't quite ready to move to Georgia, it made sense to invest in real estate there. We had a growing family and knew we would visit Georgia frequently—we could always use it as our vacation home. Or we could rent it out to offset the mortgage payments since we were still living on my income alone.

With a formal entry and three bedrooms, two baths, a spacious living room with a wood-burning fireplace, and a separate family room, it seemed like a dream home for a family. I imagined hosting Christmas parties for Filip's family, and Adem and Kendra with their kids. The kids could run around the house and play while the adults sat by the cozy fireplace, enjoying appetizers and champagne.

After consulting with Filip, I applied for the home loan by myself, given he was still unemployed, and I made an offer on the Georgia house. Within a few hours, my offer was accepted and by the following month, we had keys to our very own vacation home! It was time to celebrate.

✦

The Bay Area had a large Bosnian community, and there was never a shortage of Bosnian events on the weekends. Most of our friends, including Jasmina and Hari, who had no children yet, attended as many of these as they could. My dad planned to attend one such event. I thought we deserved a night out, so we decided to meet him there.

By that time, Dad had married a Croatian woman, whom I did not particularly care for, while Mom was dating a very kind man, Bruce. Both of my parents seemed happy with their new partners, though, which is all that mattered.

Filip and I left Amaya with Mom and Bruce, excited for our date night.

The evening started with laughter and music as we caught up with dear friends. Everyone was singing and dancing and enjoying a genuinely good time. Filip had a few beers and hung out with Hamza, Hari, and a couple of other friends at the bar while I danced nearby with Ami, Jasmina, and a few other girlfriends, occasionally stopping by Filip to steal a kiss.

Filip could be a very fun person to hang out with, but when he was drinking, there was a fine line between fun Filip and erratic, irrational, belligerent Filip, who was set off by the smallest perceived slight.

Halfway through the night I realized he might have crossed the line. He was swaying back and forth, attempting to maintain balance. To forestall another incident, I pulled him aside. "Hey babe, how're you feeling? Maybe we should call it a night soon. I'm not feeling too good." I felt fine, but I thought he might leave if it was for me.

"Why do you want to leave? You think I'm drunk? You think I'm drunk, don't you?" He had definitely crossed the line and was looking for a fight.

"No, I think you're fine," I lied to defuse him. "My stomach hurts. I don't know if it's something I ate, but I really need to lie down. Soon. Baby boy is not happy in there."

"You do think I'm drunk! I'm embarrassing you, is that it? In front of all your friends, like last time? Is that it?"

Still composed, attempting to calm him down, I replied: "Baby, look! I don't want to fight," I replied calmly, not wanting things to escalate. "If you want to stay, I can ask my dad to take me home. It's not that big a deal."

"You're going to desert me again. Just like the concert. You're going to leave me here by myself because you're 'embarrassed.' What about me? Do you know how embarrassing it is when my wife walks out on me?"

So much for not escalating. "Look Filip, I don't want to do this in front of all these people. I'm just going to go home. Good night!"

I kissed him on the lips and turned to go to Dad's table.

Filip grabbed me by the hand and pulled me back to him with some force. "Where do you think you're going?"

Standing nearby, Jasmina and Hari saw our exchange and came over quickly. Jasmina had been my best friend for years, and Hari looked out for me like I was his sister.

"Hey Annie, are you all right?" Jasmina hugged me.

Hari pried Filip away by tugging on his arm "What's going on, man?"

I knew if Filip so much as looked at Hari, Jasmina or me the wrong way, Hari, who was big and strong and not so drunk, would make it physical and who knew how that would end up? Fighting, bouncers, jail? I couldn't let that happen to either of them.

"It's really nothing guys; we're cool!" I said. "My stomach hurts, that's all, and I really want to go home. Filip didn't feel like going. If you guys could just walk us to the car, please? I want to get going."

"No, wait. Hari, buddy, I'll buy you a beer, man," Filip said, slurring his words.

"I'm good, my friend. I hit my limit. Looks like you have as well! Go home! Sleep it off! And you better not mess with Annie." Hari pointed Filip to the door, walked him out of the building.

In silence, Jasmina and I followed them with Jasmina whispering to call if I needed help later. Filip seemed docile for the moment, stumbling into the passenger seat without a word.

As we drove away, though, belligerent Filip returned, blaming me for our friends' interference and Hari making him leave. It appeared that his manhood was at stake, and that was my fault as well.

When I told him not to be ridiculous, he punched the dashboard with his fists many times in a row and so hard I thought the airbags would go off. I had never seen him this enraged—or anyone else, for that matter. And I had lived through a war. How does a person go from a nice, normal, loving guy to an unhinged stranger without rhyme or reason?

I was in a state of near shock, unable to process his behavior, let alone respond to it in any constructive way. My sweet, loving husband and father to my children could be nasty, cruel, mean, and hateful to me, his wife, his love, the one he had vowed to love forever.

I did not want that Filip anywhere near me or the babies.

This Filip. He was yelling, foam and spit coming out of his mouth like a rabid dog. I no longer felt safe alone in the car with him.

I knew I was in over my head, but it was too late to drive back to Jasmina and Hari at the party. I was terrified, but I had to keep my wits about me, so I wouldn't say anything to provoke him further. I drove as fast as I could, praying to get pulled over by the police. No such luck. We made it home.

At home, I phoned Mom to keep Amaya overnight and went straight to bed. I didn't want Amaya to see her father in this state—and I wanted to keep her safe if anything happened to me.

When Filip crawled into bed, I pretended to sleep, but I was really wide awake in panic mode, fearing what else might happen. I shoved my face into the pillow to suppress my rapid breathing. Filip, on the other hand, began to snore as soon as his head hit the pillow. I said a quick prayer of thanks, but I couldn't risk sleeping myself. I stayed up all night, alert, scared, sad, angry, and perplexed.

When Filip finally woke up in the morning, puffy eyed and sleep-deprived, I tried to talk to him about the night before, but he was up to his old tricks, offering excuse after excuse, blaming his behavior on everyone but himself, saying things that didn't even make sense. If turning tables was an art, his work would be a masterpiece. Instead of the simple apology I expected—and deserved—he called me nasty names. I sat on the couch, stunned. Filip was standing over me.

The only way I could think to respond was, "Go to hell, Filip!"

At that, Filip swung his fist at me, and in that moment, I truly thought he was about to smash my face. I closed my eyes, picturing myself in an ambulance, my head wrapped in a bandage. Instead, the punch landed on the cushion two inches away from my face.

Paralyzed with fear, I stared at him blankly. Even if I had wanted to say something, no words would have come out. Where did that come from? I remember thinking. He's not even drunk.

He nodded as if to say, How'd you like that? Then he turned around and walked out to the balcony, lit a cigarette, and sat in a chair. He took a long drag, then exhaled a long stream of smoke.

Without thinking, I ran to the balcony and shut the sliding-glass door with a loud whump, then locked it. When he heard the click of the lock, he stood up and pounded on the heavy glass with his fists, yelling to let him in. Instead, I ran back to the living room, grabbed my keys, and left the apartment. I ran to Mom's. Not ready to face her yet or explain what had happened, I wiped the tears from my face and took a minute to compose myself before entering. With a superficial hello and without saying much else, I retrieved Amaya and walked to a nearby park. Where else were we going to go?

We spent the day playing in the park. With her giggles alone, Amaya could turn my worst day into the best day. One look from those bright blue eyes, one smile, putting her little arms around my neck and saying a simple, "I love you mommy" made everything better.

We bought food for a picnic, played in the sand, fed ducks with our left-overs, walked to the library, sat on the library floor, and read together. We had the best time. I cleared my head and eventually built up enough courage to go home. I hoped Filip had taken the time to cool off, and that he wouldn't act the same way in front of Amaya.

To my surprise, I found Filip in a much calmer state of mind. After spending two hours locked out on the balcony, he was able to flag down Mom, who passed our place on her way to the laundry room. To get her help, he had to explain how he had come to be locked out and what had happened the night before. I imagine Mom would have had a few choice words for him. So, by the time I got home, he appeared docile and remorseful, and actually apologized. While I was gone, he had cleaned the dishes, done laundry, and stopped by the grocery store for flowers. Belligerent Filip had left the building, at least for now.

I was astonished by the turnaround, and I needed to strike while the iron was hot. When we sat down to talk, I got straight to the point. "I'd like you to quit drinking Filip."

"What do you mean quit drinking? Like quit quit?"

"Yeah, like quit completely. We have a child together and another one on the way, and I need to be able to rely on you. This isn't healthy for the kids. It's not healthy for anyone. You turn into an ogre when you're drunk. I don't even know who you are!"

"Yeah, but babe, how am I supposed to go to Georgia for Christmas and not have a few beers with my dad? It just won't feel like Christmas."

"There are non-alcoholic beers, Filip. You're welcome to have as many of those as you wish. But if you want to keep this family together, I need you to quit. I never want to have another fight like this."

"That's stupid. Every Christmas I have beers with my dad. Everyone's going to think I'm an idiot drinking non-alcoholic beer. It shouldn't even be called beer."

"Everyone's going to think you're an idiot if you think drinking is more important than keeping your family together. But it's your choice."

He promised that day to stop drinking and honored it, at least for a while.

We may have quit fighting about drinking, but perhaps emboldened by what I'm sure he saw as a concession, he questioned what I planned to name our son. My lifelong dream had been to name my first son Namik, after my grandpa, because I loved him, and because he died on my birthday.

"But Namik is a Muslim name," Filip argued.

"I know that," I responded. "My grandfather was a Muslim."

"No son of mine is going to have a Muslim name."

This struck me hard. I had been talking about naming my first son Namik the whole time Filip and I had been together. That he waited until then to put his foot down and in such an overbearing and intolerant way (that bordered on bigotry) felt like a betrayal. Another chink in the armor of my perfect husband.

That was a hard pill for me to swallow, and it caused a rift between us. I began having serious doubts about our marriage, and whether or not I wanted to raise my kids with this man. We were close to deal-breaker territory.

Marriage to me is meant to be a partnership: two people working together, compromising and making sacrifices for one another, based on love, mutual respect, and give-and-take. In our case, it was beginning to look like I was the giver, and Filip the taker. I was the breadwinner, while Filip stayed home to care for Amaya and play video games. After work, I cooked, cleaned, did dishes and laundry, and watched Amaya. Filip claimed exhaustion as soon as I walked in the door. And I wasn't tired from a day at work? Filip's adult responsibilities ended the moment I walked in. This became an increasing burden on my shoulders.

At the same time, I was deeply invested in our marriage. We had a child together with another on the way and a house in Georgia next door to his parents. I very much loved the good Filip.

Because I cared and genuinely wanted to support my husband and help him succeed, I added him to my checking and savings accounts, put him as a second user on my credit cards, and paid for the family medical insurance plan. He shared in every facet of my finances (except the real estate).

Perhaps blinded by love, I had always assumed we were on the same page, but as time went on, I saw that there were important differences. Much of it had to do with our families, and how we were brought up. Though my family is far from perfect, we have always worked hard, respected education, and been good with finances.

Filip seemed to have a bit of a chip on his shoulder regarding my career and the fact that I was the breadwinner of the family.

Then there was the alcohol.

Not only did Filip sometimes drink too much, Mateo was involved in his own alcohol-related traffic incident, which led to his arrest and a suspended driver's license. This incident highlighted the family's difficulties with both alcohol and finances.

One Saturday afternoon around this time, we were at lunch at Mom's. Olga called me in tears to tell us that Mateo had caused a car accident while driving under the influence and that he had been arrested. Fortunately, no one was hurt in either car, but they didn't have enough money to bail him out of jail. He had to stay there until his hearing, which meant he would miss work.

"Wait a minute," I said. "He could be in there for a while. What if loses his job? How much do you need?"

"Over $2,000. I can't ask anyone to borrow that much money."

"We're not anyone. We're family. And that's what families do." Within minutes, I logged on to a money transfer site to wire her the amount she needed.

They were family, and I wanted to help out, but these alcohol-driven crises were becoming a burden and a nuisance.

Whenever I felt overwhelmed by Filip or his family and didn't know what to do, I confided in Mom.

She'd say, "Give him some time, love. You guys are both still young. He'll come around. Everyone's been through a lot lately, and he's a good person. He just needs to do something about his drinking. He turns into a completely different person when he drinks."

No matter what, I could count on Mom to make me feel better. Mom gave me hope and strength. She inspired me to forgive, to be a bigger person, to take the high road, to try to work things out. And things did work out, for a while.

✦

Filip stopped drinking, and things between us improved tremendously. Once I started maternity leave, our daily routine consisted of taking long, relaxing strolls in the park with Amaya and feeding ducks in the nearby pond. Filip entertained her for hours by throwing pieces of bread high in the air, attracting dozens of seagulls trying to catch them in flight. On weekends, we lived a beach life with frequent trips to the Santa Cruz boardwalk where Amaya enjoyed the carousel rides and playing in the sand.

That summer was the Great Heat Wave of 2006. Bay Area temperatures in the summer don't typically exceed ninety to one hundred degrees, with most nights staying chilly in the low sixties. As a result, most residential buildings, like ours, didn't have central air conditioning.

At the onset of heat wave in mid-July, I was a few weeks shy of starting maternity leave. For three consecutive weeks, daily temperatures exceeded 110 degrees—and we were roasting! Normally, when we left our bedroom window cracked open at night, by midnight our home cooled off to a comfortable temperature. But with the heat wave, there was no relief at night either. Lows remained in the high nineties.

At eight months, I was big, bloated, and extremely uncomfortable in the heat. Amaya was cranky. Filip just wanted a cold beer. And none of us were able to get any sleep at night. Further, every hardware and home-goods store in our area were sold out of air conditioning units. You couldn't find one even if you were paying in diamonds.

Desperate to get away from the valley heat, on my first day of maternity leave, we drove to San Francisco, where it was always twenty degrees cooler since the city is surrounded by the cool Pacific Ocean breeze and on most days enveloped in a thick layer of fog.

We took Amaya to the zoo, and since it was a weekday, we practically had the place to ourselves. Amaya's big smile lit up the minute we walked in. She loved animals. She enjoyed waddling around like a penguin in front of their exhibit, but giraffes and elephants were her favorite. Pelicans did not impress her at all, however. She was afraid of their oversized bills and the bare-skin pouches flapping around as they moved.

At the end of a fun-filled day, the three of us got into my two-door Stratus and headed back home. On the way back, we stopped at the home improvement store where we found an air-conditioner—their last one.

Excited for the relief it promised, when we got home, Filip pulled the unit out of the car and carried it up two flights of stairs by himself with an injured back. But that wasn't our day. It turned out that our living room window was too small to house this heavy contraption.

"That's what happens when you buy an A/C without taking window measurements," Filip teased, taking it in stride.

"Live and learn!" was all I could say in response.

We couldn't face returning the unit, so we MacGyvered the installation. We set it up on the floor in front of the open half of the balcony's sliding glass door and hung a burgundy blanket in the space above the unit, sealing it with tape as best we could. It was an unsightly solution, but it worked! That night we dragged a mattress from the spare bedroom and parked it in front of the vent, the three of us jammed together on the mattress like sardines, the cold air tickling our feet and faces. Relief at last! At least until this heat passed.

It was also fortunate that we planned to spend our first wedding anniversary in Hawaii, and the trip was just around the corner.

CHAPTER 12

THE GIFT OF LIFE: WHAT'S IN A NAME

In Honolulu, we stayed at the same hotel, with the same group of people who had joined us on our honeymoon, minus Tina who was in Atlanta. Sitting through a six-hour flight at eight months pregnant proved uncomfortable, but once there, I healed my swollen feet in the warm sand and salt water. While we lay on the beach, my preggo-twin Ami and I drew stick figures and smiley faces on our bellies with sunblock. Hamza and Filip took care of their pregnant wives by digging holes in the sand so we could lie on our bellies. At night, we gobbled down teriyaki chicken burgers with grilled pineapple and drank virgin lava flow cocktails.

During the day, we rented two-seater buggy-carts to ride around town, while Mom and Bruce watched Amaya and Amra. Even though the carts reached top speeds of only thirty-five miles per hour, we "raced" them up the road to Diamond Head, the extinct volcano crater, laughing as the cars behind us honked at our slow pace. In the parking lot lookout, we debated who won the race, while Ami and I posed for pictures with our big bellies. Then we drove back to the city.

This was my third visit to the parking lot at Diamond Head, but I had never taken the trail up to top of the crater, and I was in no shape to do so this time either. I had to live vicariously through Mom, who gave us a run-down of her hike with Bruce.

"We began walking on a paved trail, but that quickly became a steep mountainous trail of rocks. The hike was not easy, but the 360-degree views of the Pacific Ocean and Waikiki beach were stunning and well worth it."

I promised that one day I'd hike the Diamond Head trail to see the views for myself.

Part of me secretly hoped I'd go into labor a few weeks early and bring home a little Hawaiian, but I also preferred him to be healthy and full term, so I was resigned to waiting. I was not, however, quite resigned to giving up the name Namik, and hoped that Filip, in the spirit of the fun we were all having and the love we were surrounded with, would warm up to the name.

✦

I began nesting as soon as we returned from Hawaii. With an uncontrollable urge to clean every inch of our apartment, I scrubbed floors, washed down walls and counters, cleaned out the pantry and fridge, washed baby clothes, and purged the apartment of all things unnecessary. Like a bird frantically collecting sticks to ensure her nest is ready for her to lay eggs, I was preparing to meet my handsome little man.

On the morning of September 27, my contractions started. Unlike the false alarms I had with Amaya, these felt regular and real, four to five minutes apart. Suspecting this was it, I called the hospital and was told to head over to Labor and Delivery.

Last time I made the mistake of suffering through labor pains for several hours, so I requested an epidural immediately upon check-in. Ami, in the final week of her pregnancy as well, was in the room with me as the anesthesiologist administered the epidural using a 3.5-inch needle. Ami watched their every move while I urged her to look away. The nurses joked that Ami was definitely in the right place if she went into labor as well. We all laughed.

I was distracted by the give-and-take and did not feel the pain of the needle. The numbing effects of the epidural kicked in instantly, which eased the labor pains. From that point, it was just a waiting game.

Thinking I would be in labor again for a long time, the family congregated around my bed making jokes and laughing, turning the hospital room into more of a social gathering. The men messed with the monitors attached to my belly, causing dirty looks from us women and the nurses to rush to my room to readjust them.

We were having a good old time. Periodically, a nurse came in to check my progress. After one such exam, to our absolute surprise, the nurse yelled out, "He's crowning!"

The team of doctors and nurses swarmed into the room, ushering everyone out, except Filip, Mom, and Ami.

It was time to push. The doctor shouted instructions. "Count to ten and push as hard as you can."

Everyone in the room began counting. "One, two, three, four, five, six, seven."

"Wait! Stop, stop, stop! Stop pushing!" the doctor barked.

"Why? Is everything okay? What's wrong?"

"The baby is fine. It's you I'm worried about. He's coming out too quickly," he explained. "All right, on my mark! We'll try this again. You ready?"

"Ready!"

"All right, let's go. One, two, three, four, five. Wait, stop pushing," he instructed again.

By this point I had little control. "I can't. I can't stop. I'm sorry."

"Stop, stop, stop!" he urged again.

"I'm trying, but there's a lot of press. . ." as soon as I said that, I heard my baby's loud and boisterous cry.

"Your baby is out. Congratulations, you have a healthy, beautiful baby boy!" the doctor exclaimed.

They placed him on my chest all gooey and warm. He immediately stopped crying, recognizing his mama right away. I ran my fingers across his goop-covered head and greeted him with a quick, "Hi handsome!" before the nurses whisked him away for routine clean up.

"He was in a rush to meet you," The doctor said. "Do you guys have a name yet?"

"No, we're still deciding." I looked at Filip, pleading, hoping he had changed his mind.

"No, we haven't decided yet," he said sternly.

"It will come to you. Many parents have to see the child before deciding."

As soon as nurses cleaned up our son, they handed him back to me, all bundled up. I kissed his chubby cheek and whispered, "Hi, my beautiful little man. Welcome to your family. Your big sister Amaya can't wait to meet you. She has been waiting for you like we all have."

His eyelids opened for a brief second as he stared into my eyes. Then he closed them. I noticed he was slightly cross-eyed—the cutest thing I had ever seen, but it only lasted a few hours. His itty-bitty nose looked like a button on his face and his hair was a silky, shiny black. He had less hair than Amaya did when she was born, and it was shorter. He looked like me and by default, like Grandpa Namik.

He is the cutest little boy in the world, I thought to myself as I smothered him with kisses.

Now that we had a boy and a girl, our family felt complete. I couldn't have been more grateful to God for giving us a healthy baby boy.

+

I knew many older siblings grow jealous of a new baby because they are no longer the sole focus of their parents. To prevent Amaya from resenting her brother, we bought a gift for her that we would say was from the baby. Since she loved music, it was a dinosaur-shaped green piano.

After I had recovered from labor, Mom brought Amaya to the hospital room. She gave me a long hug, like she hadn't seen me in days, even though it had only been a few hours. She lay next to me on the bed. Mom picked up the baby from the crib and handed him to me. There was nothing sweeter than watching Amaya whisper an adoring hi to her brother for the first time. She rubbed his forehead ever so gently and asked to kiss him. I snuggled her closer to him, and she bent until they were almost touching.

"Hewwo baby butter. I wuv you so much." She gave him a kiss, then sang him the lullaby I often sang to her.

"Ni-na no-chi, moye za-to pa-va. . ." This was baby Bosnian for "quiet night, my goldie is sleeping."

Awake and alert, enjoying all this attention, his eyes fixed on her. To watch them bond filled my heart. We sat there for a while, reveling in the moment, until it was time to change his diaper. Mom took Amaya and sat her down on her lap. I put the baby down in front of me on the bed and rolled up his onesie, exposing his belly so I could take off his soiled diaper.

Amaya saw the baby's belly button clip and yelled, "Lookie, Mommy, a froggy!" We all laughed. To her, the clip looked like a frog.

Filip thought that was a good time to pull out the gift-wrapped present we had hidden behind the chair, and said, "Lookie, Amaya. Your brother got you a gift."

Her eyes lit up. She tore off the wrapping paper and exclaimed, "Mommy, Daddy! Lookie, a dinosaur piano. Maya play fo' baby butter?"

"No, sweetie. We can't play this at the hospital. We'll wake up all the other babies, but you can play it for him when we take your baby brother home."

Charmed by this demonstration of sibling love, we were still chuckling when a middle-aged woman from the birth recorder's office came in, requesting that we fill out the forms for the baby's birth certificate. We had already sent her away once since we hadn't yet agreed on a name.

She was visibly frustrated. "Have you figured out the name yet?"

"No, not yet. Can you please give us another couple of hours?" I asked.

"You've had nine months to think about this, and you still don't have a name?" She rolled her eyes and left the room.

Amaya visited with us for another twenty minutes, and Mom took her home. The moment we were alone, Filip looked at me in exasperation and asked, "Why can't I have this? Why can't you give me this one thing? Why can't I name our baby what I want? Do you always have to get everything you want?"

He was turning the tables again. I could have said the same thing to him. I had just carried the baby for nine months, including one of the hottest summers on record, and pushed it out of my body in the pain of childbirth, and I owed him? "So Namik is still off the table?" My soul was crushed. "What name did you pick?"

"Aleksandar," Filip said. "Like Aleksandar Petrovic."

"The Croatian basketball player? You can't be serious. I don't get to name my son after my grandfather, who died on my birthday, but you want to name him after a Croatian basketball player?"

"What? Aleksandar is a good name," Filip said, ignoring the swell of emotions I'm sure were visible on my face.

"Fine," I said, defeated, tired of fighting. "Name him whatever you want. But at least spell it with an x, Alexander." I hoped my abject capitulation would turn him around, but that was just magical thinking.

He jumped all over it. "Are you serious? We can name him Alexander?"

"Go ahead. Do it. You're breaking my heart, but I'm done fighting over this."

"Yes!" Filip jumped out of his chair as if he had just got high score on a video game and ran out of the room to find the clerk before I could change my mind. Within seconds, he was back in the room, the clerk in tow, presenting me with documents to sign. Practically in despair, feeling like a sellout and a failure, my hormones all over the place, I scribbled my name on the birth certificate and turned away from them both to hide my tears.

Baby and I were released from the hospital shortly after we filled out the birth certificate forms.

In protest, I took up a spare bedroom at home, and for the first few months of the baby's life, I couldn't call him Alexander. I simply called him Baby. It took me a while to get over the deep hurt and be able to say Alexander out loud.

Meanwhile, I took comfort in knowing that Baby was healthy and happy. At the end of the day, that's all that really mattered. Plus, he was adorably handsome and gorgeous! A mama's boy from day one, this little angel had me wrapped around his pinky finger from the moment I met him.

Tending to a newborn was a lot easier the second time around. We quickly fell into a routine—breastfeeding, changing diapers, bathing a slippery infant. As long as he was well fed and had a dry diaper, he was a happy camper. While it's rare for babies to use their neck muscles in their first few weeks, my little guy was lifting his head and soaking in everything happening around him like a sponge.

My heart was full. Amaya was very sweet with her brother. It brought me great joy to watch her sing to him as her little fingers tenderly patted his cheek. She was a good helper too. When it was time for diaper changes, I would ask her to bring me a clean one so she could feel involved.

"Yes, Mommy!" she would happily run to the diaper bag.

"Sweetie, would you please hand me baby butter's binky too?"

"Maya want binky?" She liked to act silly, trying to put his pacifier into her mouth.

"Baby wants it baaaack," I would sing while finishing with his clothes.

In Amaya's baby talk, Alexander morphed into Ace, and the nickname grew on me. From that point on, he was Ace.

◆

Three days after Ace was born, Ami went into labor. I insisted on going to the hospital to be with her through labor and delivery. Since I had just given birth myself, the whole family thought I was nuts. But I wouldn't have missed being in the delivery room when Haris was born for the world. Like mine, Ami's second delivery was much quicker than the first, and when Haris arrived, we celebrated. He had big, sparkling dark brown eyes—a gorgeous boy, sure to break many hearts with those charming eyes when he grew up.

From birth, Haris and Ace were like twins, having been born so close together. They didn't resemble each other—Haris weighed a whole pound more than Ace—but they enjoyed each other's company from the start. It was heartwarming to see our extended family grow and expand, filling our homes with joy and laughter.

◆

When things settled down a little between Filip and me, we took Amaya and Ace to Georgia for a visit with the other side of the family. The conversation about us moving to Georgia came up again, but I wasn't ready to leave a great job. Who knew what I would find in Atlanta?

While there, we toured our house for the first time. It was everything we could hope for, but it was an older home and did need some repairs.

From time to time, Filip would tell me how sad he was about how far his family lived, and muse, "What if we moved to Georgia?"

I couldn't help but picture Amaya and Ace in our new house playing with Legos on the deck and splashing in the pool. I saw them running around the backyard with Filip, tossing a football back and forth, playing kickball. I especially loved how close we would be to Filip's parents' house; we practically shared a backyard. The kids could see their grandparents as often as they wished. And Adem and Kendra lived just twenty minutes away.

What made it harder still was that we both knew we would never be able to afford a house like that in California.

But the prospect of moving to Georgia with two little kids and no job or health insurance kept us from making the move. We decided to rent the house for the time being.

+

We had spent the last four weeks of my three-month maternity leave with Filip's family, and in January 2007, it was time to return to work where I was coming up on my seventh year. Once again, I was grateful to have a job that allowed me flexible hours. I was in the office from 6:00 a.m. to noon and finished the remaining two hours at home. It was grueling, though, and I missed my babies. This schedule had me up daily at 4:00 a.m. to express breastmilk and get ready for work. Then as soon as I got home at noon, I had to breastfeed again.

I couldn't complain. Our family was doing better than most. At least we all had jobs. The year 2007 was the beginning of the stock market crash, which sparked massive layoffs, particularly in the Bay Area, as well as the housing crisis.

I returned to work in the teeth of the financial crisis. As part of the tech team, it was my job to disable the computer accounts of the terminated employees. These events mostly took place on Fridays, which came to be known as RIF (Reduction in Force) Fridays.

On those Friday mornings, I received an email with an Excel spreadsheet attached with the names of the employees and the time of day the employee was to be released.

Some of the names were people I worked closely with and considered friends, but according to Human Resource policy, I couldn't give them any indication they were getting laid off. When it was time, an HR rep and security guard escorted the employee to a conference room where the employee's manager would be waiting. There, the employee was given their severance package and escorted out of the building by security. While their exit procedures were underway, my job, behind the scenes, was to disable the employee's company accounts in order to prevent them from logging into the system.

On one RIF Friday, an older gentleman who had helped train me, peeked into my cube on the way to his desk and joked, "Morning! Am I on the list today?"

I had read the list well before he asked me and knew his name was on it and that HR would be coming for him at 10:00 a.m. I also knew I couldn't say a word to him about it. I looked at my coworker and friend, smiled and said, "John, you know I can't tell you, even if I knew."

After that, I found it harder and harder to perform my job. I couldn't look people straight in the eyes and pretend I didn't know. That was not the person my parents raised me to be. At that point, it became irrelevant how much money they were paying me. I began looking for another job.

At first, I looked only out of curiosity to see what was out there, but when I came across a great ad for a small, but fast-growing tech company where "the sky is the limit for the next shining star," I decided to apply for the position of Operations Manager.

The next day, I had a phone call from the hiring manager. After talking on the phone for about thirty minutes, he seemed eager to meet me in person, and we set up a time. That led to a second, more formal interview with several other directors and vice presidents. I went to their headquarters where one person after another walked into the interview room with a copy of my resume, asked me some questions, and exited. After the seventh person, I had already been there for a good four hours and was ready to go home, whether I got the job or not.

I checked the time, and it was now 7:00 p.m. I thought about dinner and my rumbling stomach. Matt walked me over to another office and introduced me to the president and chief executive officer.

We exchanged pleasantries. Then he asked about my prior experience. His questions were more challenging than some of the others, and I appreciated being stretched. Then he asked a zinger of a question. "I understand you have young children. This is a fast-paced environment. How do you plan to balance your work life with family life?"

I paused. I didn't even know if he was allowed to ask that question, but I wanted the job, so I answered. "With all due respect, sir, I survived a war in Bosnia. After that, everything else is a walk in the park."

I was ready to thank him for his time when he got up from his chair and extended his hand.

"Bosnia? Okay. We're going to make you an offer! Thank you so much for coming in. Matt will be in touch with you in the next few days to go over details."

I never knew whether my answer impressed him enough to have him make me an offer on the spot, or if he had picked up on the fact that it was already 7:00 p.m. and I was still there, even though my young family was waiting at home. I got the job! And the new pay would be significantly higher.

I was excited and scared at the same time. Ace was only eight months old, and I enjoyed a great degree of flexibility with my work schedule. I came home that evening and told Filip about the interview. He seemed excited about the possibility of more money. We discussed other things at play—my professional growth potential versus being able to work from home after noon, RIF Fridays and the toll they took on my soul, and the higher pay.

I didn't have to think about it long, really, before I accepted the offer.

✦

The new job was hectic and stressful. I was new to the industry and had a lot to learn. My kids were young. Since I was a mom, a wife, a sole provider, and a full-time career woman, someone constantly needed something. Our home was in perpetual mess. While I was raised to believe that hard work pays off, there were days when I had to push myself to power through. What kept me motivated was being able to give my kids a life better than I had when I came to the United States as a refugee. What inspired me was my parents fight before me to give their kids a better life and knowing that I, at least, got to sit in a comfortable office.

Busy days were offset by relaxing lunches with Mom and Ami. Mom worked nearby, and Ami soon got an office job two blocks from where I worked. The three of us frequently met up for lunch, the only time we could have an uninterrupted conversation, and we talked about everything—the stresses of everyday life, work-related advice, and our grievances about the ever-increasing cost of living in the Bay Area.

I had no plans of ever leaving California, but the low-cost housing in Georgia looked more and more appealing. I frequented real-estate listings in the Atlanta area, admiring a multitude of spacious two-story homes for sale at a tenth of the cost of home prices in the Bay Area, and daydreaming about having a big backyard for my children to run around in. Toying with the let's move to Atlanta idea, I printed out several of those listings for our lunch dates and first floated it to Mom and Ami as an all-or-nothing idea. We would all move together, or we would all stay in California.

Homes in Georgia were spacious, with large yards, big kitchens and enough room to comfortably raise a family. We looked through dozens of pictures with longing, imagining backyard swing sets and the kids with their own rooms. These were mansions compared to the small apartments we lived in.

With five bedrooms, a quarter acre backyard, the house I set my sights on was even bigger than the house next door to Filip's parents, which we had rented to a lovely couple with three kids. On my California salary, I could easily afford to own both homes in Georgia. Before long, in my daydreams, I was planting a garden and fruit trees, pickling vegetables for the winter, and making jams and jellies while my kids happily pranced around the backyard. The more I thought about our life in California versus what our life could be like in Georgia, the more it seemed ridiculous not to move, and a loose plan began to take shape.

Mom, Ami, and I sat down one evening after work with printouts of different listings and pitched the idea to Filip and Hamza. Obviously, finding jobs in Georgia was a concern and consideration, but both seemed on board with the idea of moving—especially Filip. He could be closer to his parents and seemed convinced I could easily land a job in a fast-growing tech sector in Atlanta. We decided to do it! We would all buy homes in Georgia and move.

The next day, I made an offer on the house, which went through without issue. Filip was still unemployed, so I applied for the loan in my name only.

✦

When we broke the news to Dad, he told us he had been working on similar plans. By that time, he was retired and married to Vanesa, who owned a house and land on an island in Croatia. While Dad was not crazy about our plan, citing concerns that we were jumping into it too quickly, moving without jobs and health insurance, his plan was not much different from ours—except he had already raised his children into independent adults.

"I can't tell you not to go when I'm also already moving to Croatia. The l and Vanesa owns there has mature olive and cherry tree orchards. I always wanted to live off the land, near the sea. Island life."

I can't say I wasn't surprised at my dad's sudden desire for such a huge life change, but I understood why he would want to leave the daily grind of the Bay Area for something far more peaceful. I just assumed he would stay with us, wherever we were, but I was happy for him anyway. He had worked hard and deserved a quiet place to retire.

"So, you're going to be a cherry farmer?" I teased.

"We always joked about that, didn't we?" he smiled at me tenderly.

"I remember something about crushing rock with a sledgehammer somewhere on a lonely island in Croatia! Same idea. I never thought you'd actually go through with it!"

"Don't worry! You know God looks after your old man. What about you, kiddo?"

"God looks after me too, Dad! You're the one who taught me to follow my heart and have faith that things always work out for the best. You're the one who taught me that luck follows the brave."

I had only been at my new job a few months. Folks there liked me and appreciated the work I did, which made it that much harder to inform the president who had made me an offer on the spot know of our plans. I practiced my speech for several days before mustering up enough courage to face him. When I finally did, luck was on my side, and he made me another offer I couldn't refuse. "Why don't you stay with us? We have clients on the East Coast; it would be beneficial to have someone in their time zone, if you don't mind working remotely?"

"Are you serious?" I responded, stunned. "I would love to stay with the company and work remotely. Thank you!"

"No problem. Go see Sam. We have a brand-new laptop in his office. None of the guys want it because it's red. You'll need it in Georgia."

And just like that, I was moving with a job and health insurance for my family secured. I even kept my California salary, which would go a long, long way in Georgia.

We spent every spare minute planning our cross-country move. According to our estimations, we could easily fit two apartments worth of stuff into a twenty-six-foot rental truck. We arranged to ship one of the cars there and tow another. Filip and Hamza would switch off driving the truck and Hamza's car, while Ami, me and the kids would ride in Ami's minivan.

So, after a little under thirteen years since we came to California as refugees, it was time to say goodbye to Dad and all the friends we had made there, and start over. Early in September 2007, we loaded up the truck and set off to what we hoped would be a better future. Ami and I took turns driving the minivan with a three-year-old, a two-year-old, and two eleven-month-old babies strapped in the car. We later called it the trip from hell. It lasted five days from start to finish, and Amra and Ace took turns screaming the entire time, in protest against being confined to their car seats all day. Amaya and Haris, on the other hand, watched movies most of the trip and stayed relatively quiet.

When we pulled into the driveway of our new house, we let the kids run around in the backyard to stretch their legs while shouting and laughing with the joy of freedom. It struck us that we didn't have to shush them as we had in our thin-walled apartments in California, where we were always required to watch the noise levels.

Seeing their happy faces, and big smiles made the hard work of moving worth it. Before we entered our new house, we sat down on the front porch stairs for a moment of gratitude, taking in the heat and humidity, the sweet scent of the two soft-pink lilac trees arching over each side of the driveway, the beauty of the pine trees lining one side of the yard.

Inside the house we were greeted by a pleasant surprise. Filip's family had decorated the living room with flowers, balloons, and welcome home signs. Propped on the fireplace mantle was a card reading, "We hope your new home is filled with love, laughter, and good times!" It was a thoughtful gesture that made us feel welcome indeed.

As we toured the house, we took turns sounding off in delight.

"Wow! This house is beautiful," said Ami. "Very spacious and comfortable."

"It really is a dream come true," Filip added, smiling at me.

"A place we can watch our kids grow up. Where Filip and I can grow old." I looked at Filip lovingly as we hugged.

Hamza jumped in. "I wish you good health and many happy years under this roof!"

"Hear, hear!" we all agreed.

✦

We saw no reason to wait since we all needed beds to sleep in and a kitchen to feed the children. While the men unloaded the furniture, Ami and I unpacked boxes. Within hours, our new house looked like a home with couches set up in the living room, the TV hooked up, and the beds made.

Ami and Hamza spent their first night at our house. The following day we planned to unload the rest of the stuff in the truck at their new house. That was one of the great things about this great big new house—we had plenty of space for sleepovers.

CHAPTER 13

DISSOLUTION, END OF ILLUSION

The first several months living in Atlanta were absolutely incredible. There were many firsts in the new house, starting with Ace's first birthday party within weeks of the move. We Bosnians by nature are loud and boisterous creatures and being able to host family and friends in our spacious home without worrying about the noise was a huge relief.

Mom and Bruce flew out for the party and stayed with us for a week. Everyone pitched in to help. Mom prepared her delicious hamburgers and chicken for the barbeque, Filip grilled the meat, and I fixed snacks, drinks, and dessert. Ace's birthday party was a happy occasion, filled with love and laughter. Filip and I were elated to celebrate our son's first birthday with both of our families together—except Dad, of course, who was on his way to Croatia.

Ace was a huge fan of SpongeBob SquarePants, so we decorated the kids' table in that theme, tying balloons to birthday boy's chair. There was a larger table set up for the adults. What we thought were fairly large outdoor tables looked like miniatures in our oversized backyard.

As Mom and Filip helped me with the finishing touches, I remembered my childhood daydreams and the pictures I used to draw. "We have enough room for a pool and tennis court!"

"You always dreamed big, kid!" Mom smiled.

Perhaps it was thinking about my childhood in Bosnia, for a split second I thought about Igor and wondered how he was doing. Filip's voice snapped me back to the task at hand. "Do you think we should bring out the red car?" He meant the battery-powered ride-on Mustang Ami had gotten for the kids.

"Yes, let's bring it out. They love that thing."

The Mustang was a big hit. Children took turns speeding through the backyard, making sharp turns and leaving skid marks in the grass. They couldn't get enough of it, with, at one point, all six kids dangling off the toy car—two on the hood, Ace driving, Haris in the passenger seat, and two more sitting on the trunk. One of them was always falling onto soft grass and chasing the car to jump back on while the adults cheered from the sidelines. It was late into the night when we finally corralled the kids around the table to sing "Happy Birthday" to Ace and cut the cake. Our backyard was filled with giggles and laughter. On that day, at least, my dreams had come true. Ace's first birthday party was a huge success!

✦

Mom used the week she was visiting to apply and interview for jobs, which she believed went well. I enjoyed my full-time work-from-home arrangement, getting to spend more time with the kids and Filip that way. We even took up a few house projects. We painted Amaya's room a lively fuchsia with green-apple-colored stripes and added a border of daisies. Amaya was a fan of Dora the Explorer, so we found her a Dora toddler bed and a matching toy shelf.

We picked blue for Ace's room, adding white puffy cloud stickers to the walls and went with a Cars theme with a Lightning McQueen blanket and pillow set. Eventually, we would add the red mountain backdrop and signs for Radiator Springs, but we were in no rush. Ace still spent most nights in our bed.

Within six months of moving to Georgia, Filip picked up work at one of the hotel chains, and the kids had begun daycare. I had been thinking about Igor since the party, so on one of my slow days I emailed him.

Hi. I don't even know where to begin. It's been years. But I wanted to let you know I'm well and hope you are too. I'm in Georgia now, got married and have two kids. A girl and a boy, they're 3 and 1 years old. We bought a house here, and believe it or not, these days I enjoy planting flowers in my front yard and watching my kids play. How are you?

I hit send and within 10 minutes, a reply came.

Dear Annie, wow! It's so good to hear from you. I'm doing well (well, ha-ha I'm doing well now) and am glad to hear you are too. Hard to put many years into a single email, but I'll try. Congratulations on your new life, husband, kids, house, all of it. I did some really, really stupid stuff in the past, but I promise you, all of that is behind me now. Seeing a girl, she keeps me in line. She's studying architecture and as soon as she graduates, I'm hoping we get married too and start making babies. Hugs and kisses. Igor.

His response made me chuckle, and I followed up with another note.

You were always so charming with those hugs and kisses. It makes me happy to know you found someone who makes you happy. I'm not going to ask you about the stupid stuff you did, but please, please stay away from ALL that stupid stuff. Hugs and kisses to you too.

He quickly replied.

Don't worry! And I repeat, do not worry about any of it. I've been clean about two years now and I'm happy. Love, your other half, Igor.

Even if we hadn't married each other as we had planned all those years before when we were really just children, we remained very good friends, and the thought of knowing Igor was okay and settling down made me happy. All I wanted was the best for him. I truly did. Because I knew he was doing well, I waited several months before I reached out again.

Filip's mom, Olga, usually hosted Christmas, but for Christmas 2008, our second in Georgia, Olga and Tina were called away to Croatia unexpectedly to visit Olga's ailing mom.

It fell to us to host Christmas dinner that year for about sixteen people: Filip's dad and friends, Ami, Hamza, Kendra, Adem, and all of our kids, of course.

I had a lot to live up to. Olga was the Queen of Christmas. For Bosnian Catholics, it's customary to prepare three days' worth of food for family and any guests who may be visiting. Olga started weeks ahead of time. Her dessert repertoire alone consisted of many different kinds of holiday cookies and two or three different cakes made from scratch. Every year was a food extravaganza. She prided herself on stuffing her guests and family to the gills with her delicious dishes.

When Mateo and Filip were told about the trip, they were both disappointed to the point of dejection. "Christmas is all about the family meal, and it just won't be the same without her cooking," they both agreed.

I took that as a challenge and offered to make the Christmas meal for the family in her absence. I was excited to host our first holiday gathering. This was my chance to shine as a homemaker.

Given Olga's example, I began baking well before Christmas, making four kinds of cakes and three kinds of cookies. I also cooked several traditional dishes—stewed beef with vegetables, sauerkraut cabbage leaves stuffed with meat and rice, shepherd's pie, and a few vegetable side dishes.

It was important our home be perfectly decorated too. Our Christmas tree, adorned with red and silver ornaments and gold garland, stood out against the red accented wall. Gold garland embellished the soft-white fireplace mantle and living room and dining room walls. Wrapped boxes of Christmas gifts were stacked on the living room floor.

Filip and Mateo attended midnight mass on Christmas Eve, and we opened gifts on Christmas morning when the kids woke up. Around midday, the guests began to arrive. We had beer and wine for adults and juice for the kids. I expected Filip to refrain from alcohol since he promised not to drink. Once the party was underway, and just before I was going to serve dinner, Filip walked up behind me in the kitchen and quietly whispered, "Babe, it's Christmas. I'm going to have a couple of beers. Hope you don't mind."

The thought of it instantly made me uneasy.

"Honey, you said you were done with that." I couldn't hide my disappointment.

"Yeah babe, but it's Christmas. I just want to have a few beers with my dad and my friends. What's the problem?"

"You know how you get. I don't feel safe around you when you drink." I hoped he would stick by his promise.

At that moment, Hamza walked into the kitchen. "What are you two lovebirds whispering about?"

"Nothing, bro. I was just telling my wife here that I'm about to enjoy a nice, cold beer. Want one?" Filip grabbed two beers from the fridge, handed one to Hamza.

"All right, man! Join the party. Cheers!" Hamza raised the beer in one hand and put his other arm around Filip's shoulder. "It's about time. Merry Christmas bro!"

I was troubled by Filip's breaking his word, but I didn't want to cause a scene and ruin everyone's good time. Maybe it would be just a few beers with his friends. And that night, it was. I kept a close eye, without saying a word, and he did keep his drinking to a minimum with no violent outbursts.

Meanwhile, the kids were having a grand time, which kept me distracted from worrying about Filip too much. Once we were done with the meal, we cranked up the Bosnian music, singing and dancing with abandon. Amaya, Ace, Amra, Haris, Minnie, and Lanie stole the show dancing around the tables and stuffing themselves with dessert and juice. Big, hearty laughs reverberated through the house after the kids decorated Mateo's friend Gregg like a Christmas tree, with plastic play jewelry and stickers glued to his hands and face. Like Ace's first birthday, our first Christmas in the house was a big success.

Mateo and his friends even praised all the dishes and desserts I had made and congratulated me on rising to a big challenge. That made my day.

✦

A few days into the new year, Olga and Tina returned from Croatia. As soon as I had finished work, Filip and I strapped Amaya and Ace into their car seats and drove to his parents' house to welcome them.

The second we pulled in the driveway, Amaya unbuckled her seatbelt, jumped out of the car, and ran to her grandma in excitement, hugging and kissing her. As she draped her hands over Olga's shoulders, Olga pulled a small jewelry box from her pocket, and said, "Sweetheart, I missed you too. Very, very much. Look, Grandma got you something!"

Amaya yipped with glee as she took the box, opened it, and pulled out a gold necklace with a crucifix pendant.

Filip and I had agreed we would celebrate all religious holidays but would otherwise not impose our religious beliefs onto our children. That agreement had extended to our parents, and we made sure they were well aware of our expectations. They had all honored our wishes—until then.

When I saw the crucifix, I felt like I had been sucker punched in the gut. It wasn't the crucifix itself—we had just hosted Christmas, after all—it was the lack of respect, and the way Olga gave Amaya the gift without checking with us first. I felt like Olga was well aware of the months-long debate over our son's name, and this seemed like both a provocation and an undermining of my place in the family, a rubbing of salt in the wound.

Our religious differences had never seemed so wide as at that moment. I didn't know it then, but it would change the course of our marriage.

Filip must have noticed my silent anger. In one brisk move, he grabbed the necklace and stashed it in the glovebox. He didn't say a word, caught between his mother and his wife. Olga didn't say a word either, but she had this look on her face like she had won. I shrugged it off for the sake of harmony, and we went inside to hear about their trip.

I addressed it with Filip when we got home. Still feeling the sting, I quietly approached him. "How come Olga gave Amaya a crucifix necklace? I thought we agreed we weren't going to push either religion on the kids?"

"I don't know. It's my mom. She's crazy. It's like she's trying to start something."

"Well, that hurts. That really hurts. I couldn't name my son Namik, even though you knew what that name meant to me because it's a Muslim name. And now your family's giving our daughter a crucifix? Are we trying to erase the fact that our children are half Muslim? Because that's what it seems like."

"No, of course not," Filip said, brushing me off. "Don't make such a big deal out of it. Like I said, it's just Mom being Mom. I don't know why she did it."

"Okay, then. Can we return the pendant to your mom then? Amaya can keep the necklace."

"I don't care. If that's what you want, go ahead," he replied, by his tone implying that he wanted nothing to do with it.

I wanted him to understand. "It bothers me that she's meddling in how we raise our children—that she's meddling at all."

"If it bothers you that much, then go ahead and give it back to her." He walked away, heading to the garage to have a cigarette—and get away from me.

I knew then that when it came to a choice between me and his family, he'd choose his family. Maybe he was afraid to stand up to his mother, but I wasn't. If he wanted me to take care of it, I would do just that. But I dearly wished he had my back when I needed him.

✦

On most Friday nights, the family gathered at our house to hang out. I cherished those days with family, as they were one of the reasons we moved to Georgia in the first place, and what I had daydreamed about—raising my kids in a big family, with holiday parties and happy children running around the house.

I would talk to Olga the next Friday get together.

The evening started off with Olga and Tina opening Christmas presents from us, and Mateo boasting to Olga about the lavish Christmas dinner I had put together and how it was a huge success, all the while patting me on the back with pride.

After the exchange, Olga stepped outside on the balcony for a smoke, and I saw my chance to catch her alone, mother-to-mother. I retrieved the cross pendant and joined her on the balcony.

Apprehensive and nervous, I sat down next to her. I lit my cigarette, took a drag, then handed her the cross, saying in as calm a voice as I could muster, "It's very nice of you to get Amaya a gold necklace, but Filip and I agreed we wouldn't push any particular religious beliefs on our children. You should take this back please. I hope you understand."

Olga's face quickly transformed from a smile to rage. "How dare you? That's despicable! She is my granddaughter. I'll give her whatever I please." She stood up, flicked her cigarette off the balcony into the grass, and stomped back inside the house, slamming the balcony door behind her.

I was flabbergasted. I expected her at best to be apologetic for overstepping, at worst miffed that we couldn't accept her gift. I did not expect this Mount Vesuvius of unbridled, entitled rage. Now I knew where Filip got it.

I walked after her into the living room only to hear her command her family to leave. "Mateo, Tina, get up. Let's go! I don't want to spend another minute in this house."

"I'm sorry you feel this way, Olga," I tried to placate her. "I'm sure you agree that how we raise our children is between Filip and me."

I looked to Filip for support, but all he said was: "What the hell happened?"

Mateo and Tina were stupefied by this turn of events, and Amaya ran out of her room. "Why is Gamma mad?"

"Nothing happened!" Olga continued in rage, pointing at me. "She cannot dictate the gifts I give to my own grandkids. Get up. Let's go!"

I looked at Filip, pleading for help, but he seemed almost as angry as she was, and not at her. If Filip wouldn't stand up for me, I would stand up for myself. These were our children. This was our house. We'd decide the rules. I could not tolerate being spoken to in such manner in my own house and in front of my family and children.

"Look Olga, this is our house. It is not right for you to act this way in front of our kids."

"I am going to act however I want to act!" Her shrill voice echoed as she walked downstairs toward the front door.

"I respect that you're Filip's mom," I called after her, "but if you're going to act disrespectful to me in front of my husband and children, you are not welcome in my house anymore."

My hands trembled, and a nervous sweat came over me. I had never said anything like that to anyone before. I never had to.

But Olga wasn't ready to retreat. "This is my son's house! You can't stop me from coming to my son's house. I'll break in if I have to."

"And I will call the police if you break into my house."

It was unfathomable how this woman could have gone from smoking a cigarette peacefully on my balcony sixty seconds before to pounding her chest like a wild gorilla threatening to break into my home.

Filip remained silent.

"Mateo, Tina, let's go! I don't need your stupid gifts either!" She hurled the bag of Christmas gifts at me.

Finally, they left, and an uneasy quiet descended on the house. I asked Filip why he hadn't done anything. He shrugged, not offering much of an explanation other than "I told you she's crazy!"

"If she's crazy, I don't want her anywhere near my house until she apologizes." I was still shaking with adrenalin.

"My mother will never apologize to you," Filip scoffed.

"Why not?" I demanded.

"That's just how she is," he continued, as if anyone should know that.

"Then I don't want her around my house. I don't want her anywhere near my kids because that behavior is unacceptable. I don't care who she is."

✦

Although Filip hadn't directly attacked me for the altercation with his mother, I certainly didn't feel like he had backed me up either, and everything changed between us from then on. Filip seemed to go full-on passive-aggressive, barely speaking to me and leaving any room in the house I entered. We became two strangers living together under one roof.

It seemed like Filip took this estrangement as a release from his promise to avoid alcohol and started binge-drinking frequently. Most evenings after I signed off from work, Filip took my laptop into the garage where he sat by himself, played music, drank, and smoked. One such evening, he smashed bottles on the garage floor, then fell asleep in the chair. In the morning, he woke up to the shards of broken glass, showered, and then went to work. We had fruitless, almost daily arguments about all this. My dreams of a happy family were shattered among the broken glass and cigarette butts on our dusty garage floor.

✦

These times of marital sorrow rekindled my memories of Igor. I frequently found myself thinking about him, and how far I had drifted from the life I had once imagined for myself as a child. I longed for Igor, who represented that life for me. He had always been kind to me. Seeing me smile made him happy. Thinking about our time together back in Bosnia made me forget, at least briefly, the agony of my life with Filip.

Life was so simple back then. I liked to daydream about our class field trip to the movie theatre at the end of sixth grade. It was a humid day in June, our last summer as innocent teens filled with hopes and dreams before the war began. School was almost out, and we looked forward to summer break when we would be sleeping in, spending our days with friends, hanging out in coffee shops, and swimming in the river.

Igor and I just liked being with each other—nothing fraught or difficult about it. We assumed we would always be together. As we sat on the stairs near the theatre's box office holding hands while the teachers checked us in one by one, we made plans for the future.

I teased Igor that day about why he had never invited me to see his band practice. He looked deep into my eyes and said, "I would love for you to see me play, but before you do, we have to get better."

I never did get to watch a rehearsal before we fled Bosnia.

When Dad returned to Bosnia for the first time, five years after we had arrived in the United States, he asked me if there was anything I wanted him to bring back from home. I didn't ask for any particular toy or object from the house I grew up in. I didn't ask for any comfort food or snack item. My one and only request was simple. "Find Igor and take a picture of him. That's all I want."

Dad came through. He brought the picture home, and I cherished it, keeping it hidden in my desk wherever I was. When life got hard and I felt like crying, I would look at Igor's face smiling at me, standing next to my dad at our favorite coffee shop, and I always felt better.

Along with the photo, Igor had sent me a CD of the first album he record-ed with his band, Revolt. The album was titled In the House of Pain, written in white letters on a pink cover. A handwritten note inside read:

I'm sorry you never got to see my old band practice. This is my new band. We're edgy and I hope you like it. Love always, Igor.

I listened to it often, but it wasn't until Filip and I were constantly fight-ing that the title hit me hard. I felt as if I was indeed living in my own house of pain.

Inspired by the picture and the disk, I opened my laptop and sent Igor an email just to see how he was doing. It had been a couple of months since our last exchange. Several days went by and no response, which struck me as unusual. He usually replied to my emails within hours. I thought he was either busy with work, his band, or travelling. When a whole week went by, I got worried and reached out to a mutual friend who lived in Banja Luka to ask about him. Several hours later I received a short reply from the friend stating, "I'm sorry to be the one to tell you, but you should know. Igor recent-ly passed away. I just found out about it a few days ago too. I'm very sorry!" It was timestamped 1/11/2009 at 3:33 p.m.

For hours, I stared blankly into the note on my computer screen in disbelief, chain-smoking and crying uncontrollably. I remembered our first kiss by Vrbas River, the sheepish gaze of his gorgeous blue eyes, Igor racing across town to say goodbye to me before I left Bosnia. Then there was the very last time I saw him at dinner on my visit to Bosnia the summer of 2000 when he hugged me one final time and whispered into my ear the last words he had spoken to me in person: "I wish it was me taking you home tonight."

I cursed the bloody war, blaming it for everything—for having to flee my country, for separating me from Igor, for my parents' divorce, for Filip's drinking, and my own shortcomings. Had it not been for that stupid war, maybe my entire life would have turned out much differently. I was angry at myself for not keeping in touch with Igor more often. I regretted not telling him, at any point after I had left, how I truly felt about him.

My first love and a most beautiful and genuine soul had become my guardian angel at only thirty years young. Ironically, I would later find out from friends he died from an overdose, wanting just one last high before settling down. It was as if a part of me had died with him. I was numb and couldn't fathom never seeing him again. I clutched his picture and the CD close to my heart, embracing it as the only tangible thing I had from him. His music was his passion. I stared at the album cover and suddenly saw it in different light—a final message from Igor: "Revolt" against "The House of Pain."

It made me realize just how short life is. While the trauma of his passing triggered deeply suppressed memories of the war, it also made me look inward. I wasn't happy, and though I had two beautiful children, I hadn't achieved many of the goals I had set as a child. I was fooling myself, barely surviving.

Back then, I thought maybe I didn't deserve to be happy, or rather, that I should be happy with whatever I received. Survivor's guilt. Why should I get to be happy? Why should I get what I wanted when so many innocent people and children had lost their lives in the war? Why did I get to survive while others did not? I questioned my worthiness. I questioned my entire existence.

Acknowledging this pain was the first step on my journey to healing. I thank Igor for forcing me to take that first step every day.

✦

While in the thick of my pain, it was hard for me to see a way out. I resigned myself to drowning out my sorrows with Linkin Park played extra loudly on repeat: "Given Up," "Faint," "Numb," and "Bleed It Out." Maybe Chester Bennington screaming into the microphone with frustration and anger would be enough to tell Filip how I felt and get him to change.

It didn't.

I had a business trip to Dallas scheduled for the end of January. I was eager to get away for a little time to myself to think about what could be done to mend our marriage. All of it was weighing extra heavy on my heart.

As soon as I left home, though, Ace developed a fever. That I was far from my baby and unable to comfort to him upset me even more. I couldn't help but feel guilty. I also felt like a failure as a mother, and Filip was happy to agree with me, taking any opportunity to reproach me for being gone when a boy needed his mother most. Filip suddenly appeared to have turned into one of those old-school husbands about childcare—sure he'd help out, but now that we were fighting, the kids were primarily my responsibility and Filip took it upon himself to let me know whenever I was slacking on the job.

Filip filled in just fine, but suddenly it was like he resented every second of it. He took a day off work to take Ace to the pediatrician, who diagnosed him with an ear infection and prescribed antibiotics.

I couldn't wait to get back home and cuddle my babies. I returned early Friday morning and took the rest of the day off to spend with the kids. The time away had not helped—it certainly hadn't changed anything between me and Filip. Exhausted by life, I looked forward to a quiet weekend of rest, smiles, and cuddles with Amaya and Ace.

✦

That evening, Ami, Hamza, Adem, and Kendra came by our house to invite Filip and me to a hockey game. Ami and Hamza had tickets courtesy of their boss. Something was telling me to stay home that evening, though. Given that Filip was drinking again, going out was the last thing on my mind. I really just wanted to hang out with my kids.

Everyone else was enthusiastic about seeing the game, though, and insisted I join them, including Mom, who didn't typically encourage me to go out. She even volunteered to watch everyone's kids. "Come on, you need a break! Go have some fun," Mom said.

"Yes, come on! We have great seats! Don't be a party pooper!" the others joined in.

I reluctantly agreed.

Mom would stay at Ami's house with six kids and a puppy. Adem and Kendra had added their two young children to the mix, along with a six-week-old puppy.

After dropping off our kids and Mom at Ami's house, the six of us parents and Adem's sister, Selma, crammed into Ami's minivan. Since I was the only one who didn't drink, I was the designated driver, as usual.

Within minutes after we backed out of Ami's driveway, the guys shouted instructions to stop at a gas station for beer. Back in the car, they popped open the beer, and began drinking like a bunch of frat boys, despite my protests about the open containers.

They continued their drinking throughout the game.

Halfway through, a man who was older than we were came up to our group. He had a friendly manner and seemed to know some of us.

"Who the hell are you?" Filip yelled loudly, sloshing his beer.

"Take it easy there, tiger!" Hamza said. "That's Tom, our boss! He gave us the tickets." Then, to the gentleman he said, "Sorry Tom, Filip had a little too much to drink tonight."

"Who the hell is this guy?" Tom said, meaning Filip. "That's all right. I like him! You're having a good time. Why don't you all come to Plaka tonight?" he said, before heading back to his seat. Plaka was a Greek bar.

"We'll be there," Ami shouted after him.

I leaned into her and whispered, "I really don't want to go, Ami. Filip already had too much to drink and needs to go home."

"Oh my God Annie, relax. We're here and we're all together. We'll keep an eye on Filip, don't worry! Everyone from our office will be there. It would be rude if we don't show up."

By the end of the game, Filip was already slurring his speech. On the way to Plaka's, he downed another beer.

Once there, I avoided him altogether. Instead, I hung out and danced with the girls, but kept a close eye on him from across the room. He had moved on to hard liquor and with every shot of whiskey, he became more aggressive, sizing up other guys who walked past him like he was in a mood to start a fight.

My instincts screamed at me to call it a night. I finally worked up enough courage to walk across the room to Filip to persuade him to come home. "I think that's enough for tonight. Can we get everyone and go home please?"

"Why do you always have to be such a she-devil?" he hissed.

"Filip, I don't want to fight, okay? I miss the kids and just want to go home."

"What about all these guys checking you out? And why did Hamza touch your knee when you were dancing?" Filip's insecurities were surfacing.

Even if someone checked me out, I never paid attention. And the suggestion of anything inappropriate with my sister's husband was beyond absurd. "Filip, if you don't want to go home, you're welcome to stay, but I'm leaving."

Not a second after I turned, Filip smashed an empty shot glass on the bar in a fit of rage. Blood gushed from his fist and splattered on the bar, our friends' clothes, and Filip's shirt. All eyes turned to him. The bartender asked if he should call a cab.

As I left the bar, Filip pushed his way through the group crowding around him, saying he needed some fresh air, and came outside after me. I was walking down the street in a rush, not even sure where I was going or what I was doing. I thought I might call a cab to take me home.

I heard Filip's voice not too far behind me, yelling for me to stop. I knew this side of him. It was nasty, and I was afraid. Ignoring him, I walked faster, hoping he would give up and go back to the bar, but I heard the footsteps behind me speed up. He called my name. As fear set in, I began to run, but running was never my strong suit, and he caught up with me quickly, grabbing my waist from behind.

"Filip, stop! Let me go!" I broke down in tears as I twisted to break his grip.

"Where do you think you're going? You think you can run from me? Are you really that stupid?"

"Just let me go, please!"

"You're not going anywhere! You understand? You stupid idiot! You nasty ugly creature! I hate you! I absolutely hate you! I actually wish you were dead. You don't get to tell me how to live my life! Got that? I will drink as much as I want as often as I want! And you can't do anything about it, you understand? So, shut up already, you stupid ugly hunchback!" The whole time he was screaming these vile things, he gripped me by the arms with his bear-paw hands and violently shook me back and forth.

A police officer pumping gas at the gas station across the street saw what was happening. He banged the nozzle into its slot and jumped into his vehicle, turning on the lights and siren. The patrol car squealed through a U-turn and pulled up in front of us. The police officer ran out of his car and tackled Filip, then pressed his face against the hood of the car. Holding Filip's hands behind his back, the officer searched through his pockets for identification.

As mad as I was at Filip in that moment—and for the entire month of January—he was still the father of my children. If anything happened to him, it would hurt the kids, and they didn't deserve that.

"Officer please, he's my husband," I said. "We had a little fight. Please let him go!"

"Ma'am, please step away and let me do my job," he replied.

"Please officer, I'm so sorry. We just had a fight. We have two kids at home, and he had too much to drink. Please don't arrest him! What am I going to tell our kids? I can't let him go to jail." I'm loyal. I protect the people I care about regardless of the consequences.

Or at least that's what I thought I was doing at the time. Years later I would learn that it's common for abused women to protect their abusers. If he's this angry with me now, and I tell the officer the truth . . .

I wanted to say something oh-so-badly, but I was terrified, and I could easily imagine how infuriated Filip would be after we got home because I'd witnessed his fury before. So, in a split second, I decided to protect my husband again because I feared the next fight we'd have would be over Filip blaming me for getting him in trouble with the police.

Filip was quiet. Suddenly, he looked collected and calm. Even his slurred speech had improved.

"Ma'am, you need to step away and let me do my job," the officer repeated firmly.

I stood on the sidewalk in tears. The officer asked Filip why he had acted so aggressively. Filip apologized, saying he had one too many drinks.

He turned to me and asked, "Do you want to press charges, Ma'am?"

"No! Can you please just let him go, so I can take him home?"

I hoped this would bring Filip back to his senses. My plan was to gather the others, drive everyone home, and get Filip to bed.

With no recourse, the officer agreed to cut Filip loose, but not before giving him a lecture. "You have a beautiful young wife, Mister, who obviously deeply cares about you! I recommend you never lay a finger on her again, and I sure to God hope I don't ever see you again."

"Yes Sir! Sure thing, Officer." Filip seemed chastened in front of the police officer, but as soon as he drove away, he turned to me and muttered, "You ugly cow! You almost got me arrested."

"I almost got you arrested?" His insults didn't bother me as much as his playing the victim.

Filip was strangely subdued in the few minutes it took us to walk back to Plaka and gather most of our group. I corralled everyone into the car where we waited for Kendra to reel in Adem. Meanwhile, Filip stood outside leaning on the passenger side door, his arms resting on top of the car as he quietly smoked. Then out of nowhere, like a caged beast looking to escape, he struck the roof of the car with his fists about half dozen times, startling everyone inside. Then he took off running into a dark alley.

Caught off guard, by the time we got out of the car to go after him, Filip had already disappeared into the woods. Logically, I knew I should have just left him to himself given his excessive drinking, abusive behavior, and vile insults, but my conscience wouldn't allow it. I was not about to leave the father of my children somewhere in Atlanta, intoxicated and with no transportation home. If anything had happened to him, I would have never been able to forgive myself.

We went on a manhunt.

We called his phone; he didn't answer. As soon as Adem and Kendra turned up, we left the parking lot. Ami and Hamza enlisted their coworkers to look for Filip as well. We drove around the streets of Atlanta for nearly an hour with no luck. All the calls to his phone went to voicemail. Worried that something might have happened to him, Hamza and Adem took turns rapidly redialing his phone number as I drove aimlessly through the streets of Atlanta looking for any sign of him.

When he finally decided to answer his phone an hour later, Filip told Hamza he had been walking around and lost track of where he was. He found an intersection and gave us the cross streets to pick him up. By then, it was 5:00 a.m. Everyone in the car breathed a sigh of relief that nothing had happened to Filip. We were all ready to go home and get some rest.

I entered the cross streets into the car's GPS and without a word, drove to the location to pick him up. Then we drove home. I dropped off Kendra, Adem, and his sister at their house. Then I took Ami and Hamza home. Instead of waking Amaya and Ace, I left them with Mom for the day, and drove myself and Filip home. Still reeling from an intensely explosive and violent night, I walked straight to our bedroom and locked the doors behind me. Filip rattled the door knob a few times, realized we would not be sharing a bed that night, and crashed in Ace's room. It was 6:00 a.m.

✦

Three hours later, Mom was knocking on our door. I got out of bed, barely able to keep my eyes open to let her in. Visibly worried, Mom started off by saying she had heard about the night before and asked me to come with her to talk. Knowing Mom, she just wanted me to be safe and out of Filip's reach. While I appreciated her concern, I sent her back to Ami's house to watch the kids, promising to come by later. This wasn't Mom's battle; it was mine. I had had enough of Filip's ways and was not about to run from him.

As soon as Mom left, still reeling from the night before, I collected Filip's clothes from our closet and tossed them out in the driveway. Pile by pile, I cleared out Filip's entire section of the closet, and for the first time in months, felt liberated. After everything I had done for him and his family since we'd known each other, after having been the sole breadwinner for our family for years, I didn't deserve to be treated the way he treated me. I was done putting up with it. It was time for Filip to leave.

But before I could do anything, I had to ensure our kids' future. As a hard-working mom, I had stashed away two college tuitions worth of savings. Filip was on all the credit cards and bank accounts, and I knew he was perfectly capable of cleaning out the accounts in retaliation. I hid his wallet and planned to keep it hidden until the next business day when I could go to the banks and figure out how to protect that money.

Filip had come into the marriage with barely anything. Even his new car was purchased with cash that mostly I earned, so I hid the keys.

With the assets protected, at least temporarily, I poured an oversized glass of cold water and walked into Ace's room where Filip was still passed out. Then I poured the ice water on his face.

Filip jumped to his feet, yelling, "What the. . . ?" He rubbed water out of his eyes, then scanned the room in surprise. When he saw me standing next to the bed, he pulled himself together.

"Your stuff is outside! I've had enough of your drinking, your pushing me around, your name calling, your putting me down, enough of your mom, enough of these fights, enough of the broken glass and beer bottles! I've had enough of you, Filip! Get out of my house!"

He laughed at me, as if I were playing a joke. He didn't move or offer any kind of apology or explanation. He stood there smirking, as if he knew he had me forever, and there was nothing he could do to lose me, nothing I could do to make him leave.

I pointed to his stuff in the driveway. He walked outside, collected the clothes. I tried to block his way into the house, insisting he leave, but he pushed past me smirking still, saying he wasn't going anywhere—cool as a frosty beer on a hot summer day.

Was he so lacking in self-awareness that he didn't know the line he had crossed? I wanted to crawl out of my own skin. Or was I the crazy one, as he implied when he asked why I was acting so irrationally? He certainly made me feel like I was.

For fifteen minutes, we stood at the front door arguing. At least I tried to lay out my case. Filip made fun of me.

When he saw I wasn't going to back down, he tried his other favorite tactic, victimhood.

"Where do you want me to go?" he whined. "It's not like I can go back to my parents' place! You took care of that."

"I don't care where you go! Anywhere! I don't want to live with you anymore! This isn't healthy, and I'm not leaving. I bought this house! I pay the bills! I supported this family for years when you were out of a job. Everything we have is because I worked hard for it! I'm not handing it over to you. Get out!" I yelled and pushed at him without moving him an inch.

If I couldn't get Filip to leave that way, I had one more line of attack to try. Filip had a collection of football and hockey jerseys I had given to him as gifts for birthdays, anniversaries, and other special occasions. He was a big sports fan, and the jerseys meant everything to him. In desperation, I retrieved a pair of scissors from the kitchen and walked past Filip into the driveway where some of the jerseys were still piled. I picked up a jersey and told him if he didn't leave, I would cut it up.

He laughed. He didn't think I would do it, but he had no idea how far he had pushed me. I cut up the jersey and dropped the scraps onto the driveway. He stood there with that silly look on his face. I picked up another jersey, cut it up, dropped it on the driveway. No reaction. I cut up a third, and then a fourth. Still, he just stood there, daring me to do something more.

I looked around, thinking about what else he loved, and then cut up a pair of his leather tennis shoes. When I cut those into thin leather strips, something finally clicked with Filip that I was serious.

At that point, he retrieved two suitcases from the house, and in complete silence collected his belongings from the driveway and stuffed them into the suitcases. He asked for his wallet and car keys, but I refused to return them. With clothes tightly packed in the bags, Filip walked out of the driveway and onto the street. I locked the door behind him.

With Filip gone, I breathed a sigh of relief. I sat on the balcony, smoking to calm myself down. Thirty minutes and three cigarettes later, I locked the front door behind me and drove to Mom's to pick up Amaya and Ace. Mom had been worried sick since she left my house. She made me breakfast and coffee, and I recapped the morning.

Now that Filip had left, I felt a strange sense of calm and relief, not only that the kids and I would be okay without him, but that he could no longer hurt us. Mom and I took the kids to park to let them run around and play while she and I had a heart-to-heart. I vividly remember Amaya and Ace holding hands that day as they ran to a big blue-and-green slide, smiling without a care in the world. Amaya's pigtails bounced as she ran up the stairs to the top of the slide while Ace chased his big sister, laughing.

Without taking my eyes from my beautiful babies, I told Mom my plans to file for divorce. I felt guilty about the kids, but I was fed up with the fights, drinking, and bullying. "Marriage is not supposed to be like that. Life is not supposed to be this hard. This unhealthy, this toxic. What example are we setting for our kids? All we do is fight about his drinking—and everything else."

"I can't tell you what I think you should do, but I will support you in whatever decision you make," Mom said.

Mom stayed at the park with me and the kids until dusk, listening, letting me talk it out. She gave me comfort knowing she had my back unconditionally. The fresh crisp Georgia air of that gloomy February day gave me clarity and caused Amaya and Ace to work up an appetite. As we walked back to the car, I promised to make them grilled cheese sandwiches at home, give them baths, and go night-night together. I was determined to make their first night without their father a comfortable one.

✦

As I pulled into the driveway, I noticed the lights were on in just about every room in the house. I had left at mid-day and expected to come home to darkness in the house. Immediately suspicious, I called Filip's phone. When he answered, I said, "Hey, where are you?"

"Home, watching a basketball game. Why?"

Was he really trying to pretend nothing had happened? "I locked the door and took your keys. How did you get in?"

"Oh, I climbed up the balcony in the back. The door was unlocked." Again, he said this as if it was no big deal, as if he did this every day.

"I want you to leave, Filip! If you don't, I'm calling the police."

"Okay, then, call the police," he replied, as if he knew something I didn't.

I dialed 911 and waited nearby until a police car arrived. When an officer pulled into my driveway, I pulled up beside him and exited my car.

I explained to him what happened beginning with the night before. I even told him that I had cut Filip's jerseys into strips that morning. I wanted him to have the whole picture.

The young officer seemed sympathetic, but said I shouldn't have destroyed the jerseys and shoes—that was against the law. He asked me to wait in the driveway. Then he rang the doorbell to talk to Filip. Mom, Amaya, and Ace were still in the car.

Filip seemed casual about the whole thing. Calm even. When the officer requested he leave the house, Filip agreed, asking only for his wallet and car keys.

The officer returned to me and asked for Filip's items.

I explained that the car belonged to me, and that because Filip had access to my bank accounts and credit cards, I wasn't going to return his wallet either.

Growing visibly frustrated, the officer stopped asking me to give him the wallet and keys, and started instructing me to do so in that commanding police voice they learn.

I politely declined each time.

He said that Amaya and Ace should go in the house, and I nodded to Mom that it was okay, so she let them out of the car. The officer followed them up the drive and spoke to Filip, gesturing and periodically looking over at me.

I observed their interaction from the driveway, wondering what they could possibly be talking about. Once the children were through the door and out of sight, the officer came back to me, told me to turn around, and handcuffed me. I was dumbfounded. Was this some kind of a joke? Mom gasped and rushed out of the car.

But it was no joke. The officer escorted me to the back seat of his car. Never in my life had I been in trouble with the law. Not even in my wildest nightmares could I have imagined I would find myself in the back seat of a police car, handcuffed like a criminal, on my way to jail. My whole life I had worked hard, followed all the rules—and I mean all of them—and all I ever wanted to do was raise my children in peace.

Meanwhile, I looked at Filip as he stood framed by the front door, the front door of my house, the smirk of victory on his face. He could have saved me from this embarrassment just as I had saved him the night before, but he chose not to. And that was the difference between us. As the car pulled away from the house, Filip stepped into the foyer and closed the door on me, on our marriage, on our family.

But what hurt even more was he had done it again! He had turned the tables on me. Embarrassed, hurt, and angry, I broke into sobs. Instead of making grilled cheese sandwiches for my babies and snuggling them into bed, I was headed to jail. How could I face them now? How did he always win?

CHAPTER 14

ANGER MANAGEMENT

I was brought to city jail for processing, and I was scared. I didn't know what to expect. A younger, mean-looking female guard with her hair tightly slicked into a ponytail stood in front of me. She was short, stocky, and buff for a woman. You could imagine her gut-punching a thug to his knees. She handed me a zip-lock bag and recited the instructions she'd recited hundreds of times by now: "Remove all your jewelry, pull the tie string out of your sweatpants and shoelaces out of your shoes. Place all items in the bag. These will be returned to you upon your release."

"Yes, ma'am!" I said, mustering enough courage to reply.

She ordered me to strip out of my hoodie and undergarments, handed me an orange top, then escorted me to a cell occupied by several other females. The cell was damp, about twenty-by-twenty feet wide, its concrete walls lined with metal benches bolted to the walls. I shivered from nerves and the cold.

I sat several feet away from everyone else, my back against the concrete. A disheveled woman in her mid-thirties, who must have been strung out on drugs, was railing about the injustice of being locked up for not paying child support. "What kind of crime is that?" she asked, looking at me. I expected her to attack any moment. This is it! I thought. This is how I die! I survived the Bosnian war only for this?

I was freaking out on the inside, beating myself up for letting my life spiral this far out of control. On the outside, however, I kept my cool, face impassive, breathing deeply to calm my nerves. I had learned that much in the war surrounded by soldiers ready to kill without flinching. No matter how close you are to a screaming meltdown, show no fear.

To distract myself, I kept one eye on the crazy woman in case I had to defend myself and thought about how I had gotten to this point. In life, we set the standard for how we allow ourselves to be treated—and I had set that bar pretty low with Filip. Since he had come into my life, every decision I made was either to please Filip or to avoid displeasing him. I had a vision of what a marriage should be, of what a family should be—two parents, a tidy house with a yard, beautiful and loving children. Until then, my goal was always to preserve that, to save our marriage for the sake of the kids, so that we'd all have a "normal" life—whatever that is.

What I failed to see was that every time I gave in to Filip, every time he got drunk and bullied me, I lowered the bar even farther until he probably no longer saw me as a loving, equal partner who worked hard to support our family. It felt like he hadn't seen me as his desirable wife for a while, really. I can only guess how he truly saw me. My guess would be I alternated between being his gravy train—we certainly couldn't have been living that lifestyle on his salary—and his emasculating prison warden who expected him to help around the house and do his fair share with the children. I was the person who hated his parents and kept them from their grandchildren, who wouldn't let him drink when he felt like it, who didn't honor him as a man. But who was really imprisoned in our marriage? He seemed to do whatever he pleased and got away with it; a fact brought home in stark reality by the cold jail cell in which I found myself surrounded by actual criminals. I had to get out of this cell, and I realized that night that I had to get out of this toxic marriage and turn my life around for the sake of the children. They deserved better.

Later, and through much self-reflection, I would come to realize that Filip wasn't the only person in our marriage whose view of me had changed. I had really let myself go. After each fight, I dimmed my own light just a little more, slowly settling for the life Filip was creating for us. Over time, I had been resigning myself to this marriage, little by little lowering my expectations and diminishing myself to fit into Filip's tiny little shoebox. My self-esteem nosedived, leaving me powerless to even try to escape the marriage that chipped away at the core of who I am. That night was a wake-up call.

I can't say that I'm glad I went to jail. I regret the things I did that day— destroying Filip's clothes, refusing to return his wallet and keys, refusing to obey the police officer—and will always be ashamed of them. But sitting there that night helped me clarify how I wanted to live the rest of my life.

After I was taken away, Mom called Ami and the duo frantically called around to find out where I had been taken. Once they found out, they spent the rest of their evening in the waiting room to post bail and take me home.

Around 2:00 a.m., a different female guard opened the cell door and called my name. Without saying much, she escorted me to a glass window. Another guard sitting behind the window slid a ziplock bag with my belongings through a slit in the glass, along with some papers to sign. Wondering what was going on, I heard the guard read out the instructions, "You are not allowed any contact and are not to go within five hundred feet of him."

I was being charged with domestic violence—and "him" meant Filip. Ironic, since he was the one who shook me till I clattered. What about the kids? I broke into an ice-cold sweat thinking I might not be able to see the kids either.

Reluctantly, I signed the document, not wanting to go back to the cold cell, regained possession of my belongings, and followed the guard to the changing room. I took only the shoelaces from the ziplock bag, leaving behind the drawstring and jewelry. I stared at my wedding and engagement rings still in the clear plastic bag, and ultimately couldn't leave them behind. I shoved the bag into my pocket but vowed to never again wear the ring of a man who didn't deserve me.

I was escorted to the waiting room and freedom. Worried sick, Mom and Ami both rushed to embrace me, breathing a sigh of relief. Without wasting another moment, we hightailed it out of there. On the way to the car, they told me they had been there since shortly after I was brought in, waiting all that time for the court system to process my bail.

Ami drove us back to Mom's house. We agreed it was best that none of us have any contact with Filip from that point on, and that we'd look for an attorney to make sure I could see my kids and advise me on how to proceed.

✦

That night, I didn't sleep at all. I tried to because I had not slept in days and was exhausted, but my mind was racing, thinking of all the things I could have done differently and the repercussions of what I had done. At the first glimmer of the sun, I was looking up defense attorneys in the Yellow Pages. By 8:00 a.m., I had a consultation appointment with an experienced lawyer who confirmed my worst fears. "You can't really see your kids until the court approves a motion to modify the terms of your release order. This is fairly common practice when there are minors involved, especially very young children, as in your case. The modified order would allow contact only when you're exchanging kids, usually done in a public setting. I could draw up the paperwork today, but you're looking at about two weeks before I can get you a court date."

"Two weeks? I need to get this started right away then. You're hired. What do you need from me?" I didn't even ask him about his fees.

"Tell you what, swing by my office today. Let's get some documents signed and get the motions filed. The sooner you do it, the quicker we can get that court date set up."

Although I hadn't had a chance to say good-bye to my babies or explain to them where I was and why they couldn't see me, I was determined to do right by them.

I came out of the attorney's office with a renewed sense of optimism and called the daycare to check on my kids, hoping I could at least hear their voices on the phone. They told me that Filip had called earlier to inform them he was pulling the kids out of daycare, and that his sister would be watching them for a while. My heart sank. So much for a renewed sense of optimism.

✦

A week had gone by without hearing my kids' voices or seeing their faces, and then another. Not knowing if they were happy, sad, or just as scared as I was, all I could do was cry for hours with each passing day. Friends and family tried to console me to no avail. Even little Amra noticed my state of mind. One day she brought me a photo album, pointed to pictures of my children, and said, "Lookie auntie, we can see Ace and Amaya here! And they're happy!"

My only response was to fall to the floor, curl up in a ball, and sob for hours until there were no more tears left. I hated Filip's actions. I hated that he had kept my children from me. But most of all, I hated that neither Filip nor anyone on his side of the family found it in their hearts to bring my kids to me so I could see them. I wasn't allowed to call or go near Filip, but someone could have brought my kids to me.

After days of burgundy-red eyes and eyelids almost swollen shut from sobbing, I grew tired of feeling powerless. I missed my children, so what was I going to do about it? I vowed to get them back, no matter what it took. People make mistakes all the time—going to jail for domestic violence was a big one. But people also fix their mistakes, and I was determined to fix the biggest mistake of my life! I was not about to roll over and let it define me. Once I was cried out, my anger turned from "I hate this" into "I will prove you wrong."

+

With great anticipation, I awaited my scheduled court date because that was the first step to redemption.

I arrived an hour early. Sometime later, Filip strolled into the courtroom. After carefully scanning the room, he spotted me and sat next to me. He knew I wasn't allowed near him. It seemed like he was goading me into losing my cool. Under his breath, he said, "You look nice."

It was unsettling. I wasn't fooled by his pleasantries. Yet, I couldn't risk riling him. Without saying a word, I turned my head away, ignoring him.

But the judge noticed us together and, visibly upset, summoned my attorney. After a brief exchange, she called on me.

I said, "Your Honor, I was here first. He came and sat next to me. I wasn't even talking to him." I sounded like a teenager.

"You need to move," she ordered loudly.

"Yes, Ma'am!" I gathered my belongings and scampered to the opposite side of the courtroom. That's all I needed—turning the judge against me. I couldn't afford any more mistakes, not even little ones, if I wanted to see my kids again. Filip had everything working in his favor, on paper anyway.

When the judge called on us, I was courteous and humble, answered all the questions truthfully and respectfully, then crossed my fingers and hoped for the best. At the end of the hearing, she granted my request for the modification—and lifted an immense boulder off my chest. After the longest two weeks of my life, I would finally get to see my babies that evening.

When asked, Filip declined to press charges. The original order was modified so that Filip and I were still not allowed contact with one another except when we exchanged the kids. Filip requested we share equal visitation and alternate days. He also appealed to the court that we try marriage counseling. I agreed to any and all demands that allowed me to see my babies. My only request was for Filip to allow our kids to go back to daycare, to which he agreed. Since I had no prior record or history of violence, the judge recommended I take anger management classes, after which the case against me would be eligible for dismissal.

My first visit with Ace and Amaya that evening involved many happy tears and big mama-bear hugs and kisses. I thought I would never feel those soft, warm little arms wrapped around me or hear their beautiful voices again. Both of them cried, asking why they hadn't been able to see me. Rather than trying to explain the complexities of the legal system, I simply made a promise to my children, holding each of their cheeks in my hand, side by side, "Mommy will never, ever leave you again! I promise! I'm so sorry for everything. And I promise you, I am going to fix this."

Amaya's smile gave me lion's strength and Ace's innocence gave me a shot of willpower to keep moving forward.

✦

Over the next few weeks, I began the anger management courses required by the court, as well as the marriage counseling requested by Filip. Despite spending a couple of hundred dollars on the counseling, Filip and I weren't getting anywhere. It seemed like all he wanted to do was downplay his alcohol consumption, without showing any understanding of our situation, and generally didn't seem interested in discussing, let alone solving, our marital problems. After the three mandatory sessions I had agreed to, I declined to take it any further.

On the other hand, the anger management classes did more good for my soul than I ever could have imagined. My caseworker, Jane, was not only a great counselor, she was a wonderful being—warm, compassionate, and smart about the workings of human relationships. She was the first to open my eyes to the harsh realities of my marriage. She listened to my story intently and responded with pertinent observations and meaningful advice. With each visit, she offered pamphlets and reading assignments as homework. She also had me write in a journal, which we would review together.

Jane taught me lifelong skills that I use even today, such as how to identify feelings and put them into words when I am upset. I hadn't been able to do that in the past. She also taught me that even though I have no control over how someone behaves toward me, I have control over how I react, what my boundaries are, and whether or not I allow others to cross them.

I was grateful for these sessions and left each class looking forward to the next. Our sessions were going so well, Jane signed off on my certificate of completion after only eight sessions, rather than the usual twelve to twenty-four.

I didn't tell Filip I finished early, letting him believe I still had a few weeks to go. In fact, I seldom told Filip anything anymore. For as long as my case was pending, we were to have no contact with each other, and this was fine by me. I genuinely appreciated being apart from him and was still living with Mom. The kids stayed with me one day and with Filip the next. He would usually drop them off at daycare in the morning, and I'd pick them up in the afternoon to spend the night with me, or the other way around. Whenever I saw him on the weekends to exchange the kids, he insisted I come back home. Not only was that impossible because of the court order, being in a house with Filip was the last place on Earth I wanted to be. I was steadfast in my desire for a divorce, and I didn't want to give him any opening to convince me otherwise.

I was taking back control of my life, and if we were to even think about getting back together, it would be under very different terms—my terms. Besides, I had my work cut out for me to get back on track. Now that anger management was completed, I had to get the case dismissed and the record expunged to even out the playing field before filing for divorce.

My heart was torn, however. In those weeks and months we spent apart, it seems Filip was actually cleaning up his act. I was longing—and praying each night—to wake from a nightmare and have Filip choose his family over drinking. My heart grew heavier each time he picked up Amaya and Ace and pleaded with me about how much he wanted his wife back, and how much our kids missed having their mom at home. He probably went after my heart in this way because he knew he still had leverage there.

But I knew I had to stay the course set forth by logic and reason—this was not the time to follow my heart. My heart looked for any excuse to forgive him, but my brain knew Filip's actions rarely matched his words. To let him back in would be a disaster. Besides, I'd given him many, many chances before. I finally knew it would never work.

The final proof for me to go through with seeking a divorce came during a casual encounter when Filip arrived to pick up the kids from my mom's house, where we were staying. It was only hours after I had completed my final anger management session.

While he was casually sprawled out, resting on the freshly mowed lawn, waiting for the kids to come out, I asked Filip, "Will you at least apologize for the drinking and the night that led up to me kicking you out of the house?"

He looked at me briefly and then smirked, "I'm sorry."

I could tell he didn't mean it. In fact, it sounded snide, like a caught-out teenager hoping his parents would let him off the hook.

At that moment, I knew it was over, that Bad Filip had won out over Good Filip, and Good Filip was not coming back. I had learned too much to go back to the way it was. My heart and my head were finally in agreement.

✦

With the official anger management certificate in hand, bright and early the very next day I proudly marched back to the courthouse to clear my name. The case was dismissed! I no longer was required by law to stay away from the house.

Afterward, knowing Filip would still be at work, I ran by the house to pick up a few things since I had left without so much as a toothbrush.

I unlocked the door to our house for the first time in months and walked through the door. What I saw next stopped me short, shaking me to the core.

Piles of dirty laundry covered the stairs leading down to the basement and laundry room, with more mounds piled in front of the washer and dryer. To get to my basement office, I had to plow a path through the clothes.

My old office looked like a scene from a police show when the bad guys tear a room apart looking for drugs or money. Work documents and old family photos were scattered on the floor, drawers emptied out, picture frames broken, binders and books swept off the shelves. Upstairs in the kitchen, dirty dishes and trash covered most of the counter space. Stacked empty pizza boxes littered the kitchen floor. A pungent stench oozed from every corner of the house, as if it hadn't been cleaned since the day I was taken away.

Our home looked more like a crack house than a place where I had once lived and raised our children. Amaya's room was completely ruined. Filip had let kids draw on walls with Sharpies. Permanent black ink drawings covered walls as high as Amaya and Ace could reach. The kids' bathroom was swarming with gnats, and dead bugs lay curled in the bathtub. There were no pillowcases or bedsheets on the bed in the master bedroom, just the duvet cover with food stains and what else I didn't want to know. Trash was heaped everywhere, like a scene from Hoarders.

I started crying; I couldn't help it. All the work I had put into this house to make it a home. And the kids! They had been living in this mess the last couple of months. You'd think Filip's family at least would have wanted to keep the kids safe and clean.

I drove back to Mom's house, borrowed her video camera, and returned to record the state of the house.

When finished, still shaking in shock and disbelief, I decided to pick up the children from the daycare and take them to Mom's, even though it was Filip's day. There was no way I could have let him take them back to that filthy place. There was also no doubt in my mind that Filip would call the police to report me for kidnapping my own children. With Amaya and Ace secured, I called the non-emergency police number to understand my options.

The lady on the phone seemed kind. After I explained my situation, the house conditions and that I had my kids with me, I asked if Filip could have me arrested for taking the kids from daycare on his day.

"The situation you're describing is not considered kidnapping if you're still legally married and there's no existing custody order in place," she explained. "As their mother, you can take your kids anywhere, and you're just looking out for the best interests of your children. In fact, if you're staying with your mom, and he shows up on her property to take your kids or harass you in any way, you should know that you can have him arrested for trespassing."

I breathed a sigh of relief knowing I couldn't get arrested again, but I spent the remainder of afternoon worried and afraid, anticipating Filip's reaction and preparing for another gut punch. Around 6:00 p.m., a text message came asking where Amaya and Ace were.

"They're with me. We're at my mom's," I replied.

"Why?" he demanded.

"I came by the house today and the place is a filthy mess. I'm not letting my kids back there until you scrub that place clean."

"I'm calling the cops."

"No problem; the kids and I will be here." I was channeling Filip, trying to sound cool, collected, and confident while every muscle in my body trembled in fear, even though I had previously confirmed with police that I wasn't breaking the law. The power he held over me seems silly now, but it felt very real at the time.

A couple of hours went by and no police.

Filip texted again. "I'm coming over to pick up the kids!"

"You're not welcome here, Filip. If you come, you will be arrested for trespassing on my mom's property. You can see the kids when you clean up the house."

"You idiot. You're going to be sorry for this, Annie!"

But Filip's grip on me was weakening. I wasn't going to let this brute threaten me with my own children. Not again, not ever!

I was stunned though—was this really happening? The thought that up until a few months ago, Filip and I had shared the same bed, only to have him turn on me so viciously, as if I were his worst enemy, tormented me. As the father of my children, I prayed for him and wished him well, but it seemed as if he'd rather see me dead. The stress of it all was taking its toll on me. At five foot eight inches, I was losing weight rapidly, dropping from 125 pounds down to a mere 100 pounds and frequently breaking out in hives. I needed a good lawyer (and a good doctor, too, but I didn't realize that at the time).

✦

After I pulled the kids from daycare, I still had to work and take care of Amaya and Ace, who were now at my mom's home with me full time. Daycare was no longer an option, as Filip had access and could take them from me again in retaliation. I had to figure out the babysitting options quickly.

That's where Anela stepped in, a childhood best friend from Bosnia, who at the time had lived in Toronto, Canada. Anela and I grew up together. We had the same first name, our moms had the same first names, and Anela even shared a birthday with my mom. Anela was one of those people you can't help but love, wholeheartedly. She had two older half-brothers, but she always longed for a sister. Ami and I were like sisters she never had. For as long as I can remember, she had been part of our life.

She was at our house with her nanny when Grandpa Namik passed away. With the house crowded for the wake, Ami, Anela, and I snuck away to my room to read The Princess and the Pea. Mom gave us each a piece of cake and a glass of Pepsi.

Anela was also with us when the three of us smoked our first cigarettes. She was seven, Ami six, and I was eight. We stole cigarettes from Mom's pack and hid on the balcony, giggling like little smugglers. At the count of three, we inhaled our first puffs of cigarette smoke, coughed, got dizzy, then laughed before flicking our cigarettes off the balcony into our neighbor's yard, afraid of getting caught.

Anela was with us when we ditched school to become junior entrepreneurs, selling popcorn from the window of Dad's camper, which was parked in front of our house. She participated in other business ventures as well. One time, we collected large rocks from the river and painted faces on them. It was Anela's idea to cut hair off our Barbies and glue it on the rocks. We sold those from the camper window, too. Until the war separated us, Ami, Anela, and I were inseparable partners in mischief and giggles.

When war in Bosnia broke out in early nineties, Anela and her mom were among the first families to flee the country. We had only a day's notice before they left, and all three of us cried the whole time. When it came time to say goodbye to my childhood best friend, I had nothing to give her to remember me by, so I tied my long hair into a ponytail with a rubber band, braided it, and chopped it off as my parting gift. The following morning, Anela and her mom boarded a Red Cross jeep.

It was a cold and gloomy morning when Anela and I said our final goodbyes—not knowing if or when we'd ever see each other again. She climbed over seats to get to the far back, placing her left hand on the back window from the inside. Her face and her long, shiny curls of dark hair were wet from tears streaming down her cheeks. Standing outside, I placed my right hand over hers. For one last time, I mouthed the words "I love you" as I looked into her beautiful brown eyes. Then the vehicle drove away into the unknown, taking my best friend with it.

After our family left Bosnia, too, we lost all trace of each other. Once we settled in the U.S., I tried to reconnect with as many old friends from back home as I could find. Each time I found someone new, I would ask them if they knew anything about Anela. For years, there was no trace, and I had just about lost all hope of ever finding her when I finally caught a lucky break ten years later. I was pregnant with Amaya when someone from Banja Luka I hardly knew mentioned Anela might be living in Toronto. Within minutes, I was dialing a Canadian directory, and as luck would have it, her mom's number was listed.

Our first contact after so many years had us both in tears and screaming with joy for twenty minutes before either of us could get a word in! It turned out she was also pregnant, and her son was due within months of Amaya. From that day on, our friendship resumed as if we had never been apart.

+

Anela was the kind of friend who would hop on a plane at a moment's notice, which is what she did when she learned of my troubles. She offered to babysit indefinitely. This was a great consolation since Adem and Kendra had taken Filip's side, and it was good to have someone I loved and trusted in my corner.

The moment I brought her home from the airport, before she even got situated in her room, she went into her suitcase searching for something. I wasn't expecting a gift. Her presence alone was a gift. When she found what she was looking for, she said, "You're going to like this." She showed me a Ziploc bag with a braid of hair in it. "Remember?"

"Is that what I think it is? Wow! Just wow?"

"Yep. You gave it to me before I left."

"Jesus, I can't believe you still have that?"

"Of course, I saved it. You were my best friend. I've thought about you every day since we last saw each other."

We reminisced well into the night about our childhood, the troubles we got into, our first crushes and kisses, old friends and teachers. Renewing our friendship recharged my batteries. Seeing her eyes glow with joy as we travelled down memory lane was all the medicine I needed.

She even got me to eat again, something I had forgotten how to do since the chaos started. On her second day in Georgia, she marched into my room with a small plate of food, set it down in front of me, and said, "If you don't eat this right now, I will spoon-feed it to you! Look at you, skin and bones! Eat before you disappear!"

We both laughed and I ate a little, for her sake, before rushing off to a work-related conference call. As I sat in the other room, I heard the doorbell ring. Anela went to get it. Moments later, she walked into my room to say someone was looking for me at the door. Puzzled, and not expecting anyone, I walked to the front door, phone in hand, where a tall, strange man dressed in a brown uniform was waiting for me.

"Annie?" he asked.

"Yes?" I replied.

"You are hereby served with these documents," he announced officiously, handing me a yellow envelope.

Even though I had suspected that Filip would file for divorce before I did, that reality hit me hard—being a single mom to two kids, my family crumbling, the life I had worked so hard to build vanishing into a black hole. Even then, a tiny, tiny part of me had been hoping for a last-minute miracle—that Filip would come to his senses and choose his family over drinking. Tears rolled down my cheeks as I signed the receipt, took the envelope, and shut the door on the outside world.

I'm not one to put things off. I opened the envelope and scanned the documents. A new wave of fear shook my body. I turned to Anela. "He wants custody of the kids and some high amount of money per month in child support!"

"Can he do that?" Anela asked.

"Not if I can help it, he can't."

CHAPTER 15

MISERABILITY

Filip's filing for divorce and requesting custody of the children was a huge slap in the face, almost like a pre-emptive strike, something you'd do to an enemy, not the mother of your children. He also wanted half of all our assets, fixed and liquid, even though he had been unemployed during much of our short-lived marriage.

I guessed this was Filip's way of bullying me into going back to him. He must have figured that if there was even a sliver of a chance I could lose custody of the children, I would fall in line, and not only come back to him, but also let him do whatever he wanted. The crazy thing is, if he had wanted me back out of love, all he had to do was genuinely promise to quit the drinking and the bullying. If I believed he was sincere, I would have gone back in a second. But this didn't feel like love. It felt like a power play driven by ego and greed, the idea that somebody was taking something away from him.

Or maybe he just wanted to hurt me as bad as he could, and he knew this would do it.

Perhaps in the past, I would have given into fear and fallen for it, but that was the old me. The new me—armed with irrefutable facts—knew the kids just had to stay with me. In my opinion, Filip couldn't even keep a clean house, let alone feed them something other than store-bought mac and cheese with crackers!

When he went after the kids, I morphed into a liger, the offspring of a male lion and a female tiger! I was ready to roar! Filip was not going to take my kids from me.

With no time to waste, I retained a high-quality family attorney. My first assignment was to find a couple of friends who would write character reference letters on my behalf. Although I no longer had any close friends in Georgia who knew me well enough to provide sworn affidavits, I turned to strangers for help. The only people with firsthand knowledge of my interactions with the children were a handful of women from the daycare center. They were familiar with my situation and agreed to write letters on my behalf. In great detail, each described my relationship with my kids. A "doting, attentive, affectionate mother, who is very patient and tends to her children's needs," said one. An "involved parent who volunteers to help celebrate Fall Festival, Christmas parties and other activities," said another. Letter after letter affirmed that I was loving, gentle, and caring with not only my own children, but theirs as well.

In the alternative universe Filip was inventing, he and his army of bullies also submitted sworn affidavits to court. Before sharing those affidavits with me, Mr. Duke, my attorney, attempted to soften the blow. "Before you read these, know that they're just words, and this is not an accurate representation of who you are. Judges see this kind of stuff all the time, and they see right through it. Parties are bitter and go on the offensive. Keep in mind, however, you have some good people in your corner, people who don't even know you well, who said some wonderful things about you. These letters will only make Filip look bad. They look like they were written by a bunch of ghouls."

"Okay, Mr. Duke. Email me the letters, please."

"Ghouls" doesn't do them justice. People who I called friends, people who sat at my table and ate my food, people who slept on my couch when they couldn't make it home after an evening of heavy drinking, betrayed me beyond my wildest imagination. While Adem, Kendra, Tina, and Olga described Filip as a "loving, caring, stay-at-home dad," they painted me as a "possessive, controlling wife who was too crazy and too jealous to let Fil-

ip get a job." They also wrote "Annie once watched Ace and Amaya eat cigarette butts off the ground because she was too lazy to get up and take care of
her own children," and "she only cares about her career. She seldom hugs or
kisses her children."

My children ate cigarette butts? I seldom hug and kiss them? I only care
about my work? What? My kids are my world! My mind was spinning. How
could they say such things about me? I knew they were just words, as Mr.
Duke had said, but they were hurtful words as well as outright lies. I realized that day that I wasn't only losing a husband, but friends and family
too. I grieved those losses by crying myself to sleep for the next few months
to come.

Much later, Mom told friends and family how she felt helpless during
those times, watching me turn into skin and bones. My soul was so torn up, I
would gag at the thought of food. I wasn't trying to lose weight. I knew I had
to stay strong and healthy to see this through. I just couldn't eat. The kind
women from daycare expressed concern practically daily about my rapid
weight loss without realizing their words were causing me great sorrow.

+

I wasn't raised to fight dirty, so I didn't even try. I knew if I played that game,
Filip would win. I dreamed of him one night stomping through the mud in
a flannel shirt, knee-high rubber boots and overalls, splashing mud on my
off-white crepe blazer and crisply ironed slacks. I went shopping the next day
and bought that exact same outfit for myself. Splash your mud, Filip! That's
how I showed up at court hearings—well-dressed, prepared, and well put-
together, regardless of what Filip did or said. Sure, he brought his army of
bullies to some of our court hearings. I imagined none of what they said
about me in sworn testimony was true.

Sitting through one of those charades, I recalled a memory of Mom from
the war. A band of armed soldiers had banged on our door to kick us out
of our home. Mom stood in front of the colonel in his full military garb—
two bandoliers of ammunition draped across his chest, several hand grenades, and a handgun in his holster, and an automatic rifle hanging off

his shoulder. Mom chewed him out. "You think you're so tough, standing here in front of me and my children with your guns and your bullets? Don't you know that you can only kill me once? Have you no shame kicking an unarmed woman and her kids out into the street? What are you going to do if we don't leave? Are you going to kill us? Tell me, what are you going to do?" Mom was relentless, fed up with the constant fear of war.

She went at the Colonel for quite a while. Finally, he sighed and gave orders, then left with his unit without saying a word, never to bother us again. Countless number of times I imagined myself standing up to Filip much like Mom did to that colonel. During the divorce proceedings, I drew on her strength and example often, something Filip probably didn't expect.

I had another weapon in my arsenal, too, something much, much more powerful than any dirty trick—love! The love for my children made me want to turn the world upside down if it meant they would have a better life. Filip fought dirty. I suppose driven by spite and ego, but what he didn't know was that love beats spite every time. Love truly does conquer all! Mom taught me unconditional love that I now got to show to my children. She was a daily inspiration, a reminder and encouragement never to give up. With her as my role model, I developed the strength of will to be tenacious and unwavering, to persevere and fight until the end. Filip had no idea what a powerful force he faced.

✦

Given the character references, the video of the trashed house, my steady employment and good salary, and Filip's long history of unemployment and alleged alcohol abuse, Mr. Duke believed I had a solid chance to get custody of Amaya and Ace. Filip did not appear to have our kids' best interests at heart.

The temporary custody hearing was fast approaching, but Filip seemed busy partying with Adem and Kendra. His friends weren't shy showing off a table full of empty beer bottles on their social media pages. I gathered any evidence I could use.

Our case was assigned to Judge Bello, a woman who I imagined—and hoped—would be sympathetic to a single mother. When I saw her for the first time, however, I silently despaired. She sat behind the bench in her black robe stern, distant, and cold. She dispatched the cases before us in a manner that I found heartless, as if they were rolling past her on a conveyor belt. She seemed strict, dismissive, and impatient. She cut people off mid-sentence. It seemed like she was in a perpetually bad mood. I put my head in my hands. God, I don't want to be here! I thought to myself.

Our case was up. Filip sat with his lawyer. I sat on the other side of the courtroom next to Mr. Duke. Each lawyer had a few minutes to present their client's sides. They went first, presenting their smear campaign.

I subtly elbowed my attorney. "Don't worry!" he said. "They have nothing."

When our turn came, Mr. Duke, armed with actual evidence, laid out the numerous reasons Amaya and Ace should stay with their mother. This was the first time I saw him present a case in court. I was impressed and happy that I had hired him. The fate of my children was in good hands.

Before he even finished, Judge Bello interrupted. "I've heard enough! I'm granting temporary custody to the mother. Father shall have visitation with children on Wednesday evenings for two hours and every other weekend. Father shall vacate the family house within fifteen days, and mother shall be allowed to move back in with the children. The Father shall clean the house thoroughly!" She directed a meaningful look towards Filip. "Furniture shall stay in the home where the children will be. Anything else?"

An elephant-sized boulder fell from my chest. I took a full breath for the first time in months.

I looked over at Filip, whose expression had changed from that all-too-familiar smirk to something I didn't recognize. Shock. He seemed surprised that he had lost. Really? I thought. With the way you left the house?

Filip's attorney stood up. "Your Honor, there is one more matter. The big-screen television in the living room. The plaintiff received it as a birthday gift from the defendant during the marriage."

"And where are the children going to live, Esquire?" Judge Bello snapped.

"With the mother, Your Honor!"

"Then this court rules the TV, too, shall stay with the Mother!"

"What on the matter of the rental house the mother owns, Your Honor?"

Mr. Duke, my attorney, stood up to address the court. "Your Honor, my client is in agreement with the Plaintiff taking possession of that property. However, since it was purchased by my client, we ask that the plaintiff take over mortgage payments, upkeep, and utilities until such time as he is able to refinance the property into his name to protect my client's excellent credit score."

"Granted! Anything else?"

"We request the plaintiff undergo an alcohol evaluation. My client will cover all associated costs. We also ask that the mother be allowed to administer a breathalyzer test to the father when he is picking up and dropping off their children and to refuse visitation if the test shows a blood alcohol content above allowable legal limit to drive."

"Also granted," Judge Bello ruled.

Suddenly, I liked this woman.

Mr. Duke had been right. Filip's antics only served to his disadvantage. While our divorce ordeal wasn't anywhere near over, on that particular day, I felt the guardian angels watching out for me and my kids. Grandpa Namik—as our special Guardian Angel—was smiling proudly at me from the heavens.

For the first time in a long time, I felt protected and that I would get through this.

✦

If there was an instruction manual with a checklist of what not to do to your ex-partner while divorcing them, Filip would have checked off a lot of those boxes—and then maybe added a few of his own.

After the hearing, I assumed Filip would want to move into the rental house as soon as he could since the rental was vacant and Filip would have the time to move his belongings without being rushed. Instead, in another of his petty power plays, he waited until the final day set by Judge Bello to vacate the family house, forcing the kids and I to extend our stay with Mom. When he finally left two weeks later, I found our utilities shut off for nonpayment. To restore them, I had to pay the past two or three months' bills totaling around $500.

On account of all this, it very much felt like Filip had no desire to reconcile our differences even for the sake of the children and move forward in a healthy and respectful way. He seemed bitter and vengeful instead.

By now, I couldn't even trust Filip to do a good job cleaning the house. Before the children and I moved back in, I rewashed every dish in the kitchen, scrubbed every surface with bleach, cleaned the floors, ran all our clothes through the washer and dryer, painted the walls, and scheduled a carpet cleaning service. I picked out new beds for the three of us as well.

While I was getting our home move-in ready, Filip introduced our children to Jezika, a woman in her late twenties, and her young son Bob. Shortly after, Jezika and Bob moved in with Filip into the rental house, which was technically still my house, as Filip had not yet refinanced the loan under his name. According to Filip, Jezika was just a dear friend in need of a place to stay and was renting a room.

I heard a different story from Amaya and Ace, who peppered me with questions after they returned from visits with their father.

"Why is she sleeping in the same room with our daddy and always holding hands and kissing him on the lips, Mommy?"

"I guess you'll have to ask your daddy that, Sweetheart," was the best I could muster without breaking into tears.

⁜

Even though it pained me to see Filip move on so quickly, my priorities were Amaya and Ace, who were innocent and didn't deserve any of what was happening to them. We desperately needed a break and a change of scenery—including Mom, who had been by my side every step of the way.

⁜

I always imagined single moms struggled financially, yet oddly, after Filip and I had split up, I no longer lived paycheck to paycheck as we had since we moved to Georgia. Despite high attorney costs, I still had money left over in my account at the end of each month because I was no longer spending a large chunk of my paycheck on booze for Filip and his buddies. With extra cash and a temporary order in place, I was excited to treat my family to a weeklong vacation in Florida, thinking we could visit several places, including the Keys.

I pitched the idea to Mom. "We've never been here before. What do you think?" I asked her excitedly as I showed her pictures of the hotel room in Islamorada. "This place looks amazing. It's on the beach and affordable. Not to mention that it's next door to a place called Theater of the Sea where you can swim with dolphins. What if we take Amaya and Ace there? We could all use a break, and what an incredible experience for the kids!"

"You know I can't swim, Annie," Mom replied.

"Mom, you're not going to actually be swimming!" I explained. "I did some research, and the water is shallow. You walk in and dolphins swim up to you. Besides, they give you a life vest. Come on, say yes! This looks really cool and the kids would love it! What do you say?"

"Fine."

Over the next few days, we booked our trip.

Before leaving, Mom thought of everything. She packed the cooler with sandwiches and juice boxes for the road trip, and extra food, sand toys, and beach chairs for the hotel. With Amaya and Ace tightly strapped in their car seats, smiling ear to ear, we set off on a twelve-hour car ride to Islamorada, singing along to Justin Bieber's "Baby, baby, baby oh" blasting through our car speakers.

After the long drive to Florida, our first few days were spent getting some much needed rest and relaxation on the beach. Mom and I lounged on beach chairs soaking in warm Florida sun rays as we watched Amaya and Ace chase each other up and down the beach and make sandcastles. Seagulls circled around above us scouring for food as the gentle waves rolled off the shore.

Watching the seagulls brought back memories of much simpler times I'd had with Filip. Although I still longed for those times when we were a happy family planning a future together, I promised myself to focus on the here and now. I knew that moving forward was the best thing I could do for myself and my kids. I vowed to focus on one day at a time and to find something good in each day.

The following day we were going to swim with dolphins. From the time we woke up, Mom began suggesting alternatives. "Why don't you go with the kids? I'll just watch from the shore."

"Ha ha, no! You're coming in with us, too." I was determined to convince her to come along. The kids joined in.

"Grandma, pleeease!!" Amaya and Ace pleaded in unison.

"Grandma can't swim! Grandma is scared of water! What if a dolphin pulls me in the water, and I can't get back to shore?" Mom said.

"Mom, a dolphin cannot pull you into the deep if you don't hold on to the dolphin. I researched this place thoroughly. I promise you! You go in about chest-deep. They swim up to you, they give you kisses, and they splash you with water—that's it! There's no swimming and no pulling, okay?"

"Okay, okay, but I'm only doing this for you guys! And if they pull me into the water, you better come swimming after me!"

"We'll save you, Grandma!" Amaya and Ace couldn't contain their excitement.

Given Mom's lifelong fear of deep waters, this was a big step for her. I was proud of my mom. After breakfast and morning coffee, we strolled next door to the Theater of the Sea. After we completed our orientation and suited up in wetsuits, the trainer walked with us to the bay.

From the moment we entered the water, kids couldn't peel their eyes from Sherwin and Kona, two gentle dolphins who whistled and clicked while happily following every command instructed by the trainer. As we stood still, Kona and Sherwin swam up to us and gave us each a kiss on the cheek. The kids were elated with their first close encounter. Mom, too, was enjoying herself so much that she seemed to have completely forgotten about her fear of water. Everyone was content and joyful, beyond happy, nodding and smiling in appreciation. This was exactly what we all needed to recharge our batteries.

I had reached an inflection point, and I knew I had to move on with my life. I refused to beat myself up because I was raising two small kids by myself as a single mother. I was more than capable of providing them with the stability in life they deserved and needed.

Over the next several months, I began rebuilding my life. I discovered a Bosnian restaurant nearby and forged new connections in the Bosnian community. I even made new friends with the women from daycare, Mary-Anne and Bonnie, who both had kids the same age as mine.

Mary-Anne and her husband Josh had moved to Georgia from New York with their two kids around the same time we moved. Mary-Anne was from a large Italian family, and we bonded over a love of food and big family gatherings. She had helped me out with the character reference letters, and I knew I could trust her. Her utter dislike of Filip always made me laugh, even on days when I didn't feel much like laughing.

Bonnie was a few years older. She had a calm presence and always gave great advice. She patiently listened to all my troubles with a sympathetic ear. She and her husband Don had moved to Georgia from Indiana with their daughter and were living in the house across from Mary-Anne's.

They became our extended Georgia family. We often barbequed on the weekends at Mary-Anne's house or mine. The adults cooked out while kids played together on the swing set in the backyard. Simple things made me happy those days, and I wore that happiness on my sleeve. I wanted to show Filip I wasn't crying over spilled milk.

I think this bothered him and his new girlfriend because soon after, Jezika began calling my work phone and sending unsolicited emails and text messages. She was saying things like if Filip wanted her for his wife, she would make a better wife, mother, and lover than me. I never understood why she felt it necessary to say those things to me, but okay. Some of the voice mails seemed like downright threats, calling me crazy if I thought I can take Filip's kids away from him. "You are never going to have them!" followed by her shrill laughter. I suppose she was yet another resident of Filip's alternate reality.

This woman—who had never actually met me in person and only knew what Filip and his friends had told her of me—was acting as if I had somehow wronged her. I was the interloper in her territory. All while living with the man who was still married to me in a house that was still in my name, occasionally driving Filip's car, which I had purchased, and demanding my kids call her "Mommy."

Holy smokes! I often wondered what kind of woman would do that to another woman? Her anger seemed so outsized, so misplaced, so ridiculous that I could only conclude she was overcompensating for the guilt she felt.

Meanwhile, I considered it demeaning to argue over a man, so I asked her to stop harassing me, adding that she could keep my soon-to-be ex-husband, and I'd throw in my wedding dress and rings for good measure. Those days, the level of exasperation on my end was so high that I could only crack jokes—so I don't crack under pressure.

But I didn't stop there. Jezika's provocations lit a fire inside me. Thanks to the emails, I now had her last name, which looked Bosnian to me. I turned to my Bosnian community for help. If there's anything a Bosnian community loves, it's good gossip. As it turned out, Jezika too, was supposedly still married—to a Bosnian man, as I suspected. People who knew her had a mouthful to say, but nothing kind or flattering. Knowing this only made me feel more uneasy when she was around my children.

✦

I had another business trip coming up, this time, back to the Bay Area. It was a brief, but welcome escape from my chaotic life. Amaya and Ace stayed with Mom, who, by then, had moved in with me to help out with the kids.

Even though the company was covering my travel expenses, my friend Jasmina insisted I stay at her house, and when I arrived, we hugged each other so tight I couldn't breathe. Then she stepped back, looking troubled. "Jesus Christ Annie! How much do you weigh?"

Jasmina, who had always been a fuller-figured woman, must have felt she was hugging a malnourished child. I was now a skeletal ninety-five pounds.

"Yeah, I know. I lost a bunch of weight," I replied, hoping to stop it right there.

Her husband walked up and hugged me from behind. "Holy crap, Annie! I feel like I'm hugging myself!"

"Stop, please. You guys are going to make me cry!"

I could almost forget about the weight I had lost until I saw old faces.

With perfect timing, Jasmina's mom, whom I called Aunt Divna, rescued me when she called out from the living room. "My dear Annie, we've been expecting you. You must be tired from the trip, come in, come in! Would you like something to eat? The table is set and waiting for you," she said, gesturing toward a table full of food.

Her voice was soothing, inviting, and motherly, as it always was. Aunt Divna was not just Jasmina's mom. She was a caring, kind woman. When we were younger, after a night on the town, Jasmina invited all her friends over and refused to take no for an answer. Aunt Divna would welcome me and ten other friends into her home at 2:00 a.m. and serve up whatever was in the fridge, before joining the party herself. Despite the age difference, she was always one of us—a best friend, confidante, and a wise, trusted advisor.

Aunt Divna always set her table like a five-star restaurant, with a pure white linen tablecloth, fine porcelain plates, silverware, serving platters, and a three-tiered dessert stand. As I walked into their house that day, the smell of her homemade hamburgers and baked potatoes was enticing. Aunt Divna had even baked a cake for dessert, and for the first time in a long time, food actually appealed to me.

I don't know if my appetite had returned because I suddenly felt safe, surrounded by people who had always looked out for me and still loved me, or because I was far away from the drama and chaos. But all of a sudden, I was famished, like I hadn't eaten in months—which was fairly accurate.

We sat at the table, and I helped myself to two hamburgers and seconds on potatoes as well. For the first time in months, food tasted good, feeding my body and my soul. With a full belly and surrounded by good, good friends, I instantly felt my energy levels rise. Those few days in the Bay Area filled my soul with so much love.

✦

Although I wanted my kids to continue to see their father and have a good relationship, I could never just kick back and relax when they were with him. In fact, I often worried the whole time they were with him, waiting for their safe return from each visit.

After I returned from California, I bought a phone for Amaya so she could get hold of me in case of an emergency, or if they needed something while they were visiting Filip. I never had hard evidence, but I assumed Filip drank even when the kids were with him. Amaya had just turned six years old, and though that was young to have a phone, I couldn't shake the feeling that something terrible could happen each time my kids left for the weekend.

A mother's instinct is seldom wrong. Weeks after she started carrying a phone to her dad's house, she called. "Mommy, Mommy! Ace is hurt!" She yelled into the phone with Ace screaming in the background.

"Baby, baby, what happened?" I asked, alarmed.

"Daddy was carrying Ace and slipped and fell on top of him. Ace is screaming that his leg hurts." Her voice shook.

"What do you mean, fell on top of him? Can Ace move his leg?"

"He can't move his leg, Mommy. Daddy thinks it's broken. Ace is screaming so bad." Amaya was now sobbing in sympathy.

"Tell your dad not to move the leg and put some ice on it. He needs to take Ace to children's hospital right away. I'll meet you there in twenty minutes!"

Mom had been sitting next to me on the couch and overheard the conversation. She changed into jeans and a T-shirt, and ran downstairs to the garage with me as we rushed out of the house. I drove as fast as I could, my babies' screams echoing in my head.

When I finally got to hold Ace at the hospital, his right leg above the ankle was badly swollen and bruised. He was crying in pain. It's definitely broken, I thought as I cradled him and caressed his head. Swaying back and forth, I tried to comfort him while we waited for a doctor. Periodically, I directed a death stare toward Filip, wishing it was him rather than my sweet baby boy.

The x-rays confirmed both tibia and fibula fractures right above the ankle, which made me angry—how does a person fall on their child? Filip tried to explain. "We were outside playing. It was starting to rain a little. I was carrying Ace in my arms. Walking uphill. I slipped on a patch of wet grass, lost my balance, and fell while holding him."

"You fell! On top of my boy? You just fell? Were you drunk?" I yelled at him in frustration. "Why didn't you try to save him? Why did you fall on top of him?"

"I just fell." Filip shrugged.

I administered a breathalyzer test, which Filip passed. A social worker was called in to investigate. At the end of the ordeal, Ace was allowed to go home with Filip after receiving a full leg cast and a prescription for pain meds.

Following that incident, I hired a private investigator to tail Filip whenever the kids went to visit him.

Several weeks later, when Filip had the kids again, the private investigator called to inform me of another incident. This time, Mateo set his arm on fire. By the PI's account, he was standing too close to the barbeque while starting the fire and his arm caught on fire, landing him in the emergency room. Amaya and Ace were within feet of him witnessing the whole thing.

Were these random accidents—all within a short period of time around my children—or were they recklessness? When I tried confronting Filip about these issues, he would generally default to some worn-out phrase like, "You're crazy! I love my kids!" I never doubted he loved our kids. I doubted if he was fit to raise them. I was growing increasingly unnerved. Coupled with their family history of drinking, it was enough to keep me on edge whenever my kids were with Filip. Once again, I couldn't eat or sleep, and I worried until the moment I had my kids safely in my arms again.

As part of our divorce, the court appointed guardian ad litem—a neutral third-party attorney—to represent the best interests of our children. Filip and I would split the guardian's fees, introducing yet another set of divorce-related expenses.

The guardian would take months to complete her investigation, and I was frustrated we had to go through it. I couldn't fathom the absurdity of our situation. How could anyone think that our kids would be better off with Filip? Yet, I had no recourse but to go along with it. After all, the court didn't know us, the guardian didn't know us—divorcing parties fight, fights get dirty, tempers flare, someone has to sift through all that mud and make a decision.

I had a good income and could afford my attorney, but Filip ended up pawning the car title for his share. The car I purchased was now being used to try to take my children from me. Filip had the option of calling a truce at any time. Maybe he was hoping I would get tired of it all and concede, that I'd give up on my children. He should have known that wasn't going to happen. He greatly underestimated the power of a mother's love. All I knew was the money we were spending on court fees and attorneys was already in the tens of thousands of dollars and would have been better invested in our children's college fund.

I couldn't see Filip's side of the story. I didn't even want to try, really. In my mind, he had forfeited his rights to his side of the story when he chose drinking over his kids, and every bullying action he had taken thereafter. All I saw in Filip was this vindictive stranger, wildly lashing out to hurt me any way he could. My only recourse was to keep on fighting for my children. I simply could not imagine the kind of life they would have if, God forbid, Filip and Jezika were somehow in charge of raising them.

The thought of how dysfunctional my kids could end up, and how many years of therapy they would need to recover from living with Filip, kept me going, even on days when I prayed to God to put me out of misery. Music gave me some solace, as well as the strength and energy to keep going. Linkin Park's "Given Up" became my anthem. I played it on repeat for months in the car on my way to and from work.

✦

Amaya and Ace often came back from their visits to Filip poisoned, brainwashed, and stressed out from Filip's and Jezika's merciless and inappropriate diatribes they shared with me: "Your mom is an idiot! She's trying to take you away from your daddy because she hates him! Oh, how I wish I could have five minutes alone in the room with her! I would show her!" followed by cackling.

Back then, Amaya was six and Ace four. They didn't deserve this kind of abuse from her, and abuse is what it was. And Filip, their father, who said he loved them—what did he do to stop it? I felt like he was too busy drinking and raging to do anything.

I knew that confronting her directly would only spell trouble for me, so I resorted to showing Filip the middle finger in desperation—in front of the kids—during drop-off once. That was not my finest moment and definitely not an example I wanted my children growing up with. They needed balance and stability, and I owed it to them to rise above it all and be a better person. That became my motivation.

✦

As part of the investigation, the guardian ad litem scheduled two separate hour-long meetings, one with Filip and another with me, to get basic information. She was an older white woman who looked to me like she was part of some elite country club set. I don't know if she was, but I had my doubts about her. I wondered if these attorneys really even care about investigating facts, or if they strike deals on the side at social events while sipping a glass of wine? Regardless, the fate of my children rested in this woman's hands.

When I met her for the first time, she looked to me like she would rather be getting a root canal than talking to me, as if we were just another case file. I wanted this investigation to move faster, but I had the impression she was not very interested in my desires.

Once she completed the initial interviews, it took her a good while to schedule the two separate house visits—one with Filip and the kids, another with me and the kids.

I requested she make at least one surprise visit to Filip to look for evidence of drinking while the kids are with him. I knew of the drinking from the kids, but no one would believe two young children without thinking they were coached by me. The PI was unable to take pictures inside Filip's home due to privacy laws. Besides, Filip was clever—I imagined him drinking his cranberry vodkas in plastic cups, telling Amaya and Ace not to touch his "juice."

The guardian's visit with me was fairly straightforward. She took a tour of our house, inspected where everyone sleeps, and spent the remaining time on our living room couch in long awkward silent pauses. I'd never welcomed anyone into my home like this; it was a new experience for me. Some homey feeling inside me was telling me to be a good hostess and offer her a soda or a glass of water, but she declined. She wasn't exactly our house guest or a friend. She was a complete stranger. Maybe she's not allowed, I wondered, but at least I offered.

She observed my interactions with Amaya and Ace, all the while fidgeting with the keys to her fancy car parked in my driveway. I was sitting on the floor, playing and laughing with my kids, trying to pretend like she wasn't even there. What else was I to do? She met my mom, assessed our living arrangements, and left.

It seemed like an eternity went by before she met with Filip and the kids and wrote up her recommendation. More than a year had gone by since Filip and I had separated. I just wanted our divorce finalized, and to put the whole thing behind us so I could move on with my life. The whole process was unnecessarily drawn out and frustrating.

In the end, though, my patience paid off when Mr. Duke finally called to share the happy news—guardian-ad-litem was planning to recommend the kids stay with me! That was a relief, but until I saw it documented, filed through the court, stamped, sealed and delivered, I remained skeptical.

Just days before my thirty-second birthday, Filip and I had our final divorce hearing to settle custody and split our joint assets. I was awarded primary custody of the kids, with Filip's visitation remaining the same—two hours on Wednesday evenings and every other weekend. The primary residence went to me, while Filip kept the house he was living in, with the court reaffirming the order for Filip to refinance the loan in his name. A hefty savings account—our children's future college education—was split equally.

Financially, Filip left our marriage in a more favorable state than he entered it, but that didn't matter to me. I got what mattered most, custody of our children. That meant I could give my kids the kind of life I always dreamed of—a stable home and a family in which their needs would always come first. Even before my own! Driving home from the courtroom that day, tears of joy—and relief—rolled down my face faster than I could wipe them away. My whole body trembled with emotion. The imminent danger had passed.

✦

That birthday, I had a newfound and hard-won freedom and plenty of reasons to celebrate. On a mission to treat and pamper myself again, I rented a thirty-foot-long Humvee limo for the evening.

The timing was everything. Filip had asked to take the kids on a Thursday night instead of the usual Wednesday, and rather than bicker about switching days on my birthday, I let him have the kids as requested. He was going to pick them up from daycare and bring them to my house at 6:00 p.m. Meanwhile, Mom, Ami, Hamza, Amra, Haris, and I got dressed to the nines and waited. Everyone was wearing fancy black and white except me—I wore a glittery bright pink summer dress.

The black limo arrived about ten minutes early. It was so large the driver couldn't even park it in the driveway. While waiting outside for Filip to bring the kids home, we inspected the limousine, feeling like rock stars heading to a red-carpet event. Inside, strobe lights lit up in stars across the ceiling while purple lights glowed beneath the luxurious leather seats. Everyone was excited.

Filip pulled into the driveway to drop off the kids, his expression changing from confusion to dismay. Ace and Amaya jumped out of the car, smiling in wonder. Amaya asked, "Mommy, what is this? Can we go in the big car?"

"We're celebrating Mommy's birthday!" I replied. "And yes, baby! We all go in the big car!"

Ace jumped in. "Mommy, you look so pretty! Can I come too?"

"Aww, thank you baby! Of course, you can. We're all going to have so much fun! Hop in. I have some fancy clothes for you. You're going to look so handsome."

Elated, they both hopped into the car as Filip faded out of view. I hoped he knew what he was missing.

That evening was a blast. We drove around downtown Atlanta for a couple of hours, playing music, dancing in the limo, and singing at the top of our voices. We smiled and giggled and laughed and hugged. We stopped to take pictures and get ice cream. I couldn't have asked for a better way to celebrate my first birthday free from a marriage that had been toxic and demeaning.

When we returned that night, however, and the kids fell into bed, exhausted, the reality of my life hit me. Instead of raising a family with the man I thought I'd spend the rest of my life with, I would be the single mother of a family of divorce. I knew it had to be that way, after the betrayals and abuse, after my husband—my ex-husband—the father of my children had chosen drinking over his family. But that didn't make it any easier.

✦

One of the greatest sorrows of my life is that Filip did not step up to make Ace and Amaya a priority in his life.

I suppose it was easier for him to live in the land of victimhood, where everything bad that happens is someone else's fault. Before he met me, he blamed his parents for his upbringing and for dropping out of high school. After he and I got together, that someone else became me. Instead of taking steps to change the state of his life, he often chose self-pity and found escape in alcohol. Over the years, I felt like the chip on his shoulder only got bigger, until he eventually came to resent me.

Filip often said he didn't have any positive role models growing up, but after a while, it was all the same, sad, broken-record of an excuse. The world is full of positive role models. If we can't find them in our own lives, we can find them in books or movies or the inspiration of real-life heroes like Mother Theresa, Princess Diana, Mahatma Gandhi. Nelson Mandela is one of my heroes. A political prisoner for twenty-seven years, if anyone would have been forgiven for feeling sorry for himself, it would have been Nelson Mandela. And though I'm sure he had plenty bad days, like we all do, he chose a different path and became one of humanity's great leaders whose name will go down in history.

I'm not saying Filip should have been Nelson Mandela or some sort of saint. I'm saying he should have been a better Filip, a better husband to me and dad to his children.

I know my kids only remember the fighting, but there was a time in their lives when their mom and dad were madly in love and kind to one another. I wanted my kids to know that time too. I wanted them to know that even though their mom and dad couldn't make it work—true love does exist and that's what I want for them when they grow up. To look for a mutually loving relationship based on kindness, respect, and passion—for what is life without great passion?

Back then, I made a conscious choice to raise my children to be good people so they can find other good people. I taught them to be honest and fair, to act from a good place in their heart, with no harm or malicious intent. When facing a difficulty in a friendship or relationship, I ask them to think through their actions and anticipate how they might impact others. I ask them to look at the big picture and not act on their first impulse, out of anger, jealousy, greed, or ego-driven emotion. I tell them to sleep on it. When stuck between a rock and the proverbial hard place, I ask them to choose the lesser of two evils. I tell them to own their actions, including their mistakes.

We all make mistakes. They're inevitable. What's important is that we learn from them. How we fix our mistakes defines us. Being honest and offering a simple apology goes a long way. Everyone struggles. How we choose to weather our storms is what defines our character. It's how we measure our own greatness. Optimism is critical. I always look for the good in any situation, in any person.

Relationships should be built on a solid foundation of love, trust, and mutual respect. When we love someone, we want to see them happy. We support their life goals; we don't tear them down. We're their best friend and biggest advocate, their pillar of strength, someone to lean on when we feel at odds with the world.

And they do the same. We feel equal. Our individual strengths and weaknesses complement each other's. We feel like we can conquer the world with this person by our side. If the two of us were hungry and poor and living on the street, it would all be good as long as we had each other. That's what true love means for me today.

But it takes time to get to know someone on that level. All I ask of my children is to learn from my mistakes and truly get to know their partners before starting a family. There's an old Bosnian saying: "You never truly know someone until you've eaten a bag of salt with them." It takes years to consume a large bag of salt. That's the point. I was in my early twenties when I met Filip. I was young, foolish, naïve, and in love. I thought I had gotten to know him well enough in a few months to spend the rest of my life with him. I was mistaken, and now we are divorced and I'm raising two kids on my own.

Despite the hardships I've faced in life and in love, I choose to believe that there is more good than bad in the world, that love is all around us. I want that kind of love for my children. I want that kind of love for myself. We all deserve that kind of love.

CHAPTER 16

RUNNING FROM REALITY

When our bodies experience a traumatic injury, we don't always feel the pain immediately. A rush of adrenaline delays the onset of great pain, so we can do what we need to do to get to a safe place. It's only later on, after the adrenaline wears off, that the pain becomes unbearable.

Though my pain was emotional, that's how I felt after the divorce—as if I had been running a marathon. The adrenaline took me across the finish line, but once the race was over, I shut down and went into a kind of emotional shock.

The divorce left me bitter, resentful, and angry, though I was not really aware of how I came off to everyone at the time. What I thought was the finish line turned out to be the starting line of my next journey, the journey to healing, to becoming the person I am today. I was experiencing a kind of PTSD. Rather than face my reality and let myself grieve the loss of my marriage and the life I had imagined for our family, I opted to escape into the fantasy of a simpler time before Filip, when I was young and everything was fun and drama-free.

✦

To forget where I was, I time-traveled into the past, daydreaming about old loves, including Louie, the sailor I had met in Hawaii before I had met Filip. Although we hadn't seen each other after that week, I had thought about him often since then, remembering how he made me feel like a movie star when I was with him. He had opened my eyes to a version of myself I had forgotten, one in which I was fresh and fun and beautiful.

I needed a reminder of that person just then, so I looked him up on social media. Nine years had passed, and Louis Goodman was now a Petty Officer, First Class in the United States Navy. His profile picture revealed he was just as handsome as I remembered him.

I sent him a message. "Um, no freaking way I find you on here! Where are you now?"

Not more than twenty minutes later, a notification popped up on my phone with his response. In his message, he reminisced about the beautiful woman who smelled like J'Adore and wrote how every time he smelled that fragrance, it made him think of me, the Outrigger Reef, techno music, and a very fast ride to Diamond Head. He also said he tried to find me in San Francisco a few years ago.

My heart skipped a beat. He remembered me down to the perfume I had worn. And he had looked for me in the Bay Area!

I waited until the next day to respond.

It's crazy you remember everything! Should we plan a reunion? Hahaha. All teasing aside, I have to admit I never expected a response so sweet from a handsome sailor man who sailed off into the sunset almost ten years ago. I'm very flattered if the scent of me left such a lasting impression. I, too, remember the convertible and you speeding so fast, the car flew over the intersection. I also remember getting a story ready for the cops in my head, in case I had to bail you out of jail. That was a wild and fun night. You still look great, by the way. And where in the world are you these days? Do you have any kids? How's your life been?

He wrote back, explaining he was with his kids just then and would write more when he returned to Seattle the following week.

A week later, I received a short note with just his new email address and nothing else. Not knowing what to make of that, I sent him another message, containing only a subject line that read, "Here's my email address too."

Over the course of the next few weeks, I learned that Louie was deployed again, and he was in a relationship with someone who was also in the Navy and moving to the East Coast. They were trying out the whole long-distance thing. He didn't seem too happy about it.

I couldn't tell from his emails if he just needed a pen pal or an ego boost while deployed at sea for the next many months. I thought I needed a hero to save me, and he seemed like just the ticket. I imagined him knocking on my front door, as he had in Hawaii, and making me feel once more like the girl from the Hollywood movies. In my dreams, he always wore his Navy whites, flashing that devilish smile while he swept me off my feet again. He was Richard Gere in An Officer and a Gentleman, I was Debra Winger, and he carried me out of Georgia, far from Filip and Jezika.

Louie never showed up, of course. He had his life to live.

His next chapter took him on a mission to Italy. He was aiming for Chief Petty Officer, and I had no doubt he would get it. I promised to keep writing until the end of his deployment.

Writing to Louie was therapeutic. While I kept up my it's-all-good façade to get through the days, I was still hurting inside. Over the course of the nine months Louie was deployed, I shared my pain with him. He was my trusted confidante and a wise, old soul who gave me honest feedback without sugar-coating. He helped me rediscover myself, that carefree fun girl who had been stuffed in Filip's old shoebox for so many years, bursting to come back to life. Louie awoke the passion in me that had been long dead. He brought smiles back into my life. While I knew I still had a long road ahead of me and wasn't yet the best version of myself, he made me feel that I could still get there.

While he was stationed in Italy, Louie fell in love, proposed, married, and brought his wife to the United States. Soon after, he made Chief.

Understandably, our correspondence tailed off and then stopped altogether, until one day—out of nowhere—he sent me a note. By this time the kids and I had moved to Phoenix, Arizona.

In that message, he shared he had been meaning to write for a while to thank me for showing him there are still great women left in this world. He said I showed him I liked him for who he was, unique and different, and if it weren't for me, he never would have met Alexandra. He went on to say she was a lot like me. She accepts him for who he is and does not judge him. He appreciated my willingness to do anything for him and for never being afraid. In closing, he thanked me sincerely and said his wife also thanked me.

I ran to the bathroom and cried. Louie was a great guy and deserved all the happiness this world had to offer. Though in my fantasies, it was always me he had found it with. It took me a few minutes to compose my thoughts and respond.

+

You're welcome, Louie. I wanted to write to you as well and congratulate you for going after your dreams and making them happen, regardless of all the obstacles in your way. You have no idea how proud I am of you. And believe it or not, I learned a lot from you as well. Wishing you and your wife the best this world has to offer. And if you guys are ever in Phoenix, I would love to meet her.

+

Our move to Phoenix came at an opportune time. While the divorce was still underway, the small, privately-owned company I worked for had been bought out by a larger corporation. Shortly after my divorce was finalized, I received notice from my new employer that my position was moving to Phoenix, Arizona. I faced an important decision. I could try to stay in Georgia as a single mom, wait for my role to be terminated, then hunt for a new job. Or I could move to Arizona and keep my good-paying job.

Arizona didn't sound so bad. Georgia had always been Filip's home, and part of me felt that as long as I lived there, I was still under his influence. Moving to a new state would take us out of a still toxic environment, especially for the kids, and give us a fresh start.

The only problem was, I had to tell Filip.

Yes, I had custody of the children, but by the terms of the custody agreement, I was required to give Filip a thirty-day notice if we were moving out of state. I sent him a certified letter with all the details, and he would have received it the weekend he married Jezika. Three weeks went by without a response. If he didn't respond within thirty days, Filip waived his legal rights to keep the children in Georgia, and we would be cleared to move. I counted down the final days, but before we reached the magic thirtieth day, Filip's attorney served me the papers suing for custody—again.

To bolster my case for maintaining custody, I researched residential areas in Phoenix, looking into watchdog groups, pulling up crime rate statistics and school ratings, and comparing them to ones we had in Georgia. And there was no comparison. The area close to the new office had better schools and safer neighborhood. As an added bonus, there was a possibility of a promotion for me at work.

Leaving Amaya and Ace behind was not an option. I couldn't imagine my kids growing up with constant fighting and arguing—on top of the alcohol abuse.

The first step was mediation. On mediation day, Filip and I would try to settle our children's future out of court—a standard procedure before trial. I took a day off work to get ready and spent a whole hour doing and redoing my hair and makeup. I chose a red business suit with a black top, hoping to strike a balance between conservative and confident.

My attorney, the tested and dependable Mr. Duke, accompanied me to the hearing. We were the last to arrive. Filip and a legion of attorneys sat around the table. One represented him, another was the guardian ad litem representing our children, and the third was the mediator, a neutral third party. Sitting at the head of the table was none other than Jezika, like she was the most important person in this room. It seemed a calculated move on Filip's part to make me lose my cool.

Before Mr. Duke sat down, leaving the chair next to Jezika for me to sit in, he reached across the table and introduced himself to her. Jezika politely shook his hand and smiled, looking past me. For a split second she seemed defused, docile, civil. Normal even.

Normal enough for me to be inspired to do the same. I smiled, reached out my hand, and pleasantly said, "Hi, I don't think we've been properly introduced. I'm Annie. Pleased to meet you."

Instantly, I felt the mood shift in the room. Everything got silent for a second, even the rustling of papers. All eyes diverted to us. For a brief moment, time stood still, only to be interrupted by a wave of unusually cold air kicking in from the a/c vent. In the same breath, Jezika's expression had changed from smiling to bewildered. She let out an angry bison-like huff as she halfway stood up from her chair, all the while staring me down for a good fifteen to twenty seconds. I probably wondered the same thing everyone else was in the moment. What is she doing? If she punches me in the face, I think I'm just going to let her! Without ever saying a word, Jezika then stormed out of the room, slamming the door behind her.

"That little shit!" one of the attorneys said. "She didn't even say goodbye."

I sat down as if nothing happened. She single-handedly brought down any chance Filip had at gaining custody. For a moment, I felt bad for Filip, but only for a moment. Deep down, I could only be grateful to Jezika for showing her true colors. Anything I would have said against her would have painted me as the resentful, angry, jealous ex-wife who was trying to take Filip's kids away. I didn't have to say a word.

Then it was Filip's turn. He painted a picture of how he and his wonderful new wife Jez were the only ones who could offer a loving home to our children—the home still mortgaged under my name. No one was buying it. Then came a round of pull-your-hair-out, bang-your-head-against-the-brick-wall, mind-numbingly unreasonable requests by Filip, all with the intention of preventing the move to Arizona. The more he talked, the less my attorney and I had to do. He was making our case for us. The guardian ad litem came out and said that if Filip pursued a court hearing, she would recommend that I take Amaya and Ace to Arizona.

With the cards stacked against him, Filip folded, agreeing to spring, summer, fall, and winter-break visitation. Once the attorneys filed the revised custody order, we were free to move. I had hoped that once the kids moved to Arizona, Filip would move too and leave his enablers behind.

Jezika had taken the car (the same blue Durango I had bought for Filip while we were married). As Mr. Duke and I left the building, Filip was standing outside in December in a short-sleeved button-up shirt, shivering. I almost felt sorry for him.

Jezika was a real piece of work. Just before we left Georgia, she staged an all-out drunken cry fest: "Why can't we just be a normal family? I am your smom (short for step-mom)," inappropriately lamenting to the kids, as if only they could fill whatever void she felt in her life. Filip explained her behavior to the kids by saying, "Oh, come on, you guys. She's just insecure."

I would have felt sorry for her if she hadn't been trying to steal my children. Her disregard for their boundaries was reckless and dangerous. I feared for Ace and Amaya's mental and physical health whenever they went to Filip's. I knew that we'd all be better off in faraway Arizona.

✦

While our revised custody order was being drafted, I looked for a new place for us to live in Arizona with an extra bedroom for Mom. Within days, a dreamhouse popped up in my mailbox from the realtor: a spacious four-bedroom, three-bathroom house about a block from my new office. With separate living and family rooms, a large kitchen with a center island, an in-ground pool and enough backyard space for a big swing set and a trampoline, this house had everything I was looking for. There was plenty of room for family gatherings, birthday parties, and holiday celebrations.

We did a video walk-through with the realtor, and I made an offer on the house before I ever set foot in it. On Valentine's Day 2012, I signed the papers. Ace, Amaya, and I left Georgia the next day.

After a two-and-a-half-day car ride from Atlanta to Phoenix, my children and I walked through the front door of our new home. In person, our new place seemed even better and bigger! Although it would only be me and the kids for a while, the new house had enough room to accommodate everyone—Mom, Ami, Hamza, and their kids.

I instantly fell in love with the shiny granite countertops in the kitchen, where I envisioned many fun family gatherings. Thinking about food made me hungry, so we drove to a nearby burger place and picked up a couple of cheeseburgers with fries, then came home to eat. With furniture and boxes in disarray in every room, we sat on the floor of my upstairs bedroom for our first official meal in the new house. Amaya and Ace beamed with happiness.

I had brought little furniture from Georgia, wanting as few reminders of the painful past as possible. In fact, before we left, I had burned the sofa and my wedding dress in the backyard, feeling relieved to have left it all behind. A new house meant new furniture of my own choosing, new memories, and a fresh new start! I had brought some of Ami's furniture to use until they made their move.

After I unpacked for a while, dancing around the new house to Dean Martin's "Volare," we grew hungry again. I opened the box marked pots and pans and made French toast. Meanwhile, Amaya and Ace were happily running around the house, picking out their rooms. I dug up Amaya's and Ace's fold-up chairs from the garage, flipped a box upside down to use as a table, and set us up on the back porch. My heart was full watching the kids dip their French toast into sour cream, which left white mustaches on their smiling faces.

Later that afternoon, we took a walk to explore our new neighborhood and the park nearby. Seeing other kids playing outside, riding their bikes and running around with no supervision, brought back sweet memories of my own childhood in Bosnia before the war. It made me realize just how blessed we were to have found a safe neighborhood where the kids could do the same. Amaya and Ace made new friends immediately, and I knew, without a doubt, they would love growing up there.

I had two weeks of vacation from work to move in and get settled.

When we had first come to the States as refugees, my dad often said, "Get familiar with your new surroundings, so you can learn to love them better." I took care of the basics first—signing the kids up for school and daycare, locating the grocery stores, and finding doctors and a dentist. Everything we needed was fairly close to home.

Next came the furniture. I found a beautiful bar-height, dark cherry dinner table with a leaf insert. With eight chairs, it was the perfect size for family dinners when Mom, Ami, Hamza, and their kids moved out to Arizona. It came unassembled, though, so I needed Ace's and Amaya's help to push the table out of the car trunk while I pulled and guided the 250-pound hunk of solid wood table-top onto a duvet-comforter on the floor. Then we slid it slowly from garage into the kitchen. A couple of days and many blisters later, we had assembled the table and all eight chairs. That night, the Three Musketeers ate our very first dinner at our new dining room table.

The living room was spacious, with a slanted cathedral ceiling and a gorgeous dark-brown chandelier. The walls were a light sand color with matching tiles. I found a comfortable dark-brown leather sectional to match, with a chaise on one end and recliner on other. The good-sized room called for an entertainment center large enough to fit a big flat-screen TV, and I found just the perfect dark cherrywood unit with bookshelves on each side. Matching glass coffee tables and red-and-gold accents in the curtains, lamps, throw pillows and candles, made our living room look immaculate, warm, and inviting.

When we finished decorating, Ace and Amaya ran around the house yelling, "Mommy, Mommy, we live in a mansion!"

For Ace's bedroom, we picked an industrial-looking bed frame with a matching night table and dresser, along with sports-themed bedding and night-lamp. Amaya picked a white bed frame and matching white furniture with Minnie Mouse bedding. For both rooms, we found carved wooden letters at a craft store to spell out the kids' names on the walls.

✦

My American Dream was coming together, sans the Prince Charming or white picket fence. Getting settled in was healing and therapeutic. I felt a sense of empowerment rebuilding my life completely on my own. After that, no task could be too daunting.

I had spent much of that year in the solitude of my own thoughts, reflecting on my life and accepting all that had happened. Moving to Phoenix and adapting to the new life meant spending quality time with Ace and Amaya and doing all the things we enjoyed doing. We couldn't get enough of our new home, and even the most mundane activities gave us pleasure. We especially enjoyed baking together, sending the aroma of freshly baked cakes, muffins, and cookies wafting through the house.

Working to be happy by putting myself and my kids first brought about other positive changes in my life as well. I prided myself on having held my head high throughout the divorce and two custody battles. Even Filip seemed to acknowledge that when, one day out of the blue, he reached out to apologize. He called me the best mom he could have wished for our kids.

When I heard that, I thought to myself, Who is this guy? By that time, however, he had burned so many bridges with me that I wasn't ready to forgive him completely. The apology did provide validation and helped me see a more human side to Filip.

I wanted to remain on civil terms with him for the sake of the children. I didn't want to raise them with hate or resentment. The divorce had taught me that holding on to hate, grudges, bitterness, and resentment only hurt me. My conversations with Louie helped me come to a place where I could let bygones be bygones, which was very cleansing for the soul.

In this way, the year 2012 saw a much healthier version of me. I redis-covered my fun spirit while remaining a responsible mom who put her chil-dren's needs above all else. And after a concerned and serious Amaya sat me down to talk about the dangers of smoking, I promised to quit as a gift for her eighth birthday. Then I delivered on that promise.

In the months that followed, the rest of my family resettled from Geor-gia to Arizona. Mom moved in with me, and Ami and Hamza bought a house within walking distance. After picking out a brand-new bedroom set for Mom, she and I went to celebrate our new life together by watching fireworks on the Fourth of July.

The City of Phoenix promoted that summer's display as the biggest in twenty-six years, with live music by local bands and F-16 fly-overs. Mom and I found a spot to lay out our blanket on the lawn where the band was playing. We listened to the music, danced, and for the first time in a while, both felt really happy. We had a grand time.

That evening we saw a magnificent desert sunset, made ethereal by the reflection of the clouds in the still pond. This was followed by the most spectacular fireworks we had ever seen. With several grand finales, the display seemed to go on forever, and by the time we were finished, the percussive explosions and bright lights had us grinning ear to ear. We felt wildly blessed and happy. It was the most perfect day I had ever spent with Mom!

CHAPTER 17

THE FIRST ATTEMPT

I wish I could have ended my story in July 2012, or at least frozen in time at that picture-perfect moment with my mom. I wish that after my family made their way to Arizona, I had met the man of my dreams, and we lived happily ever after. I wish that my mom lived a long and happy life surrounded by her loving children, grandchildren, and great-grandchildren. Because that's what happens in the movies and fairy tales, and we all deserve to be happy! After an avalanche of misfortune, I was sure that life in Arizona held great things for us.

But the fairy-tale ending was not to be.

✦

My mother's life was not easy. As a child, she grew up with an alcoholic father who was known for his outbursts of violence and physical abuse. My grandmother often told us stories about having to wake her children up in the middle of the night to send them to neighbor's house for safety when her husband came home drunk.

I felt like Mom's dysfunctional siblings offered little comfort or protection—an overly dramatic older sister, Sadeta; an older brother, Sulejman, who was distant and cold; and a younger brother, Edhem, a troublemaker. I often felt they treated Mom more like an afterthought than a sister. My mother had a good heart that many people took advantage of. She was the one everyone turned to when they needed something done. But I never got the impression her siblings were willing to do much for her in return. Except, perhaps, Uncle Edhem and Aunt Enisa, Mom's sister-in-law, who was married to Uncle Edhem. She and Mom developed a close friendship and confided in each other. Mom and Aunt Enisa looked out for each other. Edhem and Enisa's two daughters were Mom's favorite nieces. They were both attentive and caring with Mom, while Mom's other nieces and nephews were distant, like their parents.

Mom married Dad at the age of nineteen. It wasn't unusual at that time to marry young. I know she loved him deeply, but I think part of her also married to escape her abusive family.

In Bosnia, it's common for extended family to live in the same household. My dad lived with his parents, his grandmother, and his older brother, who was also married and had two kids. After Mom and Dad married, Mom joined him in my grandfather's house and lived there well after Ami and I were born. Though the house was large, with eight bedrooms and three living rooms, we all lived on top of each other and sometimes that took its toll, especially after my grandfather died.

Grandpa Namik was the heart and soul of the family. He treated everyone equally and with much love. Once he passed away, his wife, Grandma T, took on the role of the family matriarch. Since Mom was the youngest in her generation, she soon became the Cinderella, expected to clean up after everyone else— vacuum, dust, do laundry, cook, and entertain guests. For whatever reason, Grandma T didn't place those same expectations on Uncle Mahir's wife. She was only a few years older than Mom. Eventually, Mom grew to deeply resent this unfair treatment.

Dad offered little help. As a male in his late twenties, raised by an affluent family who had only male children, he was a doted upon and clueless young man. He didn't really get involved with household duties and conflicts—that being the realm of women in his mind—nor did he know how to respond to women's emotional needs. While Dad was a good provider—we always had everything we needed and most of what we wanted—Mom couldn't count on Dad for either protection or consolation from her tormentors. Dad escaped conflict—and the sometimes overwhelming and overcrowded family home—either by throwing money at the issue (to distract us, he liked to buy himself and us expensive toys such as boats, campers, and so on) or by going out to bars with friends and leaving Mom to deal with everything on her own.

+

Mom and Dad separated when I was about twelve, just before the war started. Then, as I mentioned earlier, they came back together to protect our family.

These were hard times for Mom, watching over two teenage daughters in wartime, constantly worried that we would be captured, raped, tortured, and killed. Further, she couldn't always take care of her family as she was used to. There were shortages of food, running water, electricity, clothing. She had to scrape and scramble to get us through each day.

Trauma takes many forms. There's acute trauma, such as witnessing something horrible, the explosion that takes out half a neighborhood, the horrible beating by soldiers of someone you know. There's also chronic trauma, the day-to day-grind of fear, hunger, and deprivation.

Mom experienced both, yet given her background and nature, she never really talked about it, never sought help or counseling for the trauma she had endured, even after it was safe to do so once we settled in the U.S., the land of promise, rugged individualism, and self-help. She was old-fashioned about such things, as was our whole family. "Why would I need therapy? That's for crazy people."

+

Once Mom and Dad decided to flee, everything came at them at warp speed: getting back together, escaping Bosnia, living in a refugee camp, immigrating as a family to the United States, and as refugees in a foreign land.

Mom forgave Dad for cheating, but she never forgot. They began life together anew in California, where the hardships continued (though thankfully we no longer had to worry about being shot or bombed or thrown in a prison camp). Now they were raising two kids in a foreign country, unable to communicate, and taking on the worst kinds of jobs to survive, so they could both take care of the family, put food on the table, and give their children a toehold in America. Mom had no time to think about herself when she was thinking about everyone else. Life just kept steamrolling my thirty-seven-year-old mom.

I am beyond grateful for everything my parents did for us, but I honestly don't know how they did it. I often try to put myself in their shoes and marvel at how they survived—how they helped us all survive and, eventually, thrive in our new home. With grit, determination, and courage, they seemed to have conquered all the obstacles life had thrown at them, facing every challenge head-on with an abundant optimism they shared with everyone around them.

✦

In retrospect, however, the signs that Mom was struggling first appeared in her last few months in Georgia when she learned her mother was ailing. In her late eighties and still living in Bosnia, Grandma fell and broke her leg walking across the room one day. Until the fall, she had been otherwise healthy and independent, but she deteriorated rapidly from there. Mom was worried and made several trips to Bosnia within a few months, coming back each time more disheartened and exhausted than the time before.

In the next several months, Mom also became more and more withdrawn herself. When I moved my children to our new home in Arizona, whether Mom wanted to move with us or not, she felt resigned to follow. But it was a big change and took a lot of effort on her part. She was concerned that she wouldn't be able to find a new job now that she was in her fifties. She worried about becoming a burden—a legitimate worry that I regret to say I brushed off. I just didn't realize how deep-seated her need was to feel useful and wanted, to do more than her share, to carry more than her own weight, and to be independent.

She had done so much for me and the kids, I wasn't at all concerned whether she ever worked again at an outside job in her life. It was time for me to give back to her.

"You know Mom," I told her. "Maybe it's time for you to relax a little."

"What do you mean?" she asked.

"You've worked so hard all your life. I'm making good money now. Let me take care of you."

"I don't want to be a burden!"

"But you're not! You're actually a really big help. When you pick up my kids from school, that means a lot to me. I would rather they were at home with you than at some stupid daycare. They love spending time with you. If you're bored when I'm at work and the kids are in school, you can always get a part-time job, something easy and low stress. You deserve a break, Mom."

"Thank you, really. I'll have to think about it. You know I like having something to do."

Looking back, I suppose her hard work was all that kept her distracted from her demons. With time on her hands, Mom complained of tingling and numbness in the back of her head. Ami took her to see a doctor, and we used this as an opportunity to get Mom a complete checkup and physical exam. The doctor said that Mom was in perfect health. "In fact, all you have to do at this point is relax and enjoy life."

This is exactly what I had been telling her. The problem was, there were things going on beneath the surface that I, the doctor, and the rest of our family were missing.

+

In Arizona, Mom and I had a routine we stuck to like clockwork. Every workday morning, she made coffee and turned the television on to watch the news. After coffee with Mom, I dropped off Ace and Amaya at school and drove to work. Mom planned the day's meal by driving to the grocery store and picking up fresh produce. By noon, she had the food ready. I had an hour lunch break, and the office was close enough for me to come home most days to eat with Mom, when we would talk, just the two of us. That alone time with Mom was often the highlight of my day, and I thought hers as well. After I went back to work, she took a short walk to school around

2:15 p.m. to pick up Ace, Amaya, Amra, and Haris from school. Then she'd walk them back to the house until we all came home from work.

Mom had followed this routine every workday since she had moved to Arizona, except on Tuesday, October 2, 2012.

In the few weeks leading up to that day, Mom seemed withdrawn, maybe a little tired. I assumed she was worried about getting a job, but the day began like every other day with us drinking coffee together in the morning. Before I left to drop off Amaya and Ace at school, we all three kissed Mom goodbye that morning. "I've got a busy day today," I told Mom. "I might not make it back for lunch."

Sure enough, instead of going home for lunch, I grabbed a quick bite at the cafeteria in-between meetings. Around 3:15 p.m., I received a phone call from the school to let me know all four kids were waiting in the office to get picked up.

"Are you sure you have the right kids?" I said, puzzled. Mom was the most dependable person I knew. She wouldn't have left the kids at school without telling someone.

"Yes, we have the right kids."

"My mom would have called me if something came up!" I was still trying to work it out in my head.

"Amaya, Alexander, Amra, and Haris! I have all four of them in the office with me right now! No one came to pick them up."

I grabbed my car keys and ran out of the office. "Hang on! I'll be there in five minutes," I said and hung up the phone. Something was terribly wrong. I could feel it in my bones.

I dialed Mom's cell phone number as I ran. It rang all the way through, then went to voice mail. I went weak in the knees, stumbling as I ran. I dialed Hamza who had just finished his shift. On any other day, he would be driving to my house to pick up his kids. He picked up right away.

"Hamza! I just got a call from school. The kids never got picked up. Can you please go to my house and make sure Mom is okay? Right now! She's not answering her phone. I'll get the kids from school."

"Yeah, of course. I'm a block away."

Hamza and I stayed on the phone until he got to the house. I was almost at the school. We had copies of each other's keys in case of emergencies. He entered the house and found Mom unconscious on the black leather sofa with a bucket of vomit and an oversized bottle of Ibuprofen next to her.

"God, Annie, she's here, but something's really wrong! I don't know," Hamza said.

"Is she breathing? Is she alive? What's wrong with her? Call 911 right now! God, please let her be okay!" I prayed aloud while Hamza called out to Mom.

"BB, wake up! Can you hear me?" Then he turned into the phone. "Annie, she's barely conscious. Her eyes are rolling back in her head. She looks like she had a stroke or something. I need to call 911. Let me call you right back."

I hung up to let Hamza dial 911 and waited a few minutes in front of the school to compose myself. My legs were too weak to walk. I had no idea what to tell the kids. They loved her so much they would be devastated if anything happened to her! I mustered up enough strength to put on a brave face and walked into the school. I didn't say much other than apologizing to school administrators for being late.

I loaded all the kids into my minivan and while I drove the short distance to my house, I called Hamza. He told me the paramedics had arrived. "She's alive, Annie! Unconscious and unresponsive, but alive! Her pulse is weak. The paramedics are getting her onto the stretcher."

"Okay, listen Hamza. I'm pulling up to the house with a car full of kids. I don't want them to see Mom like that. Can you please come out and take my car with the kids to your place? I'll stay with Mom."

"Yeah! Good idea. Keep the car running," he said, as we pulled up to the house.

I couldn't hide the ambulance from the kids, though. All four of them started crying and calling out. "Mommy, Mommy, Auntie Annie. What's wrong? What happened to Grandma? Is she okay?"

"Guys, Grandma got a little sick, maybe from the heat, but she's going to be okay. I don't want you to worry. The ambulance is here to take her to a hospital. They're going to give her a shot and help her get better." That was the best I could offer four kids between the ages of six and eight. We had celebrated Ace's and Haris's sixth birthdays just a few days before. "Okay? So, please everybody, I need you to be brave for Grandma right now! Hamza's going to take you all to Amra and Haris's, and I'm going to check on Grandma. Then I'll call you! I promise."

As Hamza drove off in the car with the kids, I walked inside to see Mom strapped on a stretcher. She didn't respond when I gently shook her arm and called out to her. I sent lots of prayers to God, acknowledging for the first time in my life that Mom was as mortal as the rest of us. The paramedics asked me about allergies and her family medical history, then rolled her away, collapsed the wheels on the stretcher, and loaded her into the ambulance.

I stayed behind to talk to police. I vaguely remember them asking me if I had any reason to believe she may have tried to take her life.

"What? My mom? No way! Mom wouldn't do that. She loves us. She loves her grandkids. She would never do that." I didn't have to think twice about my answer.

The police and paramedics weren't sure what else could have caused Mom's condition, though. The officer pointed to an empty 200-pill bottle of Ibuprofen on the sofa. But it wasn't uncommon for Mom to get a migraine, take Ibuprofen, and lie down until it went away. I assumed that's what the pills were for.

The police finished their notes and gave me the name of the hospital. As soon as they left, I drove Hamza's car to the hospital where I found Mom hooked up to a heart monitor and intravenous fluids, still alive. Within minutes, Ami showed up as well.

Ami and I hugged each other in tears and rubbed Mom's arm, gently stroking her hair in hopes she'd wake up.

The doctors were working on the assumption that Mom had taken a full bottle of Ibuprofen and were flushing the toxins out of her body with a heavy dose of fluids. Based on her heart rate, pulse, and other indicators at the time she was admitted, the doctors decided not to pump her stomach since the pills would have already dissolved into her bloodstream. They told us she would be at risk of liver failure over the next few days as her body tried to expel the medication.

It was in that small, cold emergency room with a pale green and blue privacy curtain separating us from the nurse's station where Ami and I first faced the possibility that Mom could have attempted to take her life. Periodically, someone would come to check on her and tell us to keep calling her to try to wake her up. Ami and I paced around the hospital bed, praying Mom would open her eyes and smile at us, praying this was just a bad dream we would wake up from any minute.

But it wasn't a bad dream—it was real. I never thought we would become that family, the one who had to face a family member's suicide attempt. Those things happened to other people, far removed from us. We only saw suicide on television or read about it in newspapers. This couldn't be happening.

Five hours passed before Mom showed any signs of life by letting out a quiet mumble. Ami and I jumped to her side and started calling her. "Mom, Mom! Wake up. Mom, what happened? Do you know where you are?"

"Hmm, yeah. I'm at your house." Mom's lips moved into a crooked smile, or maybe I just wanted it to be a smile.

"You're not at my house, Mom. You're in the hospital," I said, as the nurse rushed to my side. She told us to keep talking to Mom, to ask her questions.

"I'm in the hospital?" she asked, then closed her eyes again and drifted away.

"Mom, what did you do? Please, tell us what you did?" Ami started crying.

Mom was in and out of consciousness for another two hours. When she finally came to, she admitted she had taken all the pills in the bottle. Even then, I didn't want to believe she had tried to end her life. I pushed it out of my mind, and focused, instead, on what we had to do to get her better and get her home.

Around 11:00 p.m., her attending physician informed us they would be checking Mom into the hospital's psychiatric ward under suicide watch until they could be sure she was no longer a danger to herself. My stomach flip-flopped with anxiety, but Mom was quiet, docile, and unfazed. I no longer recognized the person staring at me blankly from behind a mask of indifference.

Patients on suicide watch were issued red hospital gowns and assigned a room with minimal equipment—no cables, trays, or sharp objects—and no privacy. A human monitor was in the room with the patient at all times to make sure they didn't harm themselves. If the monitor needed a bathroom break, they called for a sub, even if a family member was in the room. This was our new normal.

It was past midnight when Ami and I left the hospital. We went back to my house to get a change of clothes for my kids so Hamza could take them to school the next day. As we entered the family room through the garage, I was telling Ami what happened. I pointed out the vomit bucket and the middle of the room where the paramedics had put Mom on the stretcher. I pointed out the black leather couch and the empty Ibuprofen bottle. That's when we found it—a letter from Mom! It seemed as if she had tried to write it after she took the pills, as her handwriting got squiggly halfway down the page. In pencil, on a single page of lined paper, she wrote:

I could not live anymore. Something stronger than me pushed me to do this. I know you will not forgive me, but I couldn't think of anything else for days and nights, other than to just be gone from this life as soon as possible. No one is to blame for whatever is wrong with me and why I wish to be gone. Take care of your babies and give them a kiss from me.

We were devastated. The letter bled with Mom's pain, but we had had no idea. None. No clue. How did we miss it? There it was in front of us, the cruel reality of her words, as if they were saying, "Now do you believe me?" My answer was, "No, I still don't really believe it." What could have possessed my mother to want to end her life? I was in complete and utter denial. It was only later, when I learned something about suicidal depression, that I could even begin to comprehend what Mom was going through. And even then, I could only understand it abstractly, intellectually, as a thought problem. How far would someone go to relieve the tremendous pain they were living in everyday? I hoped never to find out for myself. But apparently for Mom, it went as far as trying to take her own life.

✦

Depression does not discriminate. It picks on the wealthy and poor equally—those who seem downhearted and those who appear strong and smiling until their last breath. One of the complexities of major depression is that to the outside observer—even a medical professional—patients can appear to be in good health while they silently suffer.

According to the Mayo Clinic, depression is a mood disorder whose causes are not always clear. It is often brought on by traumatic external events and involves the malfunction of neurotransmitters in the brain such as norepinephrine and serotonin. People with depression have trouble performing day-to-day activities and sometimes feel life isn't worth living. Other symptoms include anger, loss of appetite, anxiety, sleep disturbances, unexplained physical problems like back pain or headaches, suicidal thoughts, and so on.[8]

If not caught and treated early, depression can be debilitating. It is most often identified by a diagnostic interview screen, but not all medical practitioners regularly conduct one. There has been some success recently using brain scans to identify depression, though this is not commonly done. After what we had gone through with Mom, I believe that all practitioners should be trained in screening for depression and that such a screen should be part of routine healthcare visits, especially wellness visits. I would also like to see additional medical research in the field of using brain scans to detect activity in parts of the brain that could help identify mental illnesses. Providing affordable access to these services would not only diagnose depression earlier and more frequently, but it would normalize mental health care and help make it a priority for public health and wellness.

---

[8] Depression (major depressive disorder), Mayo Clinic, accessed November 12, 2021. https://www.mayoclinic.org/diseases-conditions/depression/symptoms-causes/syc-20356007.

I later learned that my mom suffered from something what doctors used to call "masked depression," which is even more difficult to diagnose than clinical depression. Masked depression describes the condition of a person suffering from depression whose symptoms present as physical pain (like Mom's headaches) rather than the more traditional sadness-oriented symptoms. Instead of seeking help, people with masked depression go to great lengths to hide it from their loved ones.

We all go through life with our fair share of struggles. It's only human to feel sad or irritable and even anxious when something bad happens to us or those we care about. We all have our bad days. It's one thing to have a bad day, or two, or even three, when we don't want to see anyone and need some downtime to recharge our batteries.

However, when someone starts having ten or fifteen or twenty bad days in a row, and all they do is isolate themselves day after day, that's a red flag for them to reach out and ask for help (if they can) and for loved ones to check in on them. I wish we had known this and intervened. When someone starts losing their appetite and interest in things that they once found great pleasure in, that's also a red flag. Changes in sleeping patterns, such as insomnia or sleeping away the day; lack of energy or lethargy; slowed thinking, speaking or body movements; irritability; memory difficulties; personality changes; giving away personal belongings, and acting as if they are settling their affairs—these are also red flags.

Making it even more difficult to identify, depression for children and teens (as well as for adults with masked depression) is often described as "just a headache" or "I have a stomachache." They don't want to be a burden, so they bottle their feelings up.

The National Institute of Mental Health estimates 21.0 million American adults and 4.1 million adolescents between the ages of twelve and seventeen "had at least one major depressive episode" in 2020.[9] Depression is more prevalent among females than males. Most of those people put on their

---

[9]   Major Depression, National Institute of Mental Health, accessed February 7, 2022. https://www.nimh.nih.gov/health/statistics/major-depression.

"normal" face every day and go to work or school. Unless there is something physically and visibly wrong, they can't really take sick days. They put on a fake smile and go about their day on autopilot just to survive, not enjoying a single moment of it.

When they need a day off to get some relief, when they can't even get out of bed in the morning, they often lie to cover it up. They fake a cold or a stomach virus, because telling your boss, "Hey, I want to spend a day in bed crying" doesn't fly. There's still shame around mental illness in this country and around the globe. Depression is considered a weakness, as if it's somehow the fault of those who suffer from it.

But it's not their fault. They can't just snap out of it—they need professional help and long-term treatment. What they don't need is for us to judge or feel sorry for them. They need compassion. They need their friends, family, and coworkers to understand, to refrain from judgment, and to empathize with what they're going through. For some, a simple "Hello, are you okay?" can mean the difference between life and death that day. Their agony is often invisible. Sometimes we notice someone is acting out of character. We get a gut feeling they're a little off. Our instincts are trying to tell us something we don't quite understand. Just letting them know that we are there for them, even if we don't quite understand what's going on, goes a long way toward supporting them. Our support, in turn, might lead them to seek treatment and believe it's worth the effort.

Over time, I've learned that people experiencing depression try to tamp down their feelings and grit it out, which was exactly what my mom tried to do. She was the kind of woman who had been strong for everyone else her whole life, but she neglected herself. When she needed help, she felt like she would be a burden. The truth is, she was never a burden—she was my best friend and a tremendous help to all of us, but no matter how many times we told her that, she simply didn't believe it deep down. That was the depression talking. And I will always wonder, if I had known then what I know now, could I have done anything different to save her? That's what led her to try to take her own life that Tuesday in October.

What I know now, and what I tell my children to do if they're ever feeling really sad or upset, is to talk to me or another family member or friend they trust. There's also no shame in getting professional help. People go to doctors and medical specialists all the time for other illnesses, but mental illness continues to carry its own social taboos. And people dealing with depression may, on their own, have a difficult time reaching out to a professional for help—or they may not even know who to reach out to. In walking this journey with my mom, I know now that if you can't reach out yourself, you can enlist the aid of a friend or family member. You are not a burden. It is a matter of life and death. And your life matters!

✦

Ami and I drove back to the hospital that same night. When we arrived, Mom was fully conscious and holding down liquids, but she didn't seem to be herself. She was reviving physically, but not in spirit. Her eyes were lifeless and hollow, as if her spirit had been sucked out of her body. Her facial expressions were unfamiliar, as if she was wearing a mask of her own face. The mom I knew had checked out.

I wanted so hard to believe that she was only in shock, that if we talked to her, if we hugged her and kissed her and told her how much we loved her—how much her grandkids loved her—her spirit would be regenerated, and our mom and grandma would return to us. But days went by and nothing changed. The mom I knew died that day on my black leather couch and never came back.

Looking back, there had been warning signs, but they were hidden in the bustle of our move to Arizona. We missed them.

Mom had quit her job in Georgia to move to Arizona and as a result, lost her health insurance. To follow through on my promise to take care of her and because I loved her, I bought her private insurance as soon as her old insurance ran out. Without telling me, though, she cancelled it shortly after she arrived. She also insisted I put her minivan's title in my name, and she demanded to have her name removed from various bank accounts. Now that I've done the research, I know that depressed individuals who are suicidal give away their possessions and sort out their affairs. At the time, I thought it was a little strange, but dismissed it too easily. If we had known the signs, we could have gotten my mom the treatment that might have saved her life.

Mom had often joked that she was the best health insurance client in the world because she paid high premiums to keep her copays low. Plus, she barely ever saw a doctor. She was terrified of doctors. While we were still in Bosnia, Mom had had multiple surgeries on ovarian cysts and other types of tumors. Ultimately, she underwent a complete hysterectomy and almost died during the procedure and recovery. Whenever we suggested Mom take care of her health she would say, "Every time I see a doctor, I end up in surgery. So no, thank you; no medical exams!"

It was ironic, then, that the one time Mom actually needed insurance, she had cancelled it. Mom was diagnosed with depression and post-traumatic stress disorder, but without medical coverage, she was only able to stay at the regional hospital for the minimum required seven days before she had to leave. Because she was still considered a danger to herself, the hospital wouldn't release Mom, so she was moved to a free clinic. I was hard-pressed to believe a seven-day hospital stay had been enough for Mom to fully recover. I was angry, but there was nothing we could do.

I was even angrier when I saw that the free clinic seemed as if it was more of a halfway house than a rehab center. Homeless people and drug addicts off the street checked in for a warm bed and a free meal. Mom deserved better, yet no one cared.

My healthy mom would have been disturbed by this place—the mom who checked in was expressionless and indifferent. This new person occupying Mom's body just sat there, limp and staring off into distance.

In the days following her suicide attempt, I took time off work and spent every moment with her talking, pleading, and trying to reason with her. I begged for my mom, the one we all knew and loved, to come back. I cried and told her that we needed her, that my kids missed her and asked every day where Grandma was and when she was coming home. Nothing I said resonated; it felt like talking to a brick wall. She just drifted away, becoming increasingly more absent.

At the end of the second day at the free clinic, the social worker assigned to Mom's case told Ami and me we could take her home. We were given a list of things that needed to go on lockdown, such as weapons, kitchen knives and other sharp objects, ropes, cleaning products, medications, alcohol, drugs—anything Mom could use to harm herself. We didn't feel we had the expertise to watch over her, but we weren't going to leave her with the junkies.

We brought her home, and I sat her down on a chair in front of me— much like you would sit down a child you're about to discipline. It saddened me that I had to do this with my mother. I showed her the list from the doctor and tearfully said, "I don't know how to do this Mom! I can't lock up forks. I can't hide Clorox and Windex from you. I can't baby-proof the whole house because you're not a toddler; you're a grown woman. I can't stay here and watch you all day because I have to go back to work. And when I do, I must be able to trust you that you won't try to hurt yourself again. Can you promise me that? Please, Mom? Please! I'm begging you!"

She just stared at me blankly. I wasn't sure if she heard a word I said. She didn't come right out and say it because she didn't say much of anything those days, but I had a feeling that her only regret about that Tuesday was that she had failed, that she was still alive. Now she was just waiting for her chance to die.

It was clear Mom needed around-the-clock supervision and care, but I could only provide it for a few weeks before I had to go back to work. And I knew it would be impossible for a single mom and sole provider for two young kids who received only the usual number of days of PTO to give a suicidal parent the care she deserved. I didn't have the time, knowledge, or emotional bandwidth to provide that level of care. And though Ami was not a single Mom, she was in the same boat. I have often regretted that I couldn't do more.

Ami tried to get Mom the mental help she needed in Arizona, but without insurance, that proved to be impossible. Mental health conditions simply do not receive the same level of urgency as patients with visible, physical conditions. When Hamza was diagnosed with a life-threatening disease, within days, he had a team of best-in-class medical professionals putting together his treatment plans.

With Mom, we were knocking on closed door after closed door like lost souls. In shock and in despair, with no clear path on what to do next and no one to guide us. It seemed that for an evaluation appointment alone, all the psychiatrists we talked to were scheduling several months out. Patients like Mom who have already attempted to take their life once don't have the luxury of waiting that long, nor do their families.

Having exhausted all options in Arizona, we had Hamza contact Mom's youngest brother, Uncle Edhem, who lived in Denmark and had been re-tired for a few years. He was the only sibling Mom was still close to. Hamza made arrangements for Mom to stay with Uncle Edhem for as long as needed. Uncle Edhem promised to watch her at all times.

Edhem travelled back and forth between Bosnia and Denmark, spending several weeks at a time at our family house in Prijedor to visit my grandma and several weeks with his family in Denmark. We thought it would be good for Mom to be with her brother, their mom, and our uncle's family. Besides, access to counseling and medications in Bosnia and Denmark were more readily available and significantly cheaper. With favorable exchange rates, we were able to cover Mom's medical bills and medications in Bosnia out-of-pocket. In October 2012, Mom flew to Denmark to stay with Uncle Edhem.

Mom seemed to be bouncing back after she started seeing a doctor in Bosnia who put her on anti-depressants. It helped, too, that Mom and Uncle Edhem traveled back and forth between Bosnia and Denmark where she spent time with Aunt Enisa and Mom's nieces, all of whom she loved dearly. I was hopeful that the meds would help, and I continued to pray for her. We all did. Mom was doing so well that she bought an airplane ticket to come back to Arizona in mid-February. The grandkids were excited to see her again.

+

The night of February 4, 2013, was just another uneventful night at my mom's family house in Bosnia. After having guests over in the afternoon,

Mom, Grandma, and Uncle Edhem settled down in the living room for the evening. They watched a television show together until 11:30 p.m., after which Mom got up, said good night to her mom and brother and went to bed, much like she had every other night in Bosnia. With Arizona being eight hours behind, it would have been around 3:30 p.m. my time when Mom went to bed.

At that exact time, I was finishing up at work and getting ready to celebrate Dad's fifty-ninth birthday at my house. Dad wasn't always in the States with us for his birthday, so this was special. I planned on dinner, cake, and a bottle of champagne.

That evening, we had a lovely time filled with laughter. Haris and Ace climbed up the chairs to sit on the kitchen island to help light all fifty-nine of Dad's candles. It would have been around 3:00 a.m. in Bosnia when Dad blew out the candles, and we popped open the champagne. We hung out for the rest of the evening, catching up and laughing with Dad and the grandkids he didn't get to see very often. It was a nice break from the traumatic events of the fall. When we went to bed, we were all in good spirits.

CHAPTER 18

"MENS SANA IN CORPORE SANO"

It was precisely 3:00 a.m. in Arizona when I woke up in a cold sweat from a terrible nightmare. In my dream, Mom was driving the red minivan in Bosnia when she lost control of the car, and it flipped sideways on the road. Water came out of nowhere and flooded the car with Mom trapped inside. For a split second, I felt what Mom would have felt in that car, and I couldn't breathe. Waking up in terror, I choked and gasped for air.

I immediately sat up in bed and prayed. "Dear God, please watch over my mom. Please protect her and help her get better."

I repeated the prayer at least one hundred times and continued to toss and turn in bed for the remainder of the night. My alarm went off at 6:00 a.m. on February 5, 2013, when it was time for me to start getting ready for work. Slow to get moving and still distraught from the dream, I arrived at work around 8:30 a.m. Two hours later, I received a phone call from Dad. "Are you in a private place where you can talk, Annie?"

I didn't like the sound of his voice and was already walking to a nearby empty office. "I'm not, but I'm heading there. What's up, Dad?"

"Can you find a quiet place to sit down?" he asked.

"I can talk now. What's going on?" I closed the door behind me and sat down in a chair.

"I have some bad news, Annie. We're not sure where your mom is."

"What happened?" The dream from the night before flashed before my eyes and that terrible feeling of suffocating and gasping for air came over me again.

"Your Uncle Edhem just called Ami a few moments ago. He said Mom went to bed around 11:30 last night. When he woke up this morning, BB's bedroom door was still closed, and he went inside to check on her. She wasn't there, and her bed wasn't made. He went outside to look for her and discovered the front door was unlocked. He has already contacted the police, and everyone is looking for her, but I just wanted to let you know."

"Did they check the river, Dad?" I asked.

"Don't think the worst yet, Annie. She could have gone out for a long walk. They will find her! Okay?"

"She already tried to kill herself once! She's been missing for how many hours now? She can't swim Dad! Edhem needs to hire divers right now to search the river!"

Too many things were wrong with the universe that morning for me to remain hopeful we would find Mom alive. Mom was always the one to wake up first and start the coffee. She always made her bed and folded her pajamas neatly on the pillow. She always locked the front door behind her and carried a key. Uncle Edhem had already contacted the police and reported her missing. He and several neighbors had begun a frantic search all over town, and she hadn't yet turned up. This didn't seem like the time to remain calm. This was a time to shiver in panic in a small, dimly-lit office behind closed doors.

✦

I had a terrible, gut-wrenching, hope-to-God-I'm-wrong feeling that my mother had drowned in the River Sana. The River Sana runs through Prijedor and is one of the cleanest and most scenic rivers in Bosnia. Sana in Latin means "sound" and comes from a Latin phrase "mens sana in corpore sano" meaning "a sound mind in a sound body." Most people who grew up in Prijedor learned how to swim in that river at an early age. Parts of Sana are a deep shade of dark green surrounded by a beautiful landscape of lush green trees and wildflowers. The water itself is calm and cool, making it a perfect place for families to escape the hot summer days.

Mom was not afraid of much, but she was afraid of water. She must have been around the age of seven when one of her family members decided it was time for her to learn to swim. Back then, people thought the way to teach children to swim was to throw them into the deep end and let them learn on their own. There was usually an adult on hand to assist those who sank. That was a good thing for Mo, because once they threw her in, she sputtered and floundered and nearly drowned until they pulled her out. Because of this experience, she had developed a lifelong fear of water. The experience was so scarring that Mom never learned how to swim and spent her whole life without any desire to learn.

As a young child myself, after I learned to swim and while on one of our month-long summer vacations on the Adriatic Sea, I tried to coax Mom into swimming past waist-deep water. At that time, I was oblivious to her near-drowning experience and naively called out to her. I really just wanted to prove Mom could swim and that she should not be afraid of the water. Cheerily, I kept moving farther into deeper waters telling her, "Just a little farther, Mommy. I can still touch the rocks," even though I was well beyond the point where I could touch the rocks with my feet.

Trusting me, she swam towards me until suddenly she realized she was in too deep and screamed and flailed her arms until her head sank below the water. It all happened in a flash. Dad saw the whole thing from the shore, jumped in the water, and swam like Michael Phelps to rescue her. That experience taught me to never again take Mom's fear of water lightly.

The suspicion that she may be in the water was eating me alive, and others shared it too. Divers were hired to scour the river. To make matters worse, it was winter, and the river was muddy and cold with the water risen several feet above, flooding into grass and bushes on the banks. Fallen tree branches obstructed visibility, making search efforts extremely challenging. For several days, they searched a ten-mile range without luck.

We desperately clung to the hope we'd find her alive. Hope was all we had. Hope that Mom had had a terribly bad case of delayed puberty and that she ran away from home. Hope that she had gone for a long walk and got lost. Hope that she had hit her head and gotten amnesia and that's why she couldn't contact us. Hope that one day she'd walk through the front door of the family house and wonder what all the fuss was about. It was amazing how many elaborate scenarios we concocted to make us believe she was coming back.

In the meantime, our lives continued. They had to. We still had to go to work every day. We still had to clothe and feed our children. We didn't say anything to the children about their grandma going missing. We didn't want to upset them, and we tried to keep their lives as normal as possible. The world around us did not stop turning just because we were going through a personal tragedy. For thirty days, we desperately clung to the hope that she would return. We contacted police and Uncle Edhem several times a day. We even reached out to the U.S. Embassy in Sarajevo to enlist their help.

I was at work on March 6, 2013, sitting in a large conference room surrounded by senior company executives, when a text message from Ami came through on my phone: They found her!

Chills shook me as I walked out of the conference room without a word. I still wanted to believe the best, but if they had had better news, the message would have said she was alive.

I ran outside in a panic to call Ami. When I got through, she said, "They found a woman in her mid-fifties, brown hair, wearing a brown jacket and black Ecco shoes." These were Mom's favorite comfy shoes. "She was submerged in the Sana about forty miles downstream. Her clothes had caught on to some underwater shrubs. A man who had been out fishing discovered her. She's in bad shape. Her body is badly decomposed. Based on clothing that Uncle Edhem said she was wearing when she went missing, they believe it's Mom."

I imagined the Earth I was standing on in that moment crumbling beneath my feet and turning into a sinkhole that I was falling into.

"Why? Why, Mom why? Why, my mom, God, why? What did she ever do to you, God? What did she ever do to anyone? Why the hell did you take my mom?"

My family tried to console me. "At least we found her and can give her a proper burial. Some are never found."

"Yeah, at least we found her," I echoed, but that meant nothing to me. She still had chosen to end her life. I just wanted to scream and break things.

But I couldn't and didn't because I still had two sweet, innocent kids who hadn't done anything to deserve losing their grandma in that way. They needed a sane parent now more than ever. With my body half-limp in shock, I got into my car to drive home, numb. I don't even remember telling my boss I was leaving. I don't remember much of that whole week, other than making funeral arrangements over the phone and booking a flight to Bosnia for me and the kids. When she was healthy, Mom had told us she wanted to be buried in her hometown, and we would honor that.

Ami left for Bosnia with her family the day before me. I stayed behind to wait for my passport, which had expired. I also needed a notarized document from Filip that he had overnighted, authorizing Amaya and Ace to travel to Bosnia.

About two hours after I had dropped Ami and her family off at the airport and came back home, Aunt Sadeta, Mom's older sister, called me. I hadn't talked to her in years, and neither had Mom. If I had known it was her number, I would not have picked up, but those days many friends from San Jose called to check on us, so I picked up every time I saw a San Jose area code.

I had already taken two anti-anxiety pills before her phone call and as soon as I answered the phone, this estranged sister of my late mother began drilling me with questions. "Why did she kill herself? Why did you send her to Bosnia? Why didn't you do anything to stop her?"

All I heard was "What? Why? When? Where?" like she was poking at me with her bony finger. Finally, she went too far, and I let her have it.

"All these years you never cared about her! All these years and you never once picked up the phone to ask how she was doing. And now you care? Now you want to know what happened? Now you want to know why she killed herself? Well, guess what? She's gone now! She is gone forever, and it's too late now. Do you understand? You can't bring her back and don't ever call my number again!"

I hung up the phone in tears, my body trembling. At that moment, I felt a gush of cold wind and heard a loud thundercrack, followed by a bolt of lightning and a crackling noise. I bent my head up to the black skies, then looked around me. Marble-sized hail bounced off the patio. I shivered and cried. It felt like God himself was shedding giant ice tears, along with my own.

Shortly after, my doorbell rang and a man delivered the letters containing my passport and a notarized affidavit from Filip. I was free to lay my mom to rest.

✦

Those days were a blur, and I don't remember much of our trip to Bosnia, but I do remember the weather on March 13, 2013. The day of Mom's funeral started off grey, gloomy, and cold, much like the day before when I had left Phoenix. Mom was to be buried in the traditional way. Her funeral procession gathered at the Mosque down the street from the family house after noon prayer. With family, friends, and neighbors, about fifty people attended, including Uncle Edhem and Mom's older brother Sulejman, who, like Aunt Sadeta, hadn't spoken to Mom in years.

Mom had spent half her lifetime wishing her older siblings showed her more compassion, yet they hadn't seemed to care. Now that Mom was gone, though, Uncle Sulejman had traveled from Boise, Idaho to bury his sister in Bosnia. Aunt Sadeta, however, did not even attend the funeral, and neither did Mom's six nieces and nephews. In the end, it was Dad and our next-door neighbors from Banja Luka who came to pay their respects. They were by our side the whole time. Even though our next-door neighbors are not blood relatives, I felt more connected to them than to the entire side of Mom's family.

At the Mosque, my kids and I said our final goodbye to Mom. Most Mosques have a small room in the basement where the deceased's body is washed and prepared for the funeral by wrapping it in snow-white cotton linen. The washing is traditionally done by family members of the same sex, but given

Mom's condition when she was found, Ami and I were both strongly advised against seeing her remains. While Ami wanted to see her one final time, I talked her out of it. I did not want that image to be the last look we had of her—I wanted us to remember her by her warm smile and dimples and cherish her beauty. Ami finally agreed.

Muslims aren't buried in a casket. Instead, a wooden plank called a tabut is carved with exact measurements of the deceased. As Ace, Amaya, and I entered the basement, Mom's body lay peacefully wrapped in white linen on the tabut. A traditional green cloth with Qur'an scriptures, embroidered in gold thread, was draped over Mom's body. Ami and I, with our families, walked in first to pay our final respects, followed by the rest of the family, friends, and neighbors. Traditionally, I would have been able to kiss Mom's forehead one final time, but instead, I kissed a spot on the green cloth covering her head. Then I guided my children to do the same. It was somber as we moved toward her feet. I rubbed my fingers down Mom's arm, telling her one last time how much I loved her.

Standing at Mom's feet, my children and I quietly whispered a prayer together in Arabic, as all Muslim prayers are recited in Arabic. "Inna Lillahi wa inna ilayha raji'un." It was a verse from the Qur'an that means, "We belong to Allah and to Him we shall return."

We exited the basement up a short flight of stairs. Others went inside to pay their respects while Dad stayed close to me, Amaya, and Ace. Dad gave me the strength to maintain my composure and I, in turn, projected it onto my children.

After everyone paid their final respects, Mom's body was moved to the backyard of the Mosque where the Imam led the funeral prayer. After the prayer, a dozen men lifted Mom's tabut and carried it down a small alleyway to her final resting place. Ami and I, along with our daughters and female friends, stayed outside the gate as our male family members and friends lowered Mom's body into the ground and covered her linen-wrapped body with dirt.

For Muslim cultures, it's customary that women don't enter the burial place. In most societies, men are conditioned not to cry, but women are allowed to express their grief through tears and even wailing. Among Muslims, though, wailing loudly is not considered proper behavior at a funeral since death in Islam is simply a passage of one's soul to a much better world than this one. Lowering a person's body to rest should be dignifying to the deceased and performed in reverence while praying for their soul.

As Amaya and I watched and sobbed uncontrollably about a hundred feet away, I gripped my daughter firmly and felt my heart shattering into a million pieces. I sobbed for myself and for my children, and for the immense loss that was changing our lives irrevocably.

Everything about that day was awful. Everything but a few blessed moments when the dark grey rain-and-snow-filled clouds opened up right above Mom's grave just enough to allow a single ray of sunshine to light up the hollow pit where her body now rested, as if God himself had created a pathway to Heaven for Mom's soul.

It was important to me to find something positive on that most awful day we laid her to rest. I knew the judgment was coming—that Mom had taken her own life. Many religions condemn those who commit suicide, denying traditional burial or shunning them by burying them in a separate part of the cemetery. Islam is not different. It specifically prohibits suicide in hadiths (collected accounts of the Prophet Muhammad's words and habits), and two passages from the Qur'an state:

"And do not kill yourselves. Surely, God is Most Merciful to you." (Qur'an, Surah 4 An-Nisa, ayat 29)

"And do not throw yourselves in destruction." (Qur'an, Surah 2 Al-Baqarah, ayat 195)

✦

Even Prophet Muhammad himself (peace be upon him) described suicide as a perpetual punishment in the afterlife when he pronounced, "He who commits suicide by stabbing himself shall keep on stabbing himself in Hell Fire." (Sahih Al-Bukhari, 2.446)

Because of these pronouncements against suicide, I felt fortunate that Mom was laid to rest in a traditional manner. That decision had rested solely with the Imam. In his compassion for her and for us, he chose to see that Mom's lifelong good deeds had outweighed her final decision. I held firmly onto that single ray of sunshine that lit up her grave as a sign that those same good deeds had earned her a place in Heaven.

I messaged Jasmina in California after the funeral and couldn't stop crying about, of all things, the family house in Prijedor.

Since moving to the States, my mom had invested tens of thousands of dollars in rebuilding the house in hopes of retiring there. After the war, Mom had sent Uncle Edhem the money to pay the workers to rebuild the entire east-facing wall of the house, which had crumbled. Even as recently as the year before, she had planned to live long enough to fulfill her plan. She had sent several thousand dollars to pave an area of the yard from the street to the garage, so that those who came to visit wouldn't get their shoes dirty while walking from their car to the front door. Now Mom would never enjoy the house.

Mom's generosity was boundless and her kindness without limits. Her whole life she worked hard and selflessly helped others, but her family took her for granted—and some just plain took advantage of her. Why couldn't they just love her? I remember telling Jasmina the night of the funeral that I couldn't stand another second in that house. Everything reminded me of the sacrifices Mom had made to fix up a house she would never get to enjoy. With this vast hole in my heart, I cried myself to sleep. And that night, I vowed never to return to the family house or Bosnia ever again.

+

Death is inevitable for all of us. When a person passes away from old age, their death is expected, although still a loss to the family and friends they leave behind. Death sometimes brings relief for the departed, as well as their loved ones. It can end the agony of a terminal and painful disease, for example.

When a person passes tragically, unexpectedly, or relatively young, however, their family and friends are often left in shock and disbelief. One thing is certain, though, with most deaths, no one blames the dearly departed. We mourn their loss, but accept death as a fact of life, carrying the memory of our loved one in our hearts and minds for the remainder of our own short lives.

This is not the case when a person dies by suicide. From my experience, when a family loses someone to suicide, their grief over the person's death multiplies because it's accompanied by guilt, self-recrimination, and sometimes self-hatred. It feels like grief on steroids. And as if my own judgment wasn't enough, what's worse and what I didn't expect, is the judgment of others.

Society vilifies those who take their own lives for what they've done to themselves and to their loved ones. My mom was a gentle soul who suffered most of her life, yet she continued to be victimized in death by strangers who heard about what happened, took it upon themselves to pass judgment, and called her a coward for "taking the easy way out," as they saw it. Believe me, there was nothing easy about her suicide.

When I found out what people thought about my mom, my hero, and the bravest woman I have ever had the privilege of knowing, I sometimes wish she had died of natural causes so they could look past her death to the goodness of her life. Because she took her own life, I feel like I was never allowed to honor her, to dignify her in death, even though she was an amazing human being. Initially, this left me paralyzed and powerless in my own grief. What I came to know, unfortunately, is that I was not alone. Suicide has become the tenth leading cause of death for adults and the third for teenagers in United States. Tragically, it continues to be on the rise at an alarming rate.[10] As a society, we need to understand it better for the sake of prevention and out of compassion for those affected by it.

I'm not claiming that losing a loved one to old age, illness, or accident is any easier than losing a loved one to suicide. Loss is loss. I'm not comparing levels of death or grief. But once touched by the tragedy of suicide, my life and the lives of all the other loved ones left behind are

---

[10] American Society for Suicide Prevention, Suicide Statistics, National Institute of Mental Health, accessed February 1, 2002. https://afsp.org/suicide-statistics/.

altered forever. Bottling up our feelings, or any other traumatic experiences, does irreparable damage to the soul. From personal experience, I've learned there is no shame in talking to a mental health professional and seeking help. Because of my experience, I'm also often talking myself to people who may be thinking of suicide or who have had a loved one take their own lives and are in the throes of complicated grief. Help heals.

When I lost Mom, I felt desolate. Profound grief took me through the torment of shock, sorrow, anguish, disbelief, denial, misery, anger, guilt, shame, heartbreak, agony—all in one moment that kept repeating itself in a continuous loop. I'd ask myself, Why did she do it? Or If I had done something different, would she still be alive? Those two questions kept coming back to haunt me, along with a thousand other what-if scenarios that I'd run in my head, trying to come up with ways that I might have saved her if I'd just known the answers to my questions.

Sometimes those who take their lives leave a goodbye letter and sometimes they don't. Mom did leave a letter, but it didn't help me understand any better. I love you, but I just can't anymore. Written in pencil on a white sheet of paper in her own handwriting, all those words told me at first was that my love was not enough to save her. That whatever Mom was suffering from was stronger than me, my children, my sister, her children, and countless other people who adored Mom and wished that she could have lived. The mere thought that our love—my love—was not enough, often brought me to my knees.

The letter also made me realize something else. The intention of the person taking their life is not to hurt those left behind, at least in Mom's case. My mom would never intentionally do us any harm. Her love for us was unconditional. I have to believe that her need to silence her demons and get away from her own pain simply overpowered her.

At first, I was angry. It took me several years (and lots of therapy) to take Mom's "I love you, but I just can't anymore" at face value. Over time, I came to realize that both things could be true at the same time: she couldn't live her life anymore and she really did love us. The effort of masking what she felt inside had become too much to bear, but she had loved us and had shown us how much she loved us every day of her life until she no longer could.

In trying to understand Mom's actions, I came across the story of Kevin Hines, a suicide attempt survivor and one of the few people who have jumped off the Golden Gate Bridge and lived. Today, Hines talks openly about his state of mind prior to the suicide attempt. He talks about the darkness that drove him to jump. He talks about the regret he felt at the exact moment after he jumped. He talks about praying to God to keep him alive once he hit the freezing-cold, shark-infested waters of the bay. He talks about the miracle of life renewed when the Coast Guard pulled him out of water. For me, one of the most valuable details in Kevin's story is how alone he felt before he jumped and how desperately he wanted someone to reach out, to ask him what was wrong and how they could help.

I wish I had known to ask those kinds of questions of my mom sooner.

Instead, Mom was my safety net, someone to turn to in times of sorrow. Not being able to talk to her, to ask her for advice, or hear the sound of her soothing voice has multiplied the magnitude of my grief. What has also magnified my grief is that, for whatever reason, she felt she couldn't turn to me in the same way. Should I have tried harder? Should I have pushed her to open up? I'll never know. That is part of the pain that will never go away. The pain dulls with time, but it never goes away.

CHAPTER 19

SURVIVING GRIEF

Three days after Mom's funeral we came back home to Arizona on a Saturday afternoon. Jetlagged, exhausted, and emotionally drained, I picked up our dog and Ami's from a friend's house and returned to the airport to wait for Ami and her family. Ace and Amaya played in the back seat with our Yorkie, Bella, and Ami's big, white Lab, Buddy.

Ami's flight arrived, and I dropped them off at their house a block away from ours. When I pulled up to the garage, the house felt eerie, different somehow. Mom hadn't been there for the four or five months she had been in Bosnia and Denmark, but I always expected her to return when she felt better. Now she never would return, and the house felt emptier for it, haunted by her absence.

Yet, I could still feel her presence. Her favorite tan leather sandals were neatly arranged in the garage. The picture of her smiling and hugging Amaya and Ace was attached by a magnet to the fridge. Her bathroom towels were in the hallway closet; her bed pillows still smelled like her; and her favorite bathing suit with its yellow-and-lavender flowers, the one she had taken on every one of our family beach vacations, hung where she had left it. I broke down in tears.

I hadn't really slept for two days while travelling, and I felt all the energy sucked out of me. I walked straight to bed, even though it was only 5:00 p.m. Amaya and Ace followed. We slept a good fifteen hours and didn't wake up until Sunday morning.

On Sunday, I had just about enough energy to do our laundry and run to the store to pick up a few groceries. I spent the rest of the day hugging my kids in my bed. We cried and made each other feel better. Then we cried some more until we went back to sleep.

The next day was a Monday. Ace and Amaya went back to school, and seeing no point in staying home to wallow in misery, I went back to work.

Once there, one of the senior executives saw that I had returned already and summoned me to his office. "I wanted to touch base with you and ask if there's anything I can do for you? If you need additional time off, we can arrange that."

I fought back tears while responding. "I can't tell you how much that means to me, but I would rather be at work with something to do and surrounded by people. My kids are back in school. I can't be at home by myself right now. The house has too many painful reminders."

I didn't tell him this part, but among the painful memories was the black leather couch where we had found Mom after her first attempt. That couch haunted me, and I avoided it. As time went on, I didn't look at it, I didn't sit on it, and I didn't let anyone else sit on it. Yet for reasons I can't fully explain, I didn't get rid of it. It caused a couch-sized lump in my throat every time I looked at it, yet I kept it there in the family room. I couldn't throw out the rug Mom threw up on either. When I passed through the room, I carefully stepped around the vomit-stained patches, but I couldn't throw it away. The best I can come up with is that I wasn't ready to erase reminders of Mom, even if they were negative ones. They were the last links I had to her.

Mom's bedroom haunted me too. We had furnished it together so Mom could have a room of her own, a safe haven. A place to rest. The only thing resting in that room now was Mom's death certificate, which I deposited into her nightstand after returning from Bosnia.

When the kids and I absolutely had to be home, we distracted ourselves by staying busy with homework, yardwork, crafts, and anything else that kept our fingers moving and minds focused on something else. Spending time together in this way brought us closer.

My good friends Jasmina, Annie, and Mary-Anne frequently called to check on us. Sometimes just their friendly voice and a simple, "Hello, are you okay?" was enough to get me through the day. My response was often, "No, I'm not okay today, but tomorrow will be better." That I was able to say that to someone, to lean on a friend, was often the only thing that kept me from drowning in sorrow. But even my closest friends could not begin to comprehend the agony of losing a parent to suicide. Nor would I want them to.

+

There was one person I thought would understand exactly what I was going through, my sister Ami. But over the weeks and months and years that followed Mom's first attempt and suicide, we dealt with the tragedy very differently and drifted apart. Mom's suicide broke us each individually and broke our family apart.

This would have broken Mom's heart if she had known. Family meant everything to Mom, and she raised Ami and me to look out for one another. When she had to mediate our sibling arguments, Mom would often say, "Look at how my sister and I are. Don't become that! Don't grow up to be like me and her, to not speak to each other. You are sisters. Love one another no matter what."

Yet, after she passed, that's exactly what happened to Ami and me. We became estranged. There was an insurmountable amount of stress, coupled with paralyzing grief. Ami and I had different ideas on how to cope with it all. As time went on, the stress became greater. It all came to a head on New Year's Eve 2016 when we had a big blowout, which we wouldn't work out until years later. Although a lot could be said about that evening, portions of it are not my story to tell. It involved lifelong mutual friends and a sworn enemy.

In her own profound pain, Ami broke another jar of honey. This time, a metaphorical one. Once again, she left the sticky mess under the kitchen sink for someone else to clean up. Mom was gone. I expected Ami to take responsibility for her actions. She didn't. We both needed time to heal, and as time went on, the mess remained untouched under the kitchen sink, collecting dust.

The mess stayed there for many years. My love for Ami stayed the same despite all of it. In her own time, she owned up to her actions and apologized—and we had a good talk and cleared up old misconceptions. But until that happened, I was alone for many years. Although I considered Ami my best friend throughout life, as years went by after we stopped talking to each other, I felt deserted when I needed her most. I often wondered if she cared about me, which hurt and prevented me from reaching out first. Ami, however, needed time to work through her own pain and grief. We were both very broken, barely finding strength to pick up our own pieces and glue them back together. In the meantime, our children remained close. Mom would have been proud of that.

Coping with grief takes many forms. Some choose to believe they are unlucky or cursed, and the world is out to get them. Others choose their reactions to situations based on how much or how little control they have over it. Some try to mute their pain by self-medicating in different ways, while others seek help and attempt to make sense out of situations. I guess what I'm trying to say is it would have been easy to drown my sorrows in alcohol or a mood-enhancing drug. Who would blame me if I did, after all I had been through? My kids—that's who.

For my own healing, I struggled hard to try to understand the reasons my mom chose to end her life and whether there was anything I could have done differently to prevent her from doing so. Nothing made sense, and I always converged on the same conclusion—this was Mom's doing. I could blame myself or others, but in the end, we had absolutely no control over it, in part because Mom never asked for help, but also because when help was made available to her, she found a way to escape anyway. It took me many years to find a way to understand this, accept it, grieve my loss, and forgive Mom.

✦

Seven months after Mom passed away, my maternal grandmother left us too. She was a sweet old lady with funny stories I continue to retell to my children to the present day. Those stories still make us laugh, even though they're not half as funny when I tell them. Grandma had her fair share of a rough life, but she had lived a long one. She was ninety-two and while her passing made me sad, we all knew it was her time to go. I was not mad at her for leaving us. She had become so old and frail that I actually felt relief on her behalf, as we knew she was no longer in pain.

When Grandma passed away, I hadn't yet learned to forgive Mom, which took me at least three or four years. So I was still very angry at my mother when my grandmother died, and I felt sorry for myself. Why did all these bad things happen to me? Why did I have to grow up in a war-torn country? Why did I have to become a refugee and start over? Why did I marry an alcoholic? Why did I have to go through a nasty divorce and not one but two ugly custody battles? Why did my mom have to kill herself? After all we've been through? After everything we had survived? When were we— when was I—ever going to get a break?

Another painful aspect of my grief was that each of the bad things that had happened to me in the past had also taught me valuable lessons and made me a stronger person—except this! Something good had always come from the pain, yet this was a different kind of pain altogether. I struggled to find a single thing about my mom's death that could make me a better or stronger person. It would take me years to find healthy ways of working through the grief (and helping my children work through their own grief) to finally accept the new normal Mom's suicide forced on us and become whole again. In the process, we each became very different people than we were at the beginning of our journey.

Even though I couldn't see any good that came from her death for many years, I can now see that one of the most valuable lessons I learned from Mom's life is the importance of self-love, self-care, and to unconditionally love only those who are capable of reciprocating the same feelings. My life began changing the day I learned to cultivate only those relationships that contributed to my well-being and happiness and let go of all the ones that were toxic.

✦

For many years, I was angry with Mom, but I was also mad at God. In fact, during the days, weeks, and months after we laid Mom to rest, I lost faith in God. If God was as merciful as some say, why did He take my mom? It was a childish thought, but I often asked myself what we had done to deserve the life we were given? What did my young, innocent kids do to deserve so much sadness and pain?

As time went on, I came to a place where, even though I wasn't ready to forgive Mom, I wanted God to forgive her. After all, God is all forgiving—and I didn't want my mom in some perpetual circle of hell, if there is such a thing.

Forgiving Mom was extremely challenging for me. The pain I felt, and that my children felt, was all consuming. It was brutal and real, not something I could snap my fingers to make go away. It was the kind of pain we had to grind through in all its ugliness. One thing I learned early was to not pretend the pain wasn't there. When I felt sad, I allowed myself to cry. When my children felt sad, I didn't tell them to suck it up. I hugged them and stroked their hair while they cried. When we were done grieving for that day, I made sure we got up, washed our faces, and did something that lifted our spirits.

I felt like a hypocrite asking God to forgive Mom before I was able to forgive her myself. I knew I had to work on my own forgiveness. This is where my religious beliefs helped me find some consolation. Muslims don't see death as the end of life. It's the end of the physical body and a transition to eternal life. Crying and sadness are acceptable ways of mourning, but as a child, I remember my family preferred solitude and prayer when grieving for our grandpa Namik. My grandma often talked about the brevity of life. "We're here in this moment but could just as easily be gone in the next."

I remember Grandma praying for Grandpa's soul every night. She taught me different prayers in Arabic when we were in mourning. Having lost Grandpa Namik on my birthday, I always considered him my guardian angel, so it seemed fitting to mourn my mom in the same way we mourned him.

As a result, I began praying for Mom's soul. I wasn't very religious, in the sense of wearing a hijab and going to Mosque five times a day, but I looked up prayers online, and prayed for an hour in the morning before work and an hour at night before sleep. I discovered Qur'an recitations online, and when I was at work or tending to my children and unable to pray, I played Qur'an recitations for Mom's soul. It served a dual purpose, as listening to it also felt cleansing and soothed my soul. When the recitations stopped playing, I rushed to restart them.

I gave myself up to the mercy of God to help me and my children heal. In those days, I felt as if I had been run over by a tanker in the middle of the ocean and was drowning, alone, with two very young kids and no family to lean on for support. My physical body was on autopilot, going through the motions, my brain numb from shock. God and my children were all I had.

+

Before Ami and I grew apart, the first year was a haze, but we stuck together— Ami, Hamza, our kids and me—all through the funeral, coming back home to the states, facing life without Mom, and our very first Mother's Day without our matriarch, two months after the funeral.

I was prepared for Mother's Day to be emotionally charged and took it upon myself to be strong for the whole family. Mom would have wanted us to be happy. I woke up early and got myself, Amaya, and Ace dressed nicely, like we had done for Mom. We hopped in the car and drove to Ami's house, stopping by a nearby grocery store to pick up a bouquet of flowers for Ami.

We rang the doorbell only to find her in tears, which made me and the kids sad, too. In the first several months after Mom passed, one person's sadness rippled through the rest of the family; it didn't take much for all of us to cry. With loving hugs, a little bit of makeup, and a lot of cheering up, we managed to cover up the puffiness in our eyes and go out for lunch.

Looking back at the pictures of that day, my sad, tired, dark, and hollow eyes tell a tale of their own, even though my lips were smiling. Some people go to great lengths to hide their pain from the outside world. I know I did because I didn't want others to pity me, but our eyes are the windows to our souls, and they never deceive. Those who are genuinely happy have a twinkle in their eyes. The eyes of those experiencing deep sadness are dull, lifeless. The Gospel of Matthew puts it this way: "The eye is the lamp of the body. If your vision is clear, your whole body will be full of light. But if your vision is poor, your whole body will be full of darkness. If then the light within you is darkness, how great is that darkness!" (Matthew, 6:22)

Only those who were intimately familiar with my sadness, like my family and Jasmina, Annie, and Mary-Anne, could tell how I really felt inside, while most of the time I hid it even from myself, afraid to admit it, afraid of being sad, of feeling depressed, afraid of allowing that sadness to consume me so deeply it might tempt me to follow my mother's path. Children who lose a parent to suicide are more likely to die by the same means—that scared me. For the sake of my own kids, I knew I only had one option—to overcome.

For me to stay strong, I had to find healthy ways of coping. Seeing a therapist seemed like the most obvious approach, but I had grown up in a family whose philosophy was that only those who are crazy see a therapist. I, on the other hand, believe it's crazy not to seek help in therapy because it enables us to process our emotions and equips us with tools to do so in healthy ways. My time in anger management helped me. I chose to ignore the family stigma—in fact, I thought why do I even have to tell anyone, it's my life? Then I made an appointment to see a psychologist. I had reached out through my company's Employee Assistance Program for a referral, but most programs only offer a few sessions. Later, I found out counseling services were covered by my health insurance.

I shared with the therapist my fears of becoming depressed and ask what warning signs to look for.

"The fact that you're sitting here and talking to me about all this means you're doing what you're supposed to," he said. "Your mother never asked for help. There's depression and then there's what we psychologists call 'masked depression' when someone goes to great lengths to hide their depression because they either don't want to be a burden or don't want to leave themselves vulnerable and exposed. You're here; you're talking to me. That's a lot more than your mom ever did."

His words offered me some reassurance. "My mom was my biggest supporter over the years," I told him. "I feel like she was my foundation. I built my house—my whole life—on that foundation, which makes me feel like someone's just taken a sledgehammer to the foundation and the whole house is about to crumble."

"Why would the house crumble?" he asked. "Your mom may have been a strong support system, but you're the one who built the house! I mean, you drove yourself here today. You're the one who worked hard to build your career and make enough money to buy the house. You went to school. Your mom didn't go to college for you. You did! You built the house. You built that house all by yourself dear, including the foundation."

Hearing this gave me hope that even with Mom gone, my kids and I were eventually going to be okay. He gave me literature to read on grief and healthy coping. Having someone validate that what I was feeling was a normal response to loss helped ease my mind. Grief is awful. It never really goes away, but therapy eventually helped me accept that that pain was an integral part of me, something I could learn to live with. Grief and I had to learn to co-exist.

✦

In those initial months, I measured success in baby steps and learned to take each day in stride. The first couple of birthdays and holidays without Mom were very, very difficult, threatening to send us all back into the depths of grief. I dreaded those events days in advance, torn by two opposing forces. On one hand, I just wanted to collapse in grief on my bed with the door shut and cry myself out; on the other, I knew Mom would never want us to spend all our time in sadness. She knew my children needed me to be a healthy functioning parent. On those days, I tried hard to feel happy and excited. When I couldn't, I acted as if I were, feeling guilty the whole time, caught between the living and the dead.

I was operating on two different planes—as a responsible adult with two dependents, bills to pay, a household to run, and a career to maintain, and as a grieving child who just wanted to crawl under a blanket and cry, scream, and kick pillows. There were days when I'd put my big girl pants on by day and act like an adult, but then by night, when no one was watching, I'd curl into a fetal position and cry like a baby.

For a brief time, my doctor prescribed anti-anxiety medication to take the edge off. While that did help temporarily to calm the shock and subdue some of the emotional pain, it didn't change how I felt inside. It merely evened out my racing heart and slowed my brain enough to function. I still had to deal with all the emotions after the medicine wore off. I realized early on that medication was not a good long-term solution for me.

My therapist recommended a support group, but they seemed far and few between in our area until an accidental Facebook search for "surviving a loved one's suicide" revealed a whole community of people who might understand. The Survivors of Loved Ones to Suicide (SOLOS) group had members from all over the world united by our unique grief. The group had been founded by an amazing woman named Jennifer, who had lost her mom to suicide in 1998.

I read the members' stories and discovered a place where people were able to share and openly talk about their losses without stigma or judgment, only love, compassion, and understanding. From this group I received the support and kindness of complete strangers who were going through the same pain I was. My heart wept for each and every one of them, and they for me. We uplifted each other.

In the SOLOS group, I found people I could relate to. After years of struggling to cope with her own loss, Jennifer had made it her life's mission to help others know they are not alone. It was heartbreaking to read her story and the stories of the other members, more than 25,000 from all over the world. It was also eye-opening to learn just how little support is available to people grieving suicide loss. This was the group I first shared my mom's story with, hoping that by telling her story, it would help me overcome the loss while helping other survivors feel a little less alone. Being able to share my mom's story gave me the idea to write this book. If I can ease the pain of one person who has experienced the suicide of a family member or encourage one person who is experiencing depression to seek help, then reliving my painful experience by writing it down will have been worth it.

+

During those first months after my mother's passing, many things were happening at the same time, and other things helped me get through each day. Not only was I turning back to God after my brief quarrel with Him, but I was reconnecting with nature as another form of worship. I sought peace wherever I could find it, whether that was on a walk in the Arizona desert or attending a religious service in a house of worship. I wasn't choosy about which religious establishments I prayed in. When I felt down, if I happened to be near a Catholic chapel, I said my Muslim prayers inside that chapel. I truly believe that "We are all One."

On a particularly difficult weekend for all of us, I took my kids on a day-trip to the small town of Sedona, north of Phoenix. Friends at work frequently talked about Sedona's beautiful red rock formations, its vibrant hiking trails, and its art community, as well as the town's unique energy. We had never been there, and we needed a pleasant distraction.

Our two-and-a-half-hour road trip to Sedona offered some much-needed music therapy. The kids goofed off and rocked out in the car, making me laugh the whole way there. Once we arrived, the sights of Sedona made me stand in awe as the white puffy clouds stood in stark contrast against the blue skies, which melted into red rock formations that then further melted into vibrant greenery covering the ground.

One of the local artists told me about Sedona's vortexes. People there, and the world over, believed these vortexes to be swirling centers of energy that offer healing and enlightenment. Further, the land is considered sacred by Native American tribes of the Southwest, such as the Hopi. Visitors from all over the world come to Sedona to experience its uplifting energy, to meditate, practice yoga, and perform other rituals.

Spending just a few hours at this mystical place rejuvenated us, uplifted our spirits, and recharged our batteries. We had discovered our own little oasis in the desert that we could visit every time we felt down. As I drove around, soaking in the magnificent scenery, we stumbled on a cute little chapel, The Chapel of the Holy Cross, nestled between two red rocks.

Always ready for an adventure, I parked in the nearby lot and asked Amaya and Ace to walk up the road with me to check it out. At the entrance to the courtyard, the sound of trickling water from a nearby fountain caught my attention. When I looked more closely in the flowerbed where it sat, I saw a statue of an angel tucked within the flowers. It was holding a plaque inscribed with the words, "And He shall give his angels charge over you to keep you in all ways."

I needed to see that—a reaffirmation of a higher power looking over us, a reassurance that my children and I would be okay. It was a gift to us that day. In thanks, we prayed in the tiny chapel. It was calming and peaceful, and we fondly looked forward to our next visit.

✦

I needed moments like those in Sedona of solace and peace as a reminder to stay brave, that I wasn't alone, that I could draw strength from unexpected sources. And I would need all the strength I could muster. Life wasn't finished throwing challenges my way.

After the divorce, Filip had never gotten around to refinancing the house he was awarded. Not surprisingly, it was still in my name. About three months after burying Mom and completely out of the blue, I received a letter from the bank holding my mortgage on that house. The letter informed me that I had defaulted on the loan and the house was going into foreclosure. As our children and I grieved my mother's death, Filip had stopped paying the mortgage on the house in Georgia. Then he vacated it in secrecy. Ever the vindictive ex, he hadn't even bothered to give me a heads up.

After staring at the letter in denial for what seemed like several hours, saying no, no, no, not again, not another thing to deal with, over and over in my head, at the end of the day, I had two options. I could sit there and feel sorry for myself, or I could try to do something about it. I phoned Gordon, my realtor in Georgia, to see if he could help me list the house to stave off foreclosure.

After I explained what had happened, Gordon was almost as shocked as I was, but then he got down to business. "I'm so sorry you have to deal with that. Here's what I'm thinking. If the title is still in your name, you have every right to put it up for sale. Let me see what I can do about that foreclosure notice, kiddo!"

"I don't even have the keys to the house, Gordon," I replied in desperation. "His parents live next door. Maybe you can knock on their door and ask them for the key?"

"I'll go over there tomorrow morning and will call you with an update. Don't worry. We'll figure something out."

Gordon called me early the next day with news. "The house is vacant and locked. I went next door to Filip's parents' place. They said they didn't have the key. I could try to break in."

"Can you do that? Is that even legal?"

"Of course, I can, with your permission. I'll put a new lock on it too. Your ex-husband is a real piece of work, you know that?"

"Tell me about it."

He called me back after he did a walk through. "It's not in very good shape. They left it pretty dirty. I'll take some pictures and send them to you. I don't know how much we can get for it at this point, but it's better than having a foreclosure against your credit."

"I agree. Anything you can do. I really appreciate it."

To sell it quickly, we decided to list the house for a third of what was still owed on the mortgage. Filip had left the place in such bad shape that even with the low price, several offers fell through. After working hard to secure one sale that fell through, a disappointed Gordon forwarded me the email with the note: "Good news and bad. The bad news is we have to terminate the contract. The good news is that I got the mama kitty and five babies out of the basement."

Filip and Jezika had been in such a rush to vacate the house, they left their cat behind, and it ended up having kittens in the basement. It wasn't just me cleaning up the mess Filip left behind—now the realtors were dragged into his mess as well. Maybe the renewed anger I felt towards Filip helped me feel a little less angry at Mom. Gordon and I kept at it. The kittens were adopted and the house sold—severing the last of the material threads tying me to Filip.

This was the first summer after I lost Mom. Amaya and Ace were going to Filip's for Father's Day and a few weeks afterward, but one day he called me and said, "Why don't you keep the kids with you this summer? I just can't take them right now." Then he hung up.

I knew last-minute summertime daycare would break the bank, but Filip's actions only fueled my motivation to be a better parent, even if it meant we had to live on mac-and-cheese for the summer.

I didn't want Amaya and Ace to be sad on Father's Day. A few days before, I bought an oversized pair of glasses from a party store, along with a pink mustache, and when they woke up on Father's Day morning, I invited them to the backyard. I put on the dad gear, and when they came outside, I shouted, "Surprise. Happy Father's Day kiddos! Today, I'm your mom and dad! I grew out this special pink mustache to prove it! Arghhh!" I clenched my fists in the air, showing off non-existent biceps as we chased each other around the backyard.

When we stopped, Ace giggled. "Mommy! You look funny!"

"Where did you get those big glasses, Mommy?" Amaya said, jumping in to hug me with a big grin on her face.

"What do you think? Do I look cool?" I picked her up as I hugged her back.

"You are so cool, Mommy! Can I see your glasses?"

"Oh no, these are mine. I have a pair for you and another one for Ace. We're all wearing glasses today."

"No way! Let me see." They both beamed with excitement as I gave each of them their own pair of oversized glasses. We went on to have a fun-filled Father's Day.

The simplest things made us happy. That day, we visited a tropical bird store where we picked out a beautiful baby plum-headed parakeet. We brought him back home and named him Coco, like the budgie parakeet I had as a child. Several months later, we got a parrot, an African Grey named Zumra, who quickly learned how to talk, bringing back happy memories from my childhood when Coco performed tricks for my friends.

After Mom's passing, my goal was to simply get by from one minute to another; then from one day to the next, one week to the next, one month to the next. One baby step at a time. There was a lot of falling, followed by a lot of getting back up on our feet. Through it all, my children's smiles kept me going.

That first summer went by quickly. The kids and I explored places around Phoenix, went camping, fishing, and mini-golfing, and visited Jasmina and her family in California. When summer break ended, we did our back-to-school shopping. Financially, I don't know how we made ends meet that summer with the unexpected daycare expense, but we survived—sometimes on $20 for two weeks. But I had my kids with me, and they made me laugh. They made everything better. They were the future I was living for.

CHAPTER 20

THE MANY ROADS TO HEALING

There wasn't one thing in itself that helped us on our healing journey, but rather, a series of conscious steps, similar to hiking a treacherous trail without giving up, putting one step in front of the other.

While over the years I had come to terms with what happened and perhaps even accepted it, one thing I hadn't been able to find on any of the roads we travelled was how to forgive myself for not seeing the signs and not being able to save Mom. Why couldn't I have seen them earlier? Why did I only recognize them later, after she was gone? The truth was our family knew absolutely nothing about suicide and its warning signs. Even after it was obvious Mom had made an attempt on her life, we were still in denial. We didn't think she would try it again. Why would she? She loved us.

But even in denial, in our own way, we did everything in our power to try to save her. It was Mom who gave up fighting, who refused help from us and the professionals who knew better. It was that profound realization that neither I, nor anyone else, had the power to fix her pain if she wasn't willing to help herself that helped bring about the self-forgiveness I so desperately sought.

This self-forgiveness came rather unexpectedly, and I can recall the exact moment it arrived about three years after my mother passed. Before I could forgive myself, I was constantly running from my own thoughts and feelings, travelling to distant places as a means of distraction. I was taking another trip to Hawaii, this time with Ace and Amaya, at the end of their school year. All three of us were ready for a well-deserved break. Of course, as tradition called for, we stayed at the old Outrigger Reef on the Beach.

Our trip was fun. Besides swimming in warm turquoise waters of the Pacific Ocean and chasing each other on the soft sands of the Waikiki beaches, we explored the rest of the island. At the Polynesian Cultural Center, we learned about the culture of the Pacific Islanders, received our first tribal war paint, got a taste of exotic purple bread rolls freshly made from taro root, watched in awe as a man scaled a palm tree, and saw women weave baskets with palm leaves.

At Nu'uanu Pali lookout point, just north of Honolulu, we admired the magnificent views of the windward side of the beautiful island of Oahu. Amaya and I took pictures while wind twirled our hair into an upward spiral. Ace watched, and all three of us laughed until our bellies hurt. On the way back to the hotel, we met a cab driver who grew up in Samoa and spoke a few words of Bosnian to us. We were delighted at his surprising skill.

At the Dole plantation, we learned that pineapples did not grow on trees, but instead, on the ground from a bush. Then we tried pineapple and coconut ice cream. From there, we took a short drive to Waimea Falls Park where a free-roaming peacock stole a cheeseburger from us.

There, we strolled through the magnificent foliage in this enchanted park. Vines, densely wrapped around thousand-year-old trees, allowed just enough sunlight for exotic flowers to thrive. The garden smelled like a slice of heaven. Bright red cardinals followed us everywhere as our eyes soaked in the fairy-tale scenery. Many cultures believe that seeing a red cardinal represents the spirit of our loved ones who passed away, and we felt a deep connection to Mom throughout our trip.

After an amazing week in Hawaii reminiscing with funny stories about Mom and all the fun we had had in Hawaii as a family over the years, we decided to spend our last day hiking the Diamond Head trail where Mom had hiked by herself when I was pregnant with Amaya. I couldn't hike to the top then, but I was determined to do it this time in honor of Mom.

We left the hotel early to avoid the midday heat and took a short stroll through the park toward the trail. We left the paved road and set out on the exhausting forty-five minute hike up the treacherous crater. I reminded Amaya and Ace to drink water to stay hydrated. Halfway to the top, I second-guessed our decision, but we pushed on, climbing the slippery rocks, all while thinking about Mom and how proud she would be of us.

After reaching the platform near the top, where we rested for a few minutes, Amaya and Ace were just about ready to quit. We still had two lengthy sets of stairs to climb, one with ninety-nine steps and another with seventy-six. I didn't dare tell the kids about them. I just told them we were near the end. Huffing and puffing, we mustered up enough strength to climb the stairs and brave the 220-foot dimly lit tunnel before we finally reached the top of Diamond Head, rosy-cheeked and out of breath.

The three of us stood awestruck, admiring the far-reaching views of the Pacific Ocean with its shallow turquoise waters merging into the dark blue of the deeper water, its foamy waves crashing onto rocky shores.

As I stretched my arms in the air, feeling the warm sun on my skin and the gentle tropical breeze on my fingers, I looked up toward the blue sky lined with white puffy clouds. I was grateful we hadn't given up, that we had made it to the top. I thought of Mom. Mom was a force to be reckoned with, and when she said she was going to hike that trail, nothing was going to stop her until she got to the top. Which she did, returning with a vivid description of all she had seen.

Standing where Mom had stood, seeing what Mom had seen, I felt the deep connection I had had with her before she died. I finally felt what I had only thought before. When the will to fight left Mom, there was nothing any of us could have done to make her stay. I couldn't blame her. I couldn't blame anyone else. I saw it clearly that day and, more important, I felt it deeply. Saying a prayer for my mother, I was finally able to forgive her.

As I prayed for Mom on top of Diamond Head, I also thanked God for guiding me, my daughter, and my son through these hard times. I thanked God for blessing me with my children, my devoted friends, good health, and everything else that helped get us through. I said goodbye to bitterness, embraced forgiveness, and made a conscious choice to wholeheartedly welcome happiness back into my life. It's how Mom would have wanted it. At that moment, a burden was lifted from my shoulders.

We returned to Phoenix renewed in spirit, ready to be happy again.

✦

The idea of being happy again forced me to confront the painful reminders of Mom back home. For several years after she passed away, I had given up coloring my hair because that was something she and I had always done together. Mom had started coloring my hair blonde when I finished eighth grade. Since then I had never had it professionally colored. Mom had always done it for me, and she did an amazing job. After she applied the coloring, she would sit impatiently while I rinsed my hair, waiting to ask, "How is it? Do you like it?" as if it was the first time.

It was part of the ritual that I ran out of the shower, squealing with joy, "Oh my God, Mom, I love it!"

Her whole face would light up like a Christmas tree with happiness and relief that she had done a good job.

After we moved to Arizona, I couldn't find a stylist to cut my hair to my liking. I asked Mom to hold up a mirror behind my back while I cut and styled it myself.

Mom didn't trust anyone with her hair either. I was the only one allowed to cut and style it. The way she boasted about her haircuts to her friends, everyone thought I had professional training, but I did not. I just had a knack for it. She would stand in front of the mirror admiring her haircuts and say, "No one does it as good as you."

After she passed away, I gave up on my hair because it was what I missed most about our time together. I stopped coloring my hair blonde and let it grow out. Friends commented on how the new hairstyle made me look older, but in reality, it was my life experiences that aged me.

When we returned home from Hawaii, Amaya surprised me when she asked to color her hair black. This brought back memories of me and Mom, and I happily dusted off my old hair brushes and the coloring kit. Just as

Mom colored my hair for the first time when I was Amaya's age, that day I colored my daughter's hair. I knew Mom was smiling down on us for keeping the tradition alive.

I was also inspired to deal with my own hair. Amaya stepped in for Mom, holding a mirror to reflect the back of my head while I stood in front of another mirror. I cut my hair short; then colored it blonde. Three years after Mom had passed away, I began feeling like my old self again.

✦

Getting back to feeling good felt good, and I wanted to do more, to go the extra mile and purge everything that caused anxiety and reminded us of our grief. I wondered whether our house, where I had once envisioned our happy family celebrating holidays and birthdays forever, was plagued by the dark memories. I convinced myself we would be happier if we moved. Going back to the Bay Area, where I felt the most at home and had people I could depend on, seemed like the natural choice. I set things in motion for our move back to California.

It took a while to convince my employer to approve a transfer to our Bay Area office, but they eventually agreed. By Thanksgiving, I signed a one-year lease for a three-bedroom townhouse in Santa Clara and began looking at schools for Amaya and Ace. I even had a date set for the move, December 22, 2016—a few days after the kids left to visit their dad in Georgia for three weeks. This time alone would give me a chance to pack up the house, have the movers transfer our stuff to the new place, and unpack in time for kids to return to their new home in Santa Clara to start the spring term at school. My good friend Jasmina still lived there, and she couldn't have been happier.

The new place was smaller, so I needed to get rid of some of our furniture. The black leather couch and the area rug, which triggered many unhappy memories of Mom, were the first to go. Mom's bedroom furniture was next. I listed the stuff for free, as long as the "buyer" also hauled it away. I think I had been hanging on to these things to punish myself for not being able to save Mom. Once those painful reminders of the past were gone, our home felt lighter, and I could breathe easier.

On December 17, hours after I dropped Amaya and Ace off at the airport, I packed us up. After my last night at home, it felt as if I had barely closed my eyes when four chiseled men from the moving company rang my doorbell at five in the morning ready to load the truck.

Still not fully awake, I brewed some coffee and pointed the men to the kids' rooms first, trying to stay out of the way. Like a small army of ants, they began wrapping furniture into protective blankets, loading boxes onto dollies, and carrying things into the truck. They worked hard for several hours with no breaks until around ten when they carried the last of the things out of the house.

We planned to meet at the new place at noon the following day. Exhausted, I stayed behind to clean up and get the house ready to sell. It was 7:00 p.m. by the time I finished vacuuming, scrubbed the kitchen and bathrooms clean, steam cleaned the tile in the family room downstairs, and showered. By then, I was ready to go to sleep. Instead, I loaded the pets into my minivan and embarked on the twelve-hour road trip to Santa Clara.

I drove through the night, chugging coffee and looking forward to seeing Jasmina and her family. As I grew close to her house, I pulled over and dialed her number to tell her I would be stopping by. We both squealed with joy. When I pulled up to her house, she ran out the door to greet me. "Ahh! I can't believe you're here! How are you feeling? Are you tired? Come on in, I made you some breakfast!" Her words came at me a mile a minute.

"I'm good! Tired from all the packing and I left really late last night, but wow! I can't believe I'm here! Yay!" We hugged like we hadn't seen each other in years.

"Can you stay for a while? What's the plan for today? When are the movers getting here with your stuff?"

"I actually can't stay long. I have to get up there before noon to get the keys from my landlord and wait for the guys to arrive. But I wanted to see you, at least for a few minutes."

"I'm so glad you're here!" Jasmina hugged me.

"We'll be seeing a lot more of each other now, that's for sure!" I hugged her back.

After that brief rest stop at Jasmina's house, I made the remaining thirty-minute drive to Santa Clara where I took possession of the keys to the new townhouse we would call home and waited for the movers. They arrived as promised by noon, then unloaded everything just as quickly as they loaded it in Arizona. By 5:00 p.m., the last of my stuff was out of the truck and in the townhouse, where I could get to work.

I unpacked the kitchen, set up the Internet, cable and TV, and prepared the kids' bedrooms ready for their arrival. I was brimming with energy, running from one room to another to ensure our new home was perfect when the kids came back to me. I even prepared a little scavenger hunt for them to make their first day in our new home fun.

On Christmas Eve, Jasmina and Hari came over with their kids and Aunt Divna, a bottle of champagne in hand. Hari helped start the fireplace. We cozied up around the fire, talking well into the night and listening to the soothing sounds of the crackling fire. I was excited about starting this new chapter in my life.

When Ace and Amaya joined me several days later, they were thrilled with our new place. "Mommy, I can't believe we're living in California!" Ace chirped.

Amaya joined in from the kitchen. "Finally! This is going to be so much fun, Mommy!"

My heart finally felt content after a grueling couple of years. A new start was just what we needed, but the joy was short-lived.

✦

On her second day at her new school, while waiting in the lunch line, Amaya accidentally backed into one of the mean girls and stepped on her white sneakers. The girl shoved Amaya in the back, then screamed at her, "Are you dumb? These are $200 Nikes. What's wrong with you?"

Amaya tried to apologize, but the girl was having none of it.

"I'm gonna mess you up. Like you messed up my new shoes."

From that point on, school became close to unbearable for my sweet-hearted, nonconfrontational Amaya. Our morning drop-offs became an ordeal. With a line of cars honking behind me and the principal waving at us to hurry up, Amaya sobbed in the car while I tried to convince her that she needed to go to school.

We tried talking with the principal, but that didn't seem to help matters. Amaya's tormentor was already known for her aggressive outbursts, and the administration said they were doing the best they could. Jasmina and I tried to talk some courage into Amaya by telling her she was taller than the bully and could defend herself if attacked. That didn't help either. Amaya is a lover, not a fighter. After all we had been through, it was hard to watch my daughter go through the pain of bullying.

There were other challenges to deal with as well. We had left a life of comfort in Arizona where the cost of living was reasonable and every-thing we needed—work, schools, doctors, dentists, grocery and department stores—was within a three-mile radius. In Arizona, Ace walked to school; Amaya's bus picked her up and dropped her off by our front door.

California did not have the same kind of school bus system, and I had to take on the additional task of chauffeuring the kids to school. Mornings were easy enough, as I could drop them off on the way to work, but pick-ups in the afternoon were a challenge because they landed in the middle of the workday.

In addition, the townhouse was too small for the birds, who chattered and called out loudly throughout the day. I was constantly worried that our neighbors would complain to the landlord. As far as the landlord knew, we only had one small dog. The move was supposed to make our lives easier, not harder.

After days of trying to make our move to California work, in a moment of desperation while listening to Amaya cry about yet another encounter with the bully at school, I asked them, "What do you want me to do guys? Do you want to go back to Arizona?"

"Yeeees!" They both cried out, without hesitation.

"You do?" I was surprised. I reasoned with them, as if they were adults. "But I put the house on the market. We moved our stuff here. I told our landlord we'll stay here for a year."

"We just want to go home, Mom." They both came up and hugged me, crying.

"Let's just give it a little more time, please? You know Mommy won't stay here if you two are not happy. If you're not happy, I'm not happy. Simple as that, so please give me some time to figure something out."

Moving back to California was clearly a mistake. I wasn't sure what to do, having signed a year-long lease. Within days, I was on the phone with my dad in Bosnia in tears. "I think I made a mistake coming out here, Dad. I'm not sure what to do. The kids just want to go back home to Arizona."

"Everyone makes mistakes, kiddo," he soothed. "Calm down. You'll figure it out. If you decide to go back, I can fly out and help you move. That way, at least you don't have to pay for movers again. Can you call the realtor and find out if they can remove the listing?"

"I'll call them, but I feel bad about you coming all the way out here."

"I can't make this decision for you, but make sure you weigh all your options first. I'll support you in whatever you decide." Talking to Dad always made me feel better.

My next phone call was to the realtor. Since I had no active offers on the house, the only thing for me to do was sign a contract terminating the realtor's rights to represent me as an agent, and they would remove my house from the listing without penalties or added fees. I had the document emailed to me, signed, and sent back within ten minutes, assured that if we did end up going back, we'd at least have the same house to go back to.

My next call was to Jasmina, who I knew would be disappointed, but would support me either way. After having spent an hour on the phone discussing all options, weighing pros and cons, we agreed it was best for me and my children to move back to Arizona, provided my landlord agreed to let me break the lease, and my boss that I could transfer back to Arizona. I felt like a failure, but it was important to recognize the mistake and correct it as soon as possible.

During the Martin Luther King holiday weekend, the kids and I visited Phoenix for a few days, which only strengthened our resolve to return.

After consulting with Dad and friends, we all agreed that reversing course was our best option. Talking to my boss about going back to Tempe was easy. They liked me there. The landlord took some convincing, but after he heard me plead my case, he let me out of the lease. By the end of January, Dad had flown out to California. I reserved a moving truck, and we packed up our house again. While those forty days living in the Bay Area had felt like swimming upstream, moving back to Arizona seemed effortless. The kids were elated, and I had Dad and Jasmina to help.

And just like that, we headed home. Ace and Amaya were so excited they couldn't sleep. When we pulled up to the house in the middle of the night, they both ran inside yelling, "Yay! We're back home! We're back home!" Their voices echoed in the empty house.

"Guys, please be quiet, it's 3:00 a.m. You'll wake up half the neighborhood."

"This is our house, Mommy! We don't have to be quiet like California," Ace yelled.

Amaya ran upstairs to her room, calling back to us. "Yeah, Ace, yell all you want. We're home!"

Seeing joy return to my children's faces was all the validation I needed. This was their house. This was where they felt at home.

Was I taking the easy way out, running away when things got a little hard? I didn't think so. This was our home, and it was good to be back. We had tried a new adventure, and it hadn't worked out the way we thought it would. We acknowledged that, then did something about it. We were proactive.

After we resettled, the house felt different, as if when we emptied it out, we had discharged its negative energy. We returned with a renewed sense of gratitude. The black leather couch and the area rug were gone, as was Mom's furniture. It wasn't that we were trying to forget her. We still had pictures of her around the house and other reminders, but there was no more heaviness, nothing to pull me back into dark places. There was just our house, the home to me and my children, the home I had decorated with my own hands, the home where my children and I had created many happy memories, the home we had to leave before we could find our way back.

CHAPTER 21

BACK TO BOSNIA: WE WENT, WE SAW, WE LOVED

After Dad went back to Bosnia, the kids and I spent the next year going on weekend road trips together. Only now, I was no longer running. We were simply exploring the beauty of Arizona. We saw the majestic Grand Canyon where we learned about the power of water carving out the great canyon. We walked the trails in awe of its incredible beauty. In Tucson, we visited the Kartchner Caverns and explored the caves. We witnessed a jaw-dropping stalactite column over a 1,000 years old and standing fifty-eight feet, called Kubla Khan, named after a famous poem. On the Mogollon Rim, we rented paddle and electric trolling motor boats at Woods Canyon Lake. We picnicked on the water, took pictures of the American eagle perched on top of a tall pine tree, and soaked in warm sun. We returned to Sedona where we recharged our batteries, hiked the enchanting red-dirt trails, and admired the saguaro cactus blossoms.

While immersing ourselves in Arizona culture, rich with Native American influences, I learned about the rituals of alternative healing, smudging, crystals and stones, and the importance of balance in life. All of this helped me to not only learn to let go of the past and forgive everyone, including Filip, but also to continue to find positive energy in everyday activities.

Walking through the vendor booths one weekend at a Sedona crafts fair, I saw a handcrafted silver bracelet with three large turquoise stones. As I picked it up, the wise old silversmith explained the story behind it. "In the

Native American culture, turquoise is a stone of protection and healing. It absorbs negative energy and embodies power, bringing good fortune to the wearer. We consider it more precious than gold."

"How much is it?" I asked, holding the bracelet in my hand.

"$950," he replied.

"Well, I can't afford that, but it's beautiful!" I set the bracelet back on the table.

"It would look good on you. I'm sure it will come to you someday. What's meant for you always finds its way to you." He smiled knowingly.

A few tables over, another silversmith sold rings. I was immediately drawn to two. One had three butterflies connected together by their heart-shaped wings. They reminded me of my children and me fluttering around the world together like butterflies. I tried the ring on. It fit perfectly. The second had two hands, each holding a heart, with a crown on top of the heart. As I tried that ring on my right-hand index finger, an old man with silver hair sitting behind the table began speaking in a heavy Irish accent. "With these hands I hold your heart, and I crown you with my love."

"Pardon me?" I said, not knowing whether I should be offended.

"It's an old Irish saying. The ring you're holding is called a Claddagh ring."

"I'm sorry. I don't know what that means."

"Are you single or married?" he asked politely.

"Single, why?"

"Then you're wearing it correctly. The ring symbolizes friendship, love, and loyalty. If you wear it with the heart facing out, it shows you're single. If the heart is facing in, you're taken. You should wear it on your right hand if you're not married, on your left if you are."

"I didn't know that! I just thought they were really pretty. I'll take them both, please."

I couldn't help but call Jasmina immediately after to tell her about my peculiar experiences with the mysterious silversmiths of Sedona. By then, I had been single for nine years and missed having someone to share my life with. At the same time, meeting a man of my dreams had been the last thing on my mind during those past nine years of tragedy, struggle, and taking care of my family. Occasionally, a fleeting thought and a deep sigh served as a sad reminder of my flatlined love life. After Filip, the extensive list of things I did not want in a man was so long that the next man I fancied would have to be nearly perfect.

✦

Other areas of my life were in a state of suspended animation as well. Five years had gone by since Mom's funeral. That was the last time I had been in Bosnia. After we buried her, I vowed never to return there again, but Dad still lived overseas. My vow had no effect on him, and each time we spoke on the phone, Dad ever-so-casually made it a point to remind me of how long it had been since I last visited him.

By then, I was in a good spot, emotionally and physically. I had just begun feeling happy and acting like my old self again. I knew if I went there, I would have to visit Mom's resting place, and I wasn't sure I was ready to come face-to-face with her tombstone. I feared it would eliminate all the progress I had made toward peace of mind. But Dad requested a month-long visit in the summer. Turning him down became increasingly challenging with every conversation.

Around the same time, Dad separated from his wife in Croatia. I never particularly liked her. He moved back to Banja Luka and began dating someone I instantly clicked with over the phone. Dad's new sweetheart made him happy, and I wanted to meet her in person. Dad had even remodeled our family home. He continued to plead his case.

"I can't spend a whole month in Bosnia, Dad! I'm not ready, but I wouldn't mind visiting Europe someday," I told him.

One night over pizza I asked Amaya and Ace what they thought about a road trip through Europe. "I was thinking we would fly into Vienna, rent a car, and just drive around Europe for a week, then go to Bosnia for a week?"

"Oh, Mommy, if we go there, can we drive to Italy and see the Statue of David?"

My jaw dropped. "Wait, what? How do you know about that?"

"We learned about it in school. I really want to see it."

"You're so smart! I don't know, guys. I was just thinking out loud and don't want to make any promises."

"How cool would it be to see Italy and Austria!" Amaya chimed in enthusiastically. "Of course, we would love it, Mom."

From there, an idea was born. I began researching hotels, possible routes to take, and different sights to see. Airfare was relatively inexpensive from Los Angeles to Vienna at the start of the kids' summer break from school. We could visit Vienna for a day, drive to Italy, spend a day in Venice, another day in Florence, see the Statue of David, drive to Rome, visit the Vatican, get on a ferry boat to Croatia, and drive to Bosnia.

It seemed like a good plan to pack in as much history and culture as possible into two weeks and 3,000 miles. When I told my dad about it, he laughingly dismissed it and called me crazy. This only reinforced my desire to go. Amaya and Ace were already excited about the trip.

While making reservations, I found out we wouldn't be able to drive the rental car into Bosnia because it was still considered a hostile country. Instead, from Italy, we would return the car to Graz, Austria, have Dad pick us up there and take us to Bosnia. Dad was worried about his daughter driving around Europe for a week alone with two kids, but he reluctantly agreed to the new plan. We would leave at the end of May and return home mid-June, with our first week of hotels booked ahead of time.

A few days before we left, I ran into one of my coworkers at the office, Al. We made small talk, and I shared my plans to see as many places as I could fit into a two-week trip.

He said, "I'm jealous you're going to Vienna. I was there a few years ago with my mom and brother. We had a really good time. I'd like to go back someday."

"Really? Was it amazing? I can't wait to see it. What did you like the most there?"

"We went there at Christmas-time and the streets were decorated beautifully. I think we were at Stephansplatz square, lights and Christmas music playing everywhere. I can't remember the name of the hotel we stayed at, but we had this cake called Sacher torte. It was scrumptious. You'll have to try it. Oh, and the apple strudel," he said excitedly. Al was handsome and intellectual, though somewhat of a recluse around the office. He rarely talked to anyone, so I was pleasantly caught off guard by this conversation.

"I will, thanks! Stephansplatz is one of the places we're visiting. I'll take pictures and send them to you while you're working," I said coquettishly, though I was out of practice.

"Oh, I hate you," he said, but the smile on his face as he walked back to his desk told a different story.

I fully planned to compare notes upon my return.

✦

Our trip to Europe began with an early morning drive to Los Angeles International Airport where we boarded our flight to Warsaw, Poland, then on to Vienna. By the time we arrived, we had been travelling for over thirty hours. I had just enough energy to rent a car and drive to our hotel to check in. From there, exhausted, we went straight to bed and slept through the night.

Rejuvenated, I woke up early the next day to fresh Vienna air and sounds of classical music from a nearby coffee shop. As I opened the hotel window wider to let in the morning sunlight and wake the kids, I brewed myself a cup of coffee, excited about the next few days ahead.

The first thing on the agenda was a visit to Schönbrunn Palace, a 300-year-old Baroque-style museum, which was once a summer residence to the Habsburg monarchs. The brochure I picked up informed us that the palace had over 1,400 rooms and exquisitely groomed botanical gardens.

For me and my kids, it was our first time visiting an actual palace. As we explored it during a self-guided tour, Ace, Amaya and I pondered what life must have been like for the royals who lived in those elegantly furnished rooms.

Vienna had the home of Mozart, Beethoven, and Freud, a place where cultural events take place daily. I was inspired by its charm. It made me think of Al, a man of refined tastes. I could see why he spoke so fondly of the cultured city.

As I posted pictures to social media from various places we visited in Vienna that day, a message popped up in my inbox from one of my dear friends from elementary school. "I didn't know you were in my neighborhood. Would love to see you if you have time for coffee."

"Meli, goodness! I didn't know you lived in Vienna. I would love to see you, but don't have time for coffee." For Bosnians, coffee is a couple of hours of socializing. I would have loved to spend that time with her, but we were on a tight schedule. "I have about fifteen minutes and that's only if you're nearby."

"I'm in Westbahnhof, if you know where that is?" she replied quickly.

I looked up the address and noticed Westbahnhof station was on the way. We made arrangements to meet up for a couple of minutes. Although I didn't get to grow up with my childhood friends from Bosnia, it was gratifying to realize I now had childhood friends all over the world. After reminiscing about our elementary school teacher and old classmates, we said our goodbyes, hoping another thirty years would not pass before we saw each other again.

From there, the kids and I took off on a six-hour drive through picturesque villages of Austria and past the 12,000-foot peaks of the majestic Triglav mountains. Just as the sun began to set, we descended into Mestre, Italy, the mainland part of Venice where we retired for the evening.

As we drove through the Italian countryside the next day, the sights were simply beautiful. From medieval hill towns to rolling hills, olive orchards, citrus groves and vineyards, it was no surprise Italy's landscape left many tourists breathless and eager to come back. Even the language sounded soothing, like happy songs of love. People seemed warm, generous, and kind.

When we arrived in Florence, I got my first taste of Italian traffic. Mopeds, cars, bicycles, and pedestrians all were trying to use the same narrow winding roads. Everyone was cutting everyone off just to make it through a green light. I became extra vigilant in fear of accidentally injuring someone, including ourselves.

Luckily, it didn't take long to arrive at Galleria dell' Accademia, where we would pause to see Michelangelo's famed sculpture. We arrived at the hottest part of the day only to learn we would have to wait in line for several hours. Ace and Amaya groaned in protest. Skip-the-line tours had to be booked well in advance, so that wasn't an option. With the hot Florentine sun beating down on us, the kids lobbied to skip the Statue of David and get back on the road in an air-conditioned car.

"No way guys! We've come all this way. This was your idea, Ace. You can't give up now."

"Urgh!"

They both moaned in disapproval but stayed the course. As we inched towards the entrance, the kids found entertainment watching street artists chase pigeons away from the artwork they had laid out on the street for sale. Amaya and Ace named several pigeons and shouted out cheers of encouragement to their favorite one, Mario. Even with pigeons as our main entertainment, time flew by.

Before we knew it, we were passing through a metal detector and were guided to Galleria's first room. Inside, walls were lined with masterpieces of Florentine artists. From the art room, we proceeded to the museum of Musical Instruments where Ace located a lone air-conditioning unit delivering cold air into a stuffy, humid room and glued himself to it. Amaya studied one of Stradivari's famous violas and early versions of pianos. After taking pictures of a display of stringed instruments, she joined her brother for some cold air.

From there, we entered the rotunda, where the seventeen-foot-tall statue of David stood in all its glory and seriousness, ready to face Goliath. We admired the level of detail from his curly hair, to the hollow pupils and chiseled chest, down to the visibly pronounced veins on David's arms and hands. We wondered out loud how many hours of sweat Michelangelo had to put in to create this supernatural Biblical hero and masterpiece of anatomical perfection. Seeing one of the most famous sculptures in the world was well worth the three-hour wait.

Leaving Florence filled with awe, we set off on our drive to Santa Marinella, a beachside community about forty miles northwest of Rome. We planned to stay there for three days. Exhausted from our day of waiting in line, we crashed in our beds as soon as we checked into the room, then woke up at 2:00 p.m. the following day and decided to go out for a walk.

While walking, we passed by a fresh fruit stand. The smell of locally grown, freshly picked strawberries made my mouth water instantly and brought back memories of those sweeter-than-honey juices dripping down my hand from the strawberries I remember eating as a child in Bosnia.

I pulled the kids' hands out and placed a berry in each of them. "Smell this, you guys! I bet you've never tasted strawberries like this! These will knock your socks off, they're so good." Then I realized I didn't have any Euros and would not be able to pay the fruit seller.

"Ohh, yumm! They do smell delicious. Can we get some, please?" Amaya's eyes sparkled.

"Oh, man, we still haven't exchanged money for Euros," I replied, disappointed at myself for getting their hopes up. I put the small bucket of delicious strawberries down, then took a credit card out of my wallet and showed the seller. "Do you take Visa?" I asked in English.

"No, Visa." He shook his head.

"Oh, that's too bad. Thank you anyway," I said to the man, not knowing how much he really understood. "We'll come back here another day." I signaled the kids it was time to leave.

As we walked away, the man gently tapped me on the shoulder, pointing to the grocery bag, then pointing to us, then to the fruit, while saying whole sentences in Italian, none of which I understood. He finished the last sentence with an arm roll and saying "tomorrow" in English. I guess he was trying to say, "Take what you want and pay me tomorrow," but I couldn't be sure.

That's something Dad would have done, too, for a stranger. It made me smile, and eager to see him.

While I loved the gesture, I felt bad not being able to explain that we were going to Rome the next day and wouldn't be there tomorrow. I didn't want to just take the fruit without paying. We hand-gestured for a while, unable to communicate, after which he proceeded to place a small bucket of strawberries and cherries into a plastic bag and put it in my hand. I then put a $5 bill in his hand.

We walked away but turned back to take a picture of him. He flashed the warmest, most heartfelt, genuine smile. It was a simple exchange but served as a reminder that kindness transcends all barriers and knows no boundaries.

The fruit we got from him was so sweet and juicy, it dripped through the bag on the way back to our room. We ate the strawberries, then retired for the evening.

✦

Having learned a valuable lesson in Florence, I spent a few extra dollars to purchase the skip-the-line tours of Vatican City and the Coliseum. The English-speaking tour guide, Luigi, introduced himself to the tour group. We were to see the Vatican Museums, the Sistine Chapel, and St. Peter's Basilica.

Luigi had a doctorate in art, and he talked for three hours nonstop, sharing stories about the Vatacombs (the Vatican catacombs, the resting place of many popes) and the intricate mosaic tiles, which told tales of rich Christian history. He pointed out some of the most renowned sculptures and art masterpieces in the world. My high-end digital camera could not even begin to capture the overwhelming beauty of one of the world's largest collections of art. The lavishness of the Vatican Museums was truly astonishing.

Before we entered the Sistine Chapel, Luigi talked at length about the nine paintings. Once inside, it felt surreal for a refugee kid from Bosnia to be standing in one of the most sacred places in the world. It also seemed fitting to say a prayer for Mom.

From there, we were guided to St. Peter's Basilica. To say my children and I were in awe of this astounding place was an understatement. We felt blessed as the afternoon rays of sun breached the high rotunda windows and lit up the monumental room in all its grandeur. Our Vatican City excursion was the highlight of the trip. Rome left a lasting impression. I promised to come back again someday and spend at least a few days exploring this extraordinary city.

Considering that Ace, Amaya, and I had, by this time, walked for over six hours and covered over ten miles (and still had to walk back to our car), we didn't have the strength to walk to the Coliseum. We decided to forego the remainder of our tour and drove back to our hotel in Santa Marinella.

The next day, we drove to the city of Pisa. There we indulged in scrumptious gnocchi and pizza while sitting under a red awning for shade as we admired the Leaning Tower of Pisa before us. Recharged and refreshed, we braved close to 300 stairs and climbed to the top of the tower, soaking in marvelous views of the city and laughing about many of the memories we had made on our trip so far.

We spent our last night in Italy in Mestre. Our plans to take a gondola ride in Venice in the morning fell through. We overslept our 6:00 a.m. alarm and had very little time left to eat breakfast, pack, and get back on the road to Graz, Austria, where Dad was expecting us. One week in Italy had not been nearly enough, but we vowed to return.

✦

Reunion with Dad at the rental-car return in Graz was joyous and sweet. We hadn't seen him since he had helped us move back to Arizona. We also met Gabriela for the first time, who kept him company on the trip. She was incredibly warm and loving and welcomed my children and me with huge hugs. We instantly connected.

It was very sweet of Dad to make the six-hour drive to Graz to pick us up, then drive six hours back home, especially since he'd have to do it all over again in a week to take us to the Vienna Airport. Dad knows no limits with his kids and grandkids, however, and he did it with a smile on his face and stories to tell.

Near the border between Croatia and Bosnia, Dad pointed to a road partially blocked off by a white metal barricade, now rusty and choked by tall grass and overgrown bushes. "This is where the refugee camp was."

"That? I'd never recognize it now."

"The tents are gone," Dad continued. "They were right behind those bushes."

I flashed back to the refugee tent overcrowded with bunk beds and people, frozen port-a-potties and little running water, sleeping under tarps so we wouldn't wake up soaked to the skin. How far we had come since then, with a lot of hard work and some grief along the way. Here we were, world travelers! I turned to my children and said, "I love you. And you are very blessed."

Amaya had just finished middle school, and Ace had just finished elementary. They were perfect ages to learn about their mother's heritage and history—and their own, really. It hadn't always been happy, given the war and the refugee camps, but it was real, part of who I had been and who I had become. And we were also going to have a lot of fun with Dad and Gabriela, of course.

CHAPTER 22

HOME IS WHERE YOU FEEL THE MOST AT HOME

An ocean and a continent away from where I now live in Phoenix, Arizona, is a big brick house with a white stucco façade. It's located in the heart of Banja Luka, Bosnia and Herzegovina, tightly squeezed into a plot of land among the surrounding houses and five-story buildings, bounded by old linden trees and narrow alleyways. Since my time there, new buildings and houses have popped up in the neighborhood. On the old playground where I used to play for hours with my sister and our cousins now stands an apartment building.

Much has changed, but the old willow trees in the street in front of the house still stand faithfully, protecting it from wind and sun, proud to have weathered many storms. The old house is four stories tall, with a red shingled roof. One could easily mistake it for an apartment building if it were just a little wider.

Inside, the house has room enough for eight bedrooms, three bathrooms, and three living rooms. Amaya and Ace call it a mansion. This is the house where my father's family has lived for generations. This is the house where my father was born, grew up, and lived in with Mom when they got married. This is the house where I was born, grew up and spent most of my childhood. This is the house that holds my memories of Grandpa Namik—his study and the smell of the old cedarwood chest where he hid his gifts for us. There's a certain scent associated with this old house, a scent I haven't been able to recreate in any of my other homes. It's the aroma of my grandmother's home cooking, the lilac baby shampoo Mom used to wash our hair, the Pino Silvestre aftershave my dad splashed on his face.

I carry this house in my heart wherever I go, but I wasn't sure I'd ever see it again. I felt blessed to be able to do so.

As I walked through the front door, I was flooded with childhood memories. The upstairs rooms reminded me of the green apple-flavored candy and heart-shaped chocolate-covered cookies my mom made for us and how Ami and I always tried to sneak some before dinner.

Gabriela made Turkish coffee because that's what we drink in Bosnia. Just as my mom used to, she scurried around the kitchen, warming up food and desserts she had prepared in anticipation of our arrival. Dad proudly gave us a tour of the house, showing off the improvement projects he had completed and the vegetable garden he had started from seed. Then, to my surprise, he retrieved a jar of my grandmother's famous rose jam from the kitchen and held it out to me. He had recreated her secret recipe from memory. I shed a tear remembering those days.

Suddenly, jovial and familiar voices echoed from the front door and throughout the house. "Are they here? Where are they?" It was the next-door neighbors, who had let themselves in without knocking, the way we entered their home as well. It's been that way for generations. We're like family. They have known me since the day I was born.

Dad yelled back cheerfully, "They're here! Come in, come in." Among friends and family, Bosnians are raucous, loud, and friendly.

When the neighbors clamored into the living room, my children and I embraced them in long hugs, swaying from side to side. It had been too long. We shared many kisses and sweet tears of joy.

The first thing they said to me was "Your kids have outgrown you!"

"I know," I said, embarrassed that we didn't come back more often. "Gabriela's making dinner. Who's hungry?"

"We already ate. We're just really happy to see you. Welcome home!" Sam shouted.

Another familiar voice called out from the front door. "Have they arrived yet?"

"We're here!" I yelled. "It's so good to be back. I feel like a rock star."

The living room was soon overflowing with friends and family. Surprised and happy, Amaya and Ace whispered in my ear, "Everyone here is so nice, Mommy."

"Everyone here is family," I replied.

+

After the reunion and some rest, Dad had several road trips of his own planned. He was excited to give Amaya and Ace a tour of Bosnia, to show off the beautiful landscapes, and teach his grandkids more about where we came from.

But before that, we had one big stop to make. We went to see Mom.

It was a somber, hour-long drive from Banja Luka to Prijedor. Dad drove, Gabriela sat in the front, with the kids and me in back. We made only one stop at a local flower shop, so Amaya, Ace, and I could pick out flowers while Dad and Gabriela waited in the car.

"Grandma loved pink," Amaya said quietly, holding lovely pink gerbera daisies.

A beautiful choice, I thought to myself. They represent innocence and happiness. Out loud I said, "Oh Amaya, those are really pretty. Grandma would love those. Ace, what did you pick?"

"Grandma loved roses," Ace replied, holding several beautiful orange roses.

"Grandma would be impressed. I love those, too. Let's get a few of those."

We also picked out white, yellow, and lavender daisies and asked the woman behind the counter to arrange them into a beautiful bouquet. From there, we drove to the cemetery, passing by Mom's family home.

"Looks like your uncle's home. Do you want to stop by and say hello?" Dad asked.

"Not a chance," I replied. "What he did was awful. Mom invested so much to fix up that house and then he takes Ami and me out of the will. No thank you. She would be heartbroken."

"Okay." Dad didn't press any further.

He drove another half block and parked the car on the side of the road from where we would walk. Nervously clutching each of my children's hands in mine, all I could say was, "It's going to be okay, guys." I could feel their sadness as thick as fog and as heavy as a dark cloud.

We entered through the cemetery gate, an all too painful memory of the day we laid Mom to rest, then followed the narrow pathway to her final resting place. And there it was—a tall white marble tombstone with Mom's name and her year of birth and death written in dark green. Compared to the last gray day we had been there, the cemetery was peaceful, the weather pleasant with blue skies and cottony white clouds, the sea of marble tombstones surrounded by lush green grass.

After Mom's body had been found, I thought about having her cremated so we could bring the ashes back to the United States. I was glad we had decided not to. Mom had picked this place for herself within walking distance of the house she grew up in and several graves away from her own mom.

Amaya, Ace, and I sat down next to her tombstone to lay down the flowers and say a prayer while Dad and Gabriela stood by. I'm sure Dad's feelings about all this were complicated, and he kept them to himself. This was about me and the kids.

As the three of us hugged and kissed the cold, white marble stone, we noticed a ladybug fluttering towards us. Mom had always loved ladybugs. She thought they brought good luck. The kids noticed it, too, and one of them called out, "Look. A ladybug from Grandma."

That made us laugh. After enjoying the ladybug's company for a few moments, Amaya pulled several neatly folded sheets of paper from her pocket. She had written a letter to her grandma pouring her heart out about how she felt about her passing, about all the things she missed about her grandma, as well as the things her grandma missed about Amaya and Ace growing up. It was heartfelt and sad and brought everyone to tears. As she read, I rubbed her back in encouragement with one hand and wiped away Ace's tears with the other. I felt a gentle tap on my shoulder. Dressed in white and quietly standing above us, Gabriela was holding out three tissues in a motherly fashion. This is exactly what Mom would have done. Mom would love her kindness, I thought to myself. I knew I did. I felt a growing love and respect for her.

I couldn't say that I felt that way about any of the other women Dad was with after my mom. Gabriela even resembled Mom with her short, burgundy hair and warm, affectionate ways. I knew she could never replace what we had lost with Mom, but she was a good person in her own right. I was happy she was in Dad's life, as well as in my own and the kids'.

Facing our grief that day, surrounded by love and family, was cathartic for me and the children. Running from our trauma, masking and avoiding it, had not worked for us. I was happy Dad insisted that we visited him. We needed the closure with Mom and the assurance of Dad's ongoing love.

✦

We spent the rest of our days in Bosnia exploring its beauty and teaching the children its culture and heritage. The day after we saw Mom, we set off on a picturesque, thirty-minute drive alongside steep canyon ledges of the Vrbas River. Some fifteen miles southeast of Banja Luka lies a fairy-tale like town named Krupa. It's a hidden gem known only to locals who visit Krupa to escape the stresses of everyday life and bask in the beauty of nature. We parked the car and followed a short trail off the paved road.

We passed through a narrow passageway between two large boulders into a magical land. Lined by rich, deep green grass, shaded with the bough of the trees, and bejeweled with wildflowers, the Krupa River cascaded down a riverbed of rocks. Butterflies and dragonflies swarmed the banks seeming to play in the crystal clear waters whose cool spray we felt on our faces. We stopped to take pictures and appreciate all we saw.

Several large boulders sat in the midst of the cascading waters, draped in peat moss, a beautiful contrast to the foaming waters surrounding them. An old worn-out wooden bridge connected the two sides of the river. About a half dozen wooden mills, topped by rusty old tin-roofs, were situated along the river. For decades, these mills had been using the power of the river to turn the waterwheels that turned the millstones. Over the last 100 years, they have grown one with nature, with grass and peat moss growing through the cracks in the wood. Many of the mills were not only operational, they produced the premium flour used by local bakers to craft some of the world's best pastries. Dad bought a bag of flour from one of the mills, while Amaya, Ace, and I trailed behind him to see the milling process firsthand.

Although my kids and I had travelled to different countries throughout their lives, no place was as idyllic and welcoming as Bosnia and Herzegovina. This was a side to my heritage that I hadn't talked about much with the kids. I had told them a little about the war, but not about Bosnia's beauty. It made me happy and proud to show my kids the finer side to Bosnia, a place of remarkable beauty and warm, inviting people who would invite a complete stranger into their home, feed them a warm meal, and offer them coffee.

We made new memories with Dad that day. Perhaps having his grandkids around made him feel young again. We crossed the old bridge together to the other side of the river, but instead of going back the same way, Dad began hopping like a child from one rock to another to get across. He almost made it, but he was goofing off in an attempt to impress his grandkids, and his foot slipped into the water. We laughed as he pulled his foot out of the water and emptied his shoe.

From Krupa, we continued to our next adventure thirty miles south to the city of Jajce, home to a hydroelectric power plant that supplied the region. As a teenager growing up in the war, all I remembered of Jajce was how parts of Banja Luka went dark for weeks on end when Jajce was under attack. I did my homework by candlelight.

On this trip, I saw the city for what it was, a museum of history and a World Heritage Site. This medieval town was the last stronghold of the Bosnian Kingdom. After we drove up the windy road of an egg-shaped hill, Dad parked the car outside the fortified gates of the walled-off Old Town. Those walls had been built to protect the medieval fortress on top of the hill, which it had done effectively until the 1400s, when the Ottoman Empire conquered the kingdom, bringing with it the religion of Islam and Turkish culture.

Inside the fortified gates was Old Town, a mystical city built out of ancient stone walls. Restaurants, ice cream parlors, and cafés lined the street on both sides. Dad bought ice cream for everyone, and we took a stroll down the main street under a large old, flowering linden tree, the smell of which brought back beautiful memories of playing in my grandmother's backyard as a child.

Traditional Bosnian-style homes, with proportionate four-sided roofs sitting atop white façades, adorned by ornamental dark-wood doors and small square windows, decorated the hills ascending to the fortress. Courtyards and sometimes even entire outside walls of homes were paved with stones.

As we strolled through the city, painful reminders of the war were everywhere. In the city square we passed by a white Mosque with a memorial dedicated to hundreds of war victims. Fresh red roses lined an excerpt of a poem engraved into white marble stone and written by famed Bosnian poet, Mak Dizdar:

> *We don't live here, just to live.*
> *We don't die here, just to die.*
> *We die here, just to live.*

As I read the all-too-familiar lines, often repeated by survivors of the genocide in reference to the victims brutally executed by Serb forces, my heart was heavy still. That bloody war! That tragic, cruel, unnecessary war! Maybe it would have been easier to understand if a bloody regime had been overturned, but even then, the bloodlust and barbarism would still be incomprehensible. No one was better for it, really.

Yugoslavia had been a good place to live, idyllic in many respects. But when the republics began declaring independence, jingo Serbs saw an opportunity to enact a centuries-old desire for revenge. The Serb nationalism took something good and pure and turned it into a regime of terror, greed, corruption, discrimination, and division—the effects of which have lasted to this day.

Through the General Framework Agreement for Peace in Bosnia and Herzegovina (the Dayton Agreement), Serbian President Slobodan Milošević, empowered by Bosnian Serb political leaders to represent their interests, got a seat at the negotiating table. He was essentially part of an organized terror group (i.e. "the criminal enterprise") and along with other Serb leaders, later indicted by the UN's International Criminal Tribunal for crimes against humanity and genocide in Bosnia, Croatia and Kosovo.

While the Dayton Agreement effectively stopped the violence and preserved Bosnian sovereignty, it also gave Bosnian Serbs control over 49 percent of the territory and implemented a bicameral system of government, dividing Bosnia into two autonomous entities, Federation of Bosnia and Herzegovina and Republika Srpska (or Serb Republic). The Dayton Agreement also implemented a three-member Presidency consisting of a member from each major ethnic group, thus further decentralizing the government structure.

Organized terror and crime continue to have a strong foothold in Serbia and in Republika Srpska (RS), the Serb controlled territory in Bosnia and Herzegovina. Some believe the power of organized crime was at the center of the David Dragičević case. A social activist, Dragičević frequently attended demonstrations in Banja Luka, demanding truth and justice for a growing number of unsolved murders in the region. Ultimately, he himself became a victim of the oppressive, totalitarian, and unscrupulously manipulative regime.

Dragičević was twenty-one years old when he was brutally beaten and murdered in 2018, then left for dead by the Vrbas River in my neighborhood. Although his death was declared an accident by authorities, their public statements revealed major inconsistencies with the initial investigation. Months-long protests broke out, led by David's father, who demanded truth and justice after suspecting that authorities were trying to cover up David's murder. Instead of conducting a murder investigation, police were dispatched to the streets with clubs, shields, helmets, and black ski masks to disperse the protesters on Christmas Eve 2018. This ultimately resulted in David's father being exiled to Austria while David's murderers still freely walk the streets of Banja Luka. Basic human rights and fundamental freedoms guaranteed by the Dayton Agreement do not apply under the new regime.

I am old enough to remember the good from my childhood and all the evil that ensued in the war and after. I'm also aware that many Serbs today deny that genocide ever happened in Bosnia. To admit genocide would also imply complicity, and for some, perhaps even participation, which carries consequences.

But it wasn't a handful of generals and political leaders alone that carried out the genocide. They had support. In fact, whole armies of soldiers bought into the hate; rejoiced in it even, parading the streets of Banja Luka with bandoliers and automatic guns, thick and unkempt beards, wearing furry Četnik hats and celebrating their kills that day. Drunk, they hurled insults towards Muslims, flashing their thumb, pointer, and middle fingers in the air—the same fingers used to make the sign of the cross in prayer before battle. Priests blessed these soldiers prior to battle. But these weren't God-fearing men who simply followed their leaders' orders. They were men, thousands of them, who seemed proud of what they had done and thirsty for more.

Thus, many Serbs today don't believe their wartime political leaders were war criminals. In schools today, they teach their kids a version of history that is very different from the one I survived. In fact, these days, the streets of my hometown have been renamed after Serb Četnik "heroes." To admit they were wartime criminals would be detrimental for many.

But mass graves don't lie. Forensic science doesn't lie. The recovered bones of Aunt Enisa's older brother—who was taken from his home at gunpoint by Četnik soldiers in 1992 and had been listed as missing ever since—don't lie. His bones were found twenty years later near Prijedor in one of over 750 mass graves now uncovered. He was identified by matching Aunt Enisa's DNA samples with those from excavated bones. His killer is still free; his killer's identity unknown. And Aunt Enisa will never get to look that person in the eye in a court of law to ask, "Why did you kill my brother?"

The bones of my friend Ami's brother and father were also found in another mass grave. Their bones don't lie either. Hundreds of thousands of other people whose homes were torched don't lie. Women who were raped don't lie. Refugees don't lie.

With a heavy heart, I said a prayer for all who lost their lives because of the war and for their grieving families before continuing our journey that day.

✦

We didn't have enough time to climb the stairs leading up to the citadel for a view of the city's defining feature, the magnificent Pliva waterfall. Instead, just outside city gates, we descended the stone-paved stairs. From the stairs, we took a short stroll down an unpaved path, lined with tall, lush, green linden trees, providing heavy shade in the hot summer. There, we came eye-level with one of the most spectacular sights in the world. The fifty-five-foot waterfall plunged into the Vrbas River, which then runs through Banja Luka.

As we reveled in the waterfall's majestic beauty, I noticed Dad struggling to explain something to another man in his broken English. I didn't expect to hear English spoken in the heart of Bosnia. Intrigued, I turned around to investigate.

A casual-looking stranger in his late thirties was asking Dad to take his picture. He was handsome, had broad shoulders, and was well over six feet tall. His long brown hair was neatly braided across his back, and he was sporting a few days old beard.

Curious, I walked up to him to introduce myself and help Dad with his English. He explained he was backpacking through Europe for the summer, but lived in Melbourne, Australia.

"That's very cool. Why Bosnia?" Many foreigners still don't think of Bosnia as a safe place to visit.

"I'm trying to visit as many countries in Europe as I can. This country is unbelievably beautiful, and the people are very nice and welcoming, even when they don't speak a word of English. Where are you from?" he asked.

"Well, I was born not too far from here in Banja Luka. My family and I escaped the war in 1995. Dad moved back here about ten years ago, and I currently live in Arizona with my kids."

"I'm glad you got out safely," he continued in his charming Australian accent. "This place is really beautiful. I'm surprised tourism isn't booming here."

"Thank you, and I'm really glad to hear you say that. Things haven't been the same in Bosnia since the war. There's still a lot of corruption in the government, the economy is suffering, and young people want to leave."

"That's very sad. This place has so much potential for tourism." He pointed to the waterfall.

"I agree."

"My name is Trevor, by the way!" he smiled, extending a hand to me.

"Annie. Pleasure to meet you!" I replied, shaking his hand.

"Pleasure is all mine!"

While we talked, my family started heading back to the car, so I slowly started walking toward the stairs. Uninterrupted, the handsome Australian walked beside me, continuing our conversation about his travels. As he walked me to the car, we agreed to stay in touch and exchanged contact information before we went our separate ways.

What intrigued me the most about this man was how genuinely interested he seemed in Bosnian culture—the sights, food, traditions, and customs. He didn't seem conceited or arrogant, and he certainly didn't seem to think of Bosnia as a third-world country. On the contrary, he had a childlike curiosity about him—taking in the sights with eyes wide open in awe and soaking in his surroundings like a sponge, thirsty for more.

Compared to some of the people I had come across in the past who couldn't even place Bosnia and Herzegovina on the map, the polite Australian appeared sophisticated and cultured. My heart fluttered. Our brief interaction helped me see my own culture through the lens of someone who was not jaded by the war. At that moment, I realized how proud I was of our heritage.

By the evening, we were back at our family home in Banja Luka. Trevor and I were exchanging messages. We laughed about him photobombing one of our family pictures while he shared a lovely photo of a tasty Bosnian dish. He was enjoying for dinner that night sitting across from a finch trying to steal some of his bread.

✦

The next morning, Dad and Gabriela were taking me and the kids to the Adriatic Sea where we would meet up with Dad's cousin Zakir, whom I hadn't seen in over twenty years.

When Mom was alive, she loved telling us a funny story of Zakir and his wife Enisa from the time when they were still a young couple, and I was a baby. Mom usually set the stage saying, "Annie was a happy baby. She cooed, giggled and made everyone laugh and smile—a real joy to be around. She had those adorable little fat rolls on her arms and legs that looked like dough. Everyone loved to squeeze them." I was always glad to know I'd been a happy baby for Mom.

"One day," said Mom, "we went to see Zakir and Enisa. They held Annie and played with her for hours. Annie didn't once ask for me. Before we left, Enisa asked if they could keep Annie for the night. Like all new parents, Zahid and I were chronically sleep deprived and agreed to leave Annie overnight, thinking we could use a break and get a good night's rest."

At this point, Mom's story got even better. "Well, lo and behold, around 2:00 a.m., Zakir shows up at our door with Annie in tow. He's ringing the door-bell, waking up the whole house. Zahid and I rush to the door, thinking it was some kind of an emergency. When we opened the door, Zakir said Annie had been crying for me since we left. After unsuccessful attempts to console Annie, Zakir brought her back home. As soon as I took her, she stopped crying and went to sleep in my arms."

This incident earned me the nickname "family crier" and turned into one of those stories told at every family gathering. And there we were again, over two decades later, together with Zakir and Enisa at their new vacation home in Croatia, reminiscing about Mom and the days before the war. Their refugee journey had taken them to Sweden where they lived with their two sons, daughter-in-law, and a three-year-old grandbaby, whom they adored more than life itself.

After we ate delicious barbeque kebabs, we walked to the beach for a refreshing swim, recreating some of the best family vacation times I remember as a child. Zakir snorkeled out a couple of sea urchins, carefully holding them on the palm of his hand to show Amaya and Ace. When I was a kid, my dad used to do the same thing, but thinking it would sting me, I tried to squirm away as Dad laid the urchin on my hand. Now it was Amaya and Ace's turn to squirm when Zakir tried to place the urchins on their hands.

Amaya stayed close by, afraid to go too deep in the water, while Ace swam far away with Dad and Zakir. We had a lot of fun that day. We spent the night in Croatia, had breakfast and coffee in the morning with Zach and Enisa, then headed back to Banja Luka for one more day. Our marathon road trip through Europe was coming to an end.

✦

On our last day in Banja Luka, we visited its newly rebuilt beauty, the Ferhadija Mosque. Reopened on the same day it was demolished twenty years later on May 7, 2016, this beautiful Mosque was part of our history that I was very proud to share with my children. Up until that day, Amaya and Ace had only known the Mosque from a drawing I had made and framed many years ago that hung in our living room in Arizona.

They knew the stories about the significance of the Mosque. They knew that when I was born, the Mosque's Imam led a prayer on behalf of my parents and asked God to grant me and my parents good health, protect us, and keep us on the right path. Before the Mosque was rebuilt, it pained me to know that my children would be the first generation in my family not to see this beauty in person. That day, when I stepped inside the newly rebuilt Mosque for the first time, my heart fluttered with joy. I was proud that Ferhadija had been reborn and was now more beautiful than ever.

We said our prayers inside. As I sat there, quietly pondering the journey of life, I wondered for a second what my life could have been like if the war had never happened. Would I have grown up in Bosnia? Would my friends, now scattered all over the world, still be here? If my mom hadn't gone through the trauma of war, would she still be alive? What about Igor? Would Filip have been able to give up drinking? And would we have raised our children together? Would we have been a healthier, happier family?

The casualties of the awful war weren't only those who died in the nineties. There were also those who continued to suffer years later from post-traumatic stress disorders or from depression, addiction, and other ailments afflicting those who initially survive trauma, but end up deeply broken and scarred as a result of it, whether they want to admit it or not.

I made amends that day with God for a childhood cut short, and with it, everything I imagined my life was going to be when I grew up. I was blessed and lucky to be alive—blessed to be able to tell the stories of those who could no longer speak for themselves. I made peace with the past and am grateful for the life I have today. My kids are my best friends. I miss Mom dearly, but she's with us at all times. As I left Ferhadija, my family home and my birthplace, my heart was filled with nothing but love and gratitude.

✦

And with a heart full of family love, another kind of love came into my life quite unexpectedly. After those two astonishing weeks in Europe, my kids and I were back in the States, slowly getting over our jet lag. I was getting ready to return to work. Amaya and Ace were leaving for Atlanta to visit Filip.

My first day back at work was rough because my body was still stuck in a European time zone. Halfway through the work day I was fighting off fatigue. Around lunch hour, I walked downstairs in hopes of shaking off the jet lag. On the way to the cafeteria, I ran into Al, who cheerfully blurted out, "Welcome back! How was Vienna?"

"Oh man! It was amazing! The whole trip was amazing! I tried the famous Sacher torte you recommended and have a bunch of pictures I can show you later."

"Can't wait to see them. I'll swing by your desk in a little bit."

I had to stifle the secret crush I was developing for Al. I had a strict rule about male coworkers. I kept my professional relationships strictly professional. I didn't want to date someone I worked with for the simple reason that if things didn't work out, I would be stuck seeing that person every day. In the sea of cubicles, Al sat one row over from me. That settled it. We could only be friends.

As days went on, Al and I got friendlier. We talked to each other more frequently. We exchanged numbers and started chatting outside the office. The more I got to know him, the more I liked him. We shared similar views of the world. His intelligence was refreshing and stimulating. I lost myself in our conversations.

Al loved to travel and learn about new cultures. He was funny and sweet, soft-spoken and humble, and his kindness made me smile. He was a Chicago native, and we shared stories about the Chicago Bulls glory days. Other than the fact that we worked together, Al had many wonderful qualities—the kind of qualities that make a man effortlessly attractive. And he had the most adorable smile.

After Filip, I was overly careful about who I let into my life, and I knew what qualities I wanted in a future partner. Days before leaving for Europe, I even wrote a note specifically describing the kind of relationship I longed for.

If I can visualize it, if I could get really clear with myself and what I want, it will come true, I thought, and so I wrote:

✦

I want someone who looks at me with so much love in their eyes that it melts my heart and makes my eyes water those happy little tears of joy—which would then make me feel just a little bit silly and embarrassed, but mostly humbled to have found the kind of love that others only dream of, or read of, in romance novels. We never have to express it in words, because it is always felt—but it's nice when we say it out loud, because that just makes it all the more special. I want the fire and passion that only comes alive when two people feel the same closeness and connection, and I want the kind of romance and tenderness that makes your heart flutter like blue monarch butterflies somehow suddenly inhabited your whole chest cavity. I want to feel a thousand soft little kisses on a picnic blanket spread out somewhere in a flower field in the middle of nowhere, under the clear blue skies, as the Sun is getting ready to kiss the Earth goodnight. And I want to feel warm fingers slowly tracing little heart shapes over my heart as I breathe in the sweet scent of wildflowers. I want to look deep down into a man's eyes, to see them glow and light up and twinkle like the best, most beautiful fireworks display, because they are filled with nothing but pure happiness and joy. I want a lifetime of song, dance, happiness and laughter. I want the kind of life that even if we were hungry and poor and we lived in a tent or a refugee camp, as long as we still had each other, we would have the whole world because I truly believe you can get through anything in life with the right person by your side. And I don't mind waiting for as long as it takes to find that, because if it's not that kind of love and if it's not that kind of passion...everything else is simply a joke.

✦

Al and I had our first lunch date at a restaurant called The Perfect Pear. He arrived first and got us a table by the window in the back of the restaurant. I was late as usual, and nervous, but Al was quick to make me laugh and feel at ease. Equally awkward at flirting, we made each other smile a lot that day. Our casual Sunday afternoon quickly turned into a two-hour lunch. A few weeks later, we had our first kiss on a park bench on a hot August night.

One evening, I invited him over to my place after work, and we ended up stargazing on the trampoline in the backyard. As we lay there together under the clear skies, lit up by thousands of stars, we laughed at Al's failed attempt to point out The Big Dipper. Suddenly, I had the urge to show him the note, but I wasn't sure. Then I thought, What the heck. If I can't be my true self with him, then he's not the right guy for me.

I pulled the phone out of my pocket, and said, "I want to show you something."

"What?" he asked softly.

"Don't laugh, okay?" I handed him the phone, which was open to the note.

I sat in silence, waiting for him to finish. He handed the phone back, softly gazed into my eyes and murmured, "This is beautiful."

A warm feeling flooded through me as he said that. I felt butterflies for the first time in a long time. Al and I just clicked. He understood me, and better yet, he was someone I wasn't embarrassed to introduce to my children, family, or friends. He had come into my life for a reason.

I only had one small, final test for him. A man I dated once had saved my birthday in his phone so he wouldn't forget to wish me a happy one. Of course, he never called that day. I hate the games men play with women, which is why I wasn't crazy about dating. I loved that Al never played games with me, but I guess I needed some sort of validation. If he remembered to wish me a happy birthday, he surely was a keeper.

✦

Speaking of birthdays, I had a birthday coming up, the Big 4-0. The kids had just returned from Atlanta, and I was planning to host a party that Sunday, August 12. I invited Jasmina and Hari to come out for my birthday, but Jasmina had a work commitment and was unable to make it. Al also had a trip planned.

I called Frida, whom I knew from the Bay Area and whom I had been friends with for twenty years, to ask if she and Sam would come with their girls. They were also close friends with Jasmina and Hari.

"Oh absolutely, we would love to!" Frida said. "But I meant to ask you something too."

"Sure thing. Anything for you." They had been a great support over the years, especially after moving to Arizona.

"Well, no one knows yet, but our Gracie is pregnant again. We were planning a surprise party for Sam and since they'll know the sex of the baby by then, we'll do a gender reveal party," Frida explained.

"Oh, goodness, congratulations! Wow! Yes, my kids and I wouldn't miss it for the world. When is it?"

"Saturday, August 11. Make sure you get to our house before five. One of our friends will take Sam fishing so we can prepare the surprise. First we'll surprise him and then do the gender reveal."

"Wow, sounds like we'll be partying that whole weekend. I'm so excited for you guys. Congratulations, and yes, count on us for sure."

✦

Since I had turned thirty and had been divorced for the previous decade, most of my birthdays had been low-key. The kids and I would go out to dinner. They would write me a cute card, and we'd have a lovely quiet evening. At the end of the day, the three of us would lie in the backyard stargazing in hopes of catching a shooting star. The annual Perseid meteor shower peaks on my birthday every year. I like to think it's Grandpa Namik's parting gift to me, the one that keeps on giving.

We hadn't had a big party at our house in years. For the first time in a long time, I was looking forward to celebrating my birthday with a real party. I even invited a few friends from work.

I needed to get everything ready the day before, so we could also make it to Frida's party on Saturday. By Saturday morning, I was scurrying around the house, tidying up, decorating (a Hollywood theme with red and gold balloons), preparing some food in advance for the next day, organizing the drinks and snacks.

I slipped into my party dress and drove to Frida's house to surprise Sam. I was perpetually late to everything, and this party was no exception. I parked the car near Frida's driveway, and ushered Amaya and Ace out of the car. In a rush and out of breath, I rang the doorbell, hoping we hadn't missed the surprise, as it was already a quarter past five.

To my surprise, Sam opened the door and yelled, "Surprise!"

"What? We missed it?" I exclaimed in disappointment.

"Happy Birthday!" Frida and several other friends yelled out, smiling.

"Whose birthday?" I was so confused. Who was this party for, anyway?

"Yours! Happy Birthday!" Sam and several others yelled again.

"Oh my God, you guys! Are you serious? Where's Gracie? Is she even pregnant?"

"No, we just said that to get you to come over! Come on in!"

If my birthday surprise was not enough, as I walked into their living room, I saw a shadow in the hallway, lurking behind a wall of streamers and balloons. Jasmina and Hari popped out laughing and yelling, "Surprise!"

"Aaaaaah! You're here?" I hugged Jasmina tightly in complete shock and disbelief. "Oh my God!"

"I wouldn't miss it for the world. We planned this for months!" Jasmina said laughing.

I hadn't expected Jasmina and Hari to be there. I certainly hadn't expected Frida and Sam to throw me a surprise party. I hadn't expected Jasmina and Frida to concoct a fake story about Gracie being pregnant just to get me to show up—but Jasmina didn't want to wait a whole day before seeing me on Sunday. I absolutely hadn't expected a silver bracelet with three turquoise gemstones from Jasmina as my birthday gift—similar to the one I had described seeing in Sedona.

I hadn't expected any of that, but it had come to me, along with so much more, some of which I had worked very hard for, and some of which can only be called a gift from God.

We had a great time that night. There wasn't much that would have made my birthday weekend more perfect. I was in the company of those I cherished most, my beautiful children and lifelong friends, who had been through so much with me; they had become family. I was grateful and beyond blessed.

While I was deep in my thoughts that evening, sitting outside and gazing at the clear night sky, a shooting star lit up the hot August night just as the clock struck midnight. In response, I proposed a toast, though I didn't have a drink in hand. "Here's to hoping the next forty years of my life are filled with an abundance of health, wealth, love, success, and happiness!"

"Hear! Hear! Cheers!" everyone else joined in.

Within minutes, my phone rang. I pressed yes to answer.

"Happy Birthday!" Al sang from the other end of the line.

"You remembered?" I smiled.

"Of course! How could I forget?"

I smiled. Things were definitely looking up.

EPILOGUE

LIVING A BLESSED LIFE

I often get asked: "What would you tell your sixteen-year-old self?" If I could go back in time, I would give her a big hug and tell her: "You will survive! Even when things get tough and the future looks bleak or like there is no tomorrow, keep moving forward. The darkest of nights are filled with stars and moonlight. Sometimes the storm clouds may obstruct the view, but they, too, eventually clear up. Just keep going because you will survive the darkest of nights. And when the darkness is gone, the sunshine-filled days ahead will be more than worth it."

That's the thing about turning forty—having many life lessons. I have learned to laugh and cry in the same sentence. At times I cried happy tears of joy, and at other times, life was so hard, all I could do was laugh. It seems crazy, I know, but it was the only thing I could do to cope. I have learned not to expect anything but to treat each day as a gift and a blessing, not an entitlement. I have learned to appreciate everything I have instead of focusing on everything that has been taken from me. I know who I am, what my priorities are, what I am willing and not willing to tolerate. Most importantly, I have gained the kind of self-confidence that only comes with overcoming life's challenges. I wear a smile on my face every day, or at least I try to.

The fact is, many of my childhood dreams did not come true. I never got to marry my school sweetheart Igor or name my baby boy Namik. I didn't go to college in my hometown or grow up with my childhood friends. I didn't even get to grow up in my hometown. I didn't become a doctor who delivers babies. And as for our large extended family, we were dispersed around the world as refugees from a bloody war. During many of life's challenges, I felt very much alone. My parents, both of whom I love dearly, split up not once but twice. My father lives across the ocean, and my mother tragically took her own life.

My teenage years were far from ordinary. By the time I turned fourteen, atrocious war raged in Bosnia. By sixteen, my family and I were living in a refugee camp. My worries weren't about doing well in classes or who had a crush on whom, but how we were going to share the sparse military meals they doled out and whether I would ever shower again. After that ordeal, we left the life we knew and fled to another continent where we had to learn a new language, understand a new culture, and rebuild our lives financially to survive. What didn't kill me, gave me lifelong survival skills.

I have many scars and bruises, no question. They're my battle wounds. Perhaps because of my experiences, or perhaps despite them, I don't fit a particular mold. I am a Muslim woman with short blond hair. When I'm not at work dressed for business, you can most often find me in jeans and a T-shirt. I practice my religion and pray daily to God, but I don't wear a hijab and was once married to a Catholic man. I love to have a good time, but I don't drink, and I gave up smoking at my daughter's request. I am a single mom with two beautiful children, a daughter and a son, for whom I am eternally grateful. I am raising them on my own, and they make my life worth living every day.

When I was a kid, my favorite movie was Annie. Annie was a kind-hearted, tough-minded redhead. No one messed with her. I spent countless hours watching replays of the rebel orphan-girl who no one wanted to adopt. She was my childhood hero, holding her fists in the air after beating up the boys, and saying, "All right, who's next?"

That's me—I grew up to be Annie! I always had a vision of what life should be, that there was always something better out there, and if I kept working hard, I'd find it. This was always my beacon, often the only thing that kept me going. But don't get me wrong. I'm not saying there's a secret out there, and if you find that secret, all will be well. If there is a secret, the secret is that you have to make your own way. Disney and Hollywood have it wrong. There are no knights in shining armor that will ride in and rescue the princess in distress. The princess rescues herself and writes her own happy ending. I think we need more stories like that.

Despite everything, I've had success in life, fists swinging and all. Today, I work for a Fortune 500 payments processing company. I am a Director for the Information Security Project Management Office. I love my career, not only because it pays the bills and puts food on our table, but also because I'm good at what I do, and it gives me satisfaction. I'm also the chief engineer of my own household, ensuring the home repairs are done, the garden and fruit trees are watered daily, the pantry and fridge are stocked, the clothes clean. My life is full and blessed, and I am grateful. I believe that for true happiness, we need very little—good health, self-love, a positive attitude, a loving family, and a few close friends.

It hasn't always been easy. I've worked hard to make amends with my past. I wear a smile on my face every day because I believe the most beautiful woman in the world is a happy one. She doesn't need make-up. Her light shines from within, her inner joy radiates outwardly, makes her skin glow and shimmer naturally. There's a twinkle in her eye. Each time she smiles, she lights up the whole room. Her confidence demands respect. Her wit, charm, and intelligence captivate everyone she meets. Her positive attitude is infectious.

I strive to be that woman every day in spite of the curveballs life has thrown my way. Some days, it feels like the most natural thing in the world. Other days, it's a work in progress. And that's okay too. But every morning I wake to my family, friends, work, and love, I know this much: I am living a blessed life.

ACKNOWLEDGMENTS

I wrote this book knowing that I don't have a perfect memory. Some of my recollections may be different from other people's. This book portrays what it was like to be a refugee, a daughter, a sister, a wife, a single mother from my perspective. My parents, my kids, my relatives, friends, and acquaintances will all feel and interpret our life experiences uniquely and individually.

This book comes from many life stories I shared with friends and colleagues over the years. After each story, those close to me often encouraged me to write a book about my life. I journaled; I dabbled in writing here and there; I always wanted to write a book. But I never felt safe to tell my whole story. And if I couldn't speak my truth, I saw no point in writing a book.

Growing up amid the horrors of war, for many years, I felt silenced. I felt that my voice, and the voices of my people, were taken away by the psychological warfare that went on in parallel to the war. In Banja Luka, I sometimes had to introduce myself as "Ana" or "Aleksandra" because it wasn't safe for me to say my real name. Even though I was later safe in the U.S., my new country, those irrational fears stayed with me for many years. Sharing pieces of my life with those I trusted (like my friends Judy B., Michelle H., and Amy A.) allowed me to slowly overcome those fears. I can't thank them enough for being there, for hearing me, and for encouraging me to write.

Writing about my life has been a cathartic experience, a way for me to heal. I've often read that to heal, one has to lean into the pain. I did the opposite for many years, running from the hurt instead. It wasn't until I sat down one summer, writing pages and pages of this book, that a heavy load began to lift.

I'm not sure I would have had enough willpower to heal had it not been for my kids, Mia and Tony. From the moment they were born, I knew I had to live each day setting a good example for them. They still inspire me to strive every day to be a better person today than I was yesterday. I am proud of the people they are becoming and am excited about what the future holds for us. At the same time, despite my past with their dad, that's all water under the bridge now. I want our kids to know only love. It gives me great joy when we all get together to celebrate our kids' birthdays and graduations, hanging out as a family and joking around.

I would not be where I am today without the unconditional love and support from my parents, my sister and her family, and my best friends who ended up becoming my sisters too, Aida and Lejla. I'm also indebted to those like our family friend Buco, and many others, who helped my own and many other families survive those early refugee days in the U.S. And my friends from the Bosnian music scene in California, whose lyrics and energy, at times, felt like just the right medicine.

I'm very grateful to Laura Bush and Charles Grosel for working tirelessly to edit my book and provide invaluable advice along the way. I'm also grateful to Jana Linnell for turning my vision of a book cover into a beautiful work of art.

Professionally, I would not be who I am today had I not had positive role models and mentors, such as Keith B., Mike L., Tracy M., Penny L., Laura H., Christina S.P., and Mr. Shah, who believed in me and took a chance on a refugee kid from Bosnia.

ABOUT THE AUTHOR

Aida Šibić survived the genocide in Bosnia to become a Muslim refugee in the United States where she earned a degree in computer science and is finishing a degree in computer information technology. While working her way up the corporate ladder, she became a certified project management professional, eventually responsible for implementing multimillion-dollar strategic integration initiatives with a Fortune 500 FinTech company. Currently, Aida works as Senior Director of a corporate cybersecurity program. She lives with her two teenagers in Phoenix and volunteers for organizations that provide education and services to the homeless, veterans, single moms, children, and domestic abuse survivors.

Because Aida and her family lived for five months in two different refugee camps before getting placed in the United States by the International Rescue Committee (IRC), she knows what it's like to rebuild a life after tremendous loss. Once in the US, she has also had to cope with domestic abuse and the grief of losing a loved one to suicide while balancing a full-time career and becoming the sole provider for her children, with little-to-no family support.

As a result of challenges in her own life, Aida seeks opportunities to serve others. For example, she has helped clean and remodel a veteran's home for

"House of Heroes," and she was a guest speaker for "Children's First Academy" on the importance of education. Aida has led a team of volunteers to organize a toy warehouse for W. Steven Martin 911 Toy Drive, and she has served meals to the homeless at St. Vincent De Paul.

Aida's book is another act of service. She wrote it for two main reasons: (1) to seek truth and justice for the victims of genocide in Bosnia, ensuring their story is not forgotten; (2) to help remove the stigma surrounding mental health and death by suicide. Specifically, Aida's writing seeks to normalize the topic of mental health awareness and suicide prevention. By telling her family's story, she hopes others who have lost loved ones in this manner will feel less alone. She also wants to encourage readers to learn and recognize the early warning signs of suicide, helping to prevent others from experiencing such grief.

Made in United States
North Haven, CT
23 September 2022

24461302R00200